Global Issues in Criminal Law

By

Linda E. Carter
Professor of Law
University of the Pacific,
McGeorge School of Law

Christopher L. Blakesley
The Cobeaga Law Firm Professor of Law
William S. Boyd School of Law
University of Nevada, Las Vegas

Peter J. Henning
Professor of Law
Wayne State University Law School

AMERICAN CASEBOOK SERIES®

THOMSON
™
WEST

Mat #40355673

American Casebook Series and West Group are trademarks
registered in the U.S. Patent and Trademark Office.

© 2007 Thomson/West
      610 Opperman Drive
      P.O. Box 64526
      St. Paul, MN 55164–0526
      1–800–328–9352

ISBN–13: 978–0–314–15997–7
ISBN–10: 0–314–15997–5

*TEXT IS PRINTED ON 10% POST
CONSUMER RECYCLED PAPER*

*To all those who work for justice in every
part of the world
L.C.*

*To Suzy, Chantalle, Angelique, and Christopher,
who make me whole
C.B.*

*To John Feeley, a courageous man
P.H.*

*

Preface

This book is part of a series that was conceived by Professor Franklin Gevurtz of Pacific McGeorge. Several years ago, he suggested that we incorporate transnational, comparative, and international law into all of the core courses in the law school curriculum. As a means to this end, Professor Gevurtz proposed a series of books that would supplement the primary textbooks in the core courses and provide professors with the materials necessary to teach with a global focus. From that initial idea, we now have books, either in print or in progress, in most of the main areas of the curriculum.

Global Issues in Criminal Law is designed to allow students to study issues surrounding transnational crimes, terrorism, and genocide. Students will be able to gain knowledge of basic concepts of international law, extraterritorial jurisdiction, and international tribunals that are part of the legal landscape in today's world.

We are grateful for the support of our universities, Pacific McGeorge School of Law, the University of Nevada, Las Vegas, Boyd School of Law, and Wayne State University Law School. At McGeorge, Dean Elizabeth Rindskopf Parker, Associate Deans John Sprankling and Christine Manolakas, and Professor Ruth Jones, Chair of the Faculty Research and Development Committee assisted with support and resources. At UNLV Boyd School of Law, Dean Richard J. Morgan, Associate Dean Joan Howarth assisted with support and resources.

The "Globalizing the Law School Curriculum" conference, held in August 2005 at Lake Tahoe and sponsored by Pacific McGeorge was a great source of ideas. We would especially like to acknowledge the Criminal Law and Procedure group from the Tahoe conference, which included the three of us, Professor Roger Clark, Professor Bill Pizzi, and Professor Stephen Legomsky. Their thoughts and comments inspired many aspects of the book. And, great appreciation goes to Professor Gevurtz for his tireless efforts in organizing the conference and the whole series of books.

Others who were invaluable to the development of the materials in the book include those who reviewed the materials or tried them out and provided us with feedback. Our appreciation goes to Professor Roger Clark, Professor David Sloss, and Professor Lynne Henderson.

We would also like to acknowledge the students and administrative staff without whose assistance no book could have been written. At McGeorge, they include the faculty secretaries, Denai Burbank, Paul Fuller, Stella Obillo, Cathleen Reis, Sharleen Jackson, and Sally Snyder, and research assistants, Ben Eilenberg and Andy McClelland, who worked with Professor Carter. Professor Carter would additionally like to thank the students in her Criminal Law and International Criminal Law classes who experimented with the genocide materials, providing invaluable feedback and inspiration. At UNLV, research assistants who worked with Professor Blakesley include Christine Brady, Peter Nuttall, and Caroline van der Harten. Professor Blakesley would also like to thank students in his criminal law, international law and international criminal law classes for their insight and inspiration. Professor Henning appreciates The Izumi Family Fund through Wayne State University that provided valuable support in this project, and Ms. Olive Hyman and Melissa Michaelis ('08) assisted greatly.

LINDA CARTER
CHRISTOPHER BLAKESLEY
PETER HENNING

November 2006

Acknowledgements

Portions of the following copyrighted works are preprinted by permission:

Christopher L. Blakesley, Edwin B. Firmage, Richard F. Scott and Sharon A. Williams, THE INTERNATIONAL LEGAL SYSTEM: CASES AND MATERIALS, (5th ed. 2001).

Christopher L. Blakesley & Dan Stigall, *Wings for Talons: The Case for the Extraterritorial Jurisdiction over Sexual Exploitation of Children Through Cyberspace*, 50 WAYNE L. REV. 109 (2004).

Christopher L. Blakesley & Dan Stigall, *The Myopia of* U.S. v. Martinelli: *Extraterritorial Jurisdiction in the 21st Century*, 38 GEO. WASH. INT'L L. REV. ___ (2006).

David Luban, *Calling Genocide by Its Rightful Name: Lemkin's Word, Darfur, and the U.N. Report,* 7 CHI. J. INT'L L.303 (2006).

William A. Schabas, *Problems of International Codification—Were the Atrocities in Cambodia and Kosovo Genocide?*, 35 NEW ENG. L. REV. 287 (2001).

Sharon A. Williams, *The Rome Statute on the International Criminal Court: From 1947-2000 and Beyond*, 38 OSGOODE HALL L.J 298 (2000).

*

Global Issues Series

Series Editor, Franklin A. Gevurtz

Available for Spring 2007 Classes

Global Issues in Civil Procedure by Thomas Main, University of the Pacific, McGeorge School of Law
ISBN 0–314–15978–9

Global Issues in Contract Law by *John A. Spanogle, Jr.,* George Washington University, *Michael P. Malloy,* University of the Pacific, McGeorge School of Law, *Louis F. Del Duca,* Pennsylvania State University, Keith A. Rowley, University of Nevada, Las Vegas, and *Andrea K. Bjorklund* University of California, Davis
ISBN 978–0–314–16755–2

Global Issues in Corporate Law by Franklin A. Gevurtz, University of the Pacific, McGeorge School of Law
ISBN 0–314–15977–0

Global Issues in Criminal Law by Linda Carter, University of the Pacific, McGeorge School of Law, Christopher L. Blakesley, University of Nevada, Las Vegas and Peter Henning, Wayne State University
ISBN 978–0–314–15977–7

Global Issues in Property Law by John G. Sprankling, University of the Pacific, McGeorge School of Law, Raymond R. Coletta, University of the Pacific, McGeorge School of Law, and M.C. Mirow, Florida International University College of Law
ISBN 0–314–16729–3

For Fall 2007 adoption, we also expect to have titles available in Constitutional Law, Employment Discrimination, Family Law, Labor Law, and Professional Responsibility.

*

Summary of Contents

Table of Contents

Table of Cases

The principal cases are in bold type. Cases cited or discussed in the text are roman type. References are to pages. Cases cited in principal cases and within other quoted materials are not included.

xv

Table of Statutes and Treaties

*

Global Issues in Criminal Law

*

Chapter I

INTRODUCTION

A. INTRODUCTION TO THE CONCEPT AND STUDY OF GLOBAL ISSUES

What are global issues in criminal law? Why is it important to study global issues? The starting point is an understanding of the terminology. *Global* is an umbrella term for *transnational, international* and *comparative* issues.

Transnational law is a broad category, encompassing at least criminal actions that cross national boundaries and crimes whose elements include actions in foreign countries or foreign law. Typical criminal actions that cross national boundaries include drug trafficking, money laundering, and cybercrime. In each case, the *actus reus* of the crime is likely to occur in multiple national jurisdictions. Money laundering, for example, could involve the transfer of money from an American bank to a Paraguayan bank to a Swiss bank. Crimes whose elements include acts in foreign countries or foreign law are more specialized than general crimes whose acts cross borders. For example, there is a federal crime that penalizes the importation of fish or wildlife *in violation of foreign law.*[1] An element of the crime will require proof of what violates the foreign law. One unfortunate defendant, for example, imported spiny lobsters in violation of packing laws in the Honduras and was sentenced to federal prison. Another federal crime penalizes anyone who travels in foreign commerce and engages in illicit sexual conduct abroad.[2] In today's global society, crimes increasingly in-

---

1. The Lacey Act prohibits the importation of "fish or wildlife taken, possessed, transported, or sold in violation of ... any foreign law." 16 U.S.C. § 3372(a)(2)(A). For an interesting discussion of the spiny lobster case, see Ellen S. Podgor, A New Dimension to the Prosecution of White Collar Crime: Enforcing Extraterritorial Social Harms, 37 McGeorge L. Rev. 83 (2006).

2. This statute is discussed *infra* in Chapter 2 on Transnational Crimes.

1

volve actions crossing borders and the definition of crimes is quickly keeping pace with the international nature of the criminal acts. Consequently, knowledge of transnational aspects of crimes is important for those studying and practicing in the field of criminal law today.

International is often used as an umbrella term in a similar way in which we are using the term "global." For the purposes of our study of global issues, however, international will refer to 1) international law that is applicable in domestic criminal cases in the United States, and 2) international law that is applied in international criminal tribunals. International law is defined by treaties, customary international law, and general principles of law. For instance, genocide is a crime under international law through the Convention on the Prevention and Punishment of the Crime of Genocide (Genocide Convention) that most countries of the world have ratified. Genocide is also a crime as a matter of customary international law in that most, if not all, nations of the world recognize genocide as a crime as a matter of legal obligation. Moreover, genocide is a crime that has been recognized as an especially safeguarded norm, called *jus cogens*. A *jus cogens* norm is one that is non-derogable—no nation or group may violate it, no treaty, legislation or judicial decision may derogate from the rule. We will consider this concept later in this introduction and in the chapters on terrorism and genocide.

International crimes typically have an impact both domestically and internationally. The Genocide Convention requires countries to adopt domestic legislation if necessary in order to prosecute genocide. Many nations have promulgated such laws. In the United States, there is a federal statute that penalizes the crime of genocide, 18 U.S.C. § 1091. With certain statutory limitations that the crime occur within the United States or that the perpetrator be a U.S. citizen, our federal courts could adjudicate genocide cases. In addition to the possibility of prosecutions within national court systems, there are international tribunals for adjudicating crimes such as genocide that occur in a particular country or across borders. For example, the United Nations Security Council established the International Criminal Tribunal for the former Yugoslavia (ICTY) in 1993 to adjudicate genocide, crimes against humanity, and war crimes that occurred in the former Yugoslavia during the conflict in the early 1990s. The ICTY is a temporary tribunal, but the International Criminal Court, established in 1998 and operational in 2002, is a permanent international tribunal for the adjudication of genocide, crimes against humanity, and war crimes (all *jus cogens* offenses) that occur anywhere in the world. Today's law student and lawyer should be aware of the existence of international criminal tribunals and the crimes within their jurisdiction.

Comparative refers to the law of other countries. Comparative global law is important on two levels: 1) as a general background for all American lawyers about other systems of law, and 2) as a means to understand better the reasoning and policy underlying American criminal law. In the United States, our system is a "common law" legal system. Common law is the foundation of approximately 28% of national legal systems throughout the world. Many of the world's legal systems are based on a different foundation, "civil law." Civil law is the basis of approximately 45% of national legal systems (the other 27% are based on traditional or religious law).[3] Today's lawyer should have a basic understanding of both common law and civil law traditions. While the focus of this book is on transnational and international issues, the courts use a comparative approach in deciding some of the cases that you will read.

In addition to understanding the terminology of comparative, transnational, and international issues, two other terms are necessary for your study of global issues in criminal law. Countries are referred to as **states.** This can be confusing since we refer to each of our 50 states within the United States with the same term. In order to avoid confusion, we will refer to countries as *states*, *nation-states, or states-parties* (if referring to parties to a treaty) and to our individual 50 states as a "U.S. state" or by name, such as "California." Another term that you may encounter is **municipal.** While we commonly refer to a "municipality" as a city or town within a U.S. state, "municipal" law in international law refers to the domestic law of a country.

This book is divided into three chapters that will introduce you to global issues in criminal law. They are: Chapter II—*Transnational Crimes;* Chapter III—*Terrorism;* and Chapter IV—*Genocide.* Each chapter presents a problem based on hypothetical or real facts that you will be asked to analyze based on the cases and other materials in the chapter. You will be applying many of the concepts that you are studying, such as the *actus reus* and *mens rea* of the crime, affirmative defenses, and accomplice and conspiratorial liability. In addition, you will be learning new crimes and sources of law.

Some issues and background are common to all three chapters. These common areas include concepts of jurisdiction, sources of law, and the forums in which international or transnational cases may be adjudicated. The next three subsections will provide you

---

3. *See* World's Legal Systems, University of Ottawa, http://www.droit civil.uottawa.ca/world-legal-systems/eng-generale.php.

with a background in an understanding of domestic jurisdiction (Section B), an introduction to international jurisdiction (Section C), an overview of key players and forums (Section D); and a description of sources of law (Section E).

B.   FEDERAL AND STATE JURISDICTION

"Jurisdiction may be defined as the authority to affect legal interests—to prescribe rules of law; to adjudicate legal questions; and to compel, induce compliance or take any other enforcement action. The term 'jurisdiction' derives from *juris* (law) and *dictio* (saying), meaning 'the implication being an authoritative legal pronouncement.' Jurisdiction is the means of making law functional; it is the way that states and legal institutions make law a reality. Any definition of crime and any institution that calls for the law's application to its subjects or objects necessarily includes a jurisdictional breadth—the temporal and spatial scope of that application." Christopher L. Blakesley & Dan E. Stigall, *The Myopia of U.S. v. Martinelli: Extraterritorial Jurisdiction in the 21st Century*, 38 GEO. WASH. INT'L L. REV. ___ (2006).

In the United States, there are two levels of government that may be authorized to pursue criminal charges: the federal government and each of the fifty U.S. states (plus the District of Columbia). Each level of government has authority to punish criminal conduct that comes within its *jurisdiction*, which involves two or three aspects: first, *prescriptive jurisdiction*, the power to enact a statute designating conduct as criminal; second, *enforcement jurisdiction*,[4] the authority to exercise the power of the state over the perpetrator or alleged perpetrator of a crime; and third, *adjudicative jurisdiction*, the authority to prosecute a person in that government's courts and impose punishment for a violation.

It is likely that most of the cases that you read in your Criminal Law course arise in U.S. state courts. You have probably not focused extensively on jurisdiction because most prosecutions easily satisfy the jurisdictional requirements for the specific U.S. state. For example, if a victim is murdered in California, it is clear

---

4. Some commentators include adjudicative jurisdiction within the rubric of enforcement jurisdiction. Whether separate or combined, enforcement and adjudicative jurisdiction are dependent on prescriptive jurisdiction. Hence, a state first prescribes a rule, which is to say that either by act of the legislature, decree of the executive, administrative regulation, or decision of a court, it declares a principle or legal norm. Second, the state enforces the rule; it arrests, extradites, subpoenas witnesses and documents, tries, or punishes a person for violation of the rule. A court enters a judgment vindicating the rule. Where the judiciary decides questions of law and fact and metes out the punishment or remedy, jurisdiction to adjudicate is often carved out of enforcement jurisdiction as a separate category. When prescriptive jurisdiction obtains, generally adjudicative and enforcement jurisdiction follow.

that California can prosecute the defendant for the acts that occurred within California's borders. Even if criminal actions cross U.S. state borders, there is rarely a significant jurisdictional issue. For instance, if the defendant steals a car in Indiana and drives it into Michigan, both Indiana and Michigan would be able to prosecute the defendant for theft-related crimes. For group crimes, such as conspiracy, the acts of one conspirator give the courts in that location jurisdiction over the entire criminal enterprise.

Federal jurisdiction to proscribe and prosecute crimes is far more limited than the jurisdiction of U.S. state courts. With regard to the first aspect of jurisdiction, the Constitution gives the federal government only a limited power to regulate and punish conduct in most areas. All federal criminal statutes must be based on a specific grant of authority to the Congress, augmented by the Necessary and Proper Clause. While the federal government has limited power to enact criminal laws, U.S. states retain the broad "police power" recognized as inhering in all sovereign nations to adopt regulations "to define the criminal law and to protect the health, safety, and welfare of their citizens." *Gonzales v. Raich*, 545 U.S. 1, 125 S.Ct. 2195, 162 L.Ed.2d 1 (2005). In determining the contours of the relationship between the federal government and U.S. states, the Supreme Court noted in *United States v. Morrison*, 529 U.S. 598, 120 S.Ct. 1740, 146 L.Ed.2d 658 (2000), that "we can think of no better example of the police power, which the Founders denied the National Government and reposed in the States, than the suppression of violent crime and vindication of its victims." U.S. states in turn may delegate a portion of their authority to local jurisdictions, such as counties or municipalities.

The federal government has the leading role in enacting statutes to address transnational and international criminal conduct. Only the national government negotiates and ratifies treaties, and legislation implementing a treaty may call for the enactment of criminal laws to aid the enforcement of obligations under the instrument. The Constitution grants Congress the authority under the Commerce Clause "[t]o regulate Commerce *with foreign Nations*, and among the several States, and with the Indian Tribes." U.S. CONST. ART. I, § 8, cl. 3 (emphasis added). The Foreign Commerce Clause power has been used by Congress in recent years to enact provisions making it a crime for United States citizens and residents to travel abroad for the purpose of engaging in illegal sex acts. The commerce power supports a number of important criminal laws applicable to international and transnational prosecutions involving terrorism, drug trafficking, and money laundering.

The federal government has the equivalent of a U.S. state's police power to legislate on property it owns or administers, including military installations outside the United States. The same authority applies to conduct occurring within the "admiralty and maritime jurisdiction," including ships and aircraft from the United States even if the crime occurs in another country. The Constitution also grants Congress power to "define and punish Piracies and Felonies committed on the high Seas, and Offences against the Law of Nations." U.S. CONST. ART. I, § 8, cl. 10. This is the source of authority for the Maritime Drug Law Enforcement Act, 46 App. U.S.C. § 1903, that has been used to prosecute drug trafficking involving vessels seized on the high seas with no connection to the United States. It could also provide the authority for jurisdiction over terrorism. This is because terrorism may be considered to be a crime against the Law of Nations.

The second aspect of jurisdiction is the authority of a nation (or a U.S. state) to impose its laws on a particular defendant in a criminal prosecution in its courts. There are different grounds on which a government can assert jurisdiction to apply laws to an individual defendant for conduct that may have violated one of its statutes. The fundamental basis for criminal jurisdiction is the *territoriality* principle, that conduct within the confines of a state or nation is subject to its criminal (and civil) laws. This was the basis for jurisdiction under the common law in England and has been recognized in the United States. In *American Banana Co. v. United Fruit Co.*, 213 U.S. 347, 29 S.Ct. 511, 53 L.Ed. 826 (1909), the Supreme Court described the classic principle for a nation to assert its jurisdiction:

> No doubt in regions subject to no sovereign, like the high seas, or to no law that civilized countries would recognize as adequate, such countries may treat some relations between their citizens as governed by their own law, and keep, to some extent, the old notion of personal sovereignty alive. They go further, at times, and declare that they will punish anyone, subject or not, who shall do certain things, if they can catch him, as in the case of pirates on the high seas. In cases immediately affecting national interests they may go further still and may make, and, if they get the chance, execute, similar threats as to acts done within another recognized jurisdiction. An illustration from our statutes is found with regard to criminal correspondence with foreign governments. And the notion that English statutes bind British subjects everywhere has found expression in modern times and has had some startling applications. But the general and almost universal rule is that the character of an act as lawful or unlawful must be determined wholly by the law of the country where the act is done. * * * For another jurisdiction, if it should happen to lay hold of the actor, to treat him according to its own notions rather than those of the place where he did the acts, not only

would be unjust, but would be an interference with the authority of another sovereign, contrary to the comity of nations, which the other state concerned justly might resent.

Although the notion of respecting the sovereignty of other states is still an important doctrine, the next section explores an increasing tendency for states to extend their jurisdiction over persons and actions that are in whole or in part outside their own territory.

C. INTERNATIONAL AND EXTRATERRITORIAL JURISDICTION

International law has not developed a set of rules relating to legislative, judicial, and enforcement jurisdiction in the international criminal setting that is as comprehensive, precise, or developed as the parallel domestic laws of the various nations. As a result, various theories, definitions, and applications of jurisdiction have emerged in international settings.

It is generally accepted that there are five traditional, theoretical bases of jurisdiction over international and transnational crime: **territorial**, **protective**, **nationality**, **universal**, and **passive-personality**. These bases provide the foundation upon which a state may assert jurisdiction over extraterritorial and international criminal conduct.

The **territorial theory** allows for jurisdiction over conduct an element or the effect of which takes place within the territorial boundaries of the state. It actually can be sub-divided into two forms, which may overlap. **Subjective territoriality** applies when a material element of an offense occurs within the territory (e.g., the pulling of a gun's trigger in one territory that results in harm in a second territory). **Objective territoriality** obtains when a significant effect of an offense is intended to impact and impacts the asserting state's territory. For example, if a bullet shot from the United States mortally wounds the victim, who is across the border in Mexico, Mexico would have objective territoriality jurisdiction, while the United States would have subjective territoriality jurisdiction.

The **nationality theory** (*personalité active*) bases jurisdiction on the allegiance or nationality of the perpetrator. This has long been recognized in the United States and around the world. The nationality principle allows for the laws of the home nation to apply to conduct outside its territorial boundaries. In *Skiriotes v. Florida*, 313 U.S. 69, 61 S.Ct. 924, 85 L.Ed. 1193 (1941), the Supreme Court stated:

[A]side from the question of the extent of control which the United States may exert in the interest of self-protection over waters near its borders, although beyond its territorial limits, the United States is not debarred by any rule of international law from governing the conduct of its own citizens upon the high seas or even in foreign countries when the rights of other nations or their nationals are not infringed. With respect to such an exercise of authority there is no question of international law, but solely of the purport of the municipal law which establishes the duty of the citizen in relation to his own government. Thus, a criminal statute dealing with acts that are directly injurious to the government, and are capable of perpetration without regard to particular locality is to be construed as applicable to citizens of the United States upon the high seas or in a foreign country, though there be no express declaration to that effect.

Congress relied on the nationality principle, for example, for jurisdiction in enacting the Military Extraterritorial Jurisdiction Act, 18 U.S.C. § 3261 *et seq.* The statute makes it a crime to engage in conduct outside the United States that would be punishable by a prison term of more than one year when committed by members of the armed forces, those employed by the armed forces, and by individuals "accompanying" a member of the armed forces outside the United States.

The **passive personality principle** (*personalité passive*) extends jurisdiction over offenses where the *victims* are nationals of the forum state. It applies simply and solely on the basis of the victim's nationality. Passive personality jurisdiction is not widely accepted and has been roundly rejected in the United States, except, perhaps, in relation to terrorism against U.S. nationals, where it is combined with the protective or universality theories. Because of the primary nature of the territorial principle in U.S. criminal law, extradition has traditionally been refused when the sole basis of jurisdiction is the victim's nationality, unless a treaty provision allows it.

The **protective principle**, or "injured-forum theory," is applicable whenever the criminal conduct has an impact on or threatens the asserting state's sovereignty, security, or some important governmental function. The "protective principle" emphasizes the effect or possible effect of the offense and provides for jurisdiction over conduct deemed harmful to specific national interests of the forum state.

The distinction between the protective principle and the territorial theories was clearly articulated by the Second Circuit Court of Appeals in *United States v. Pizzarusso,* 388 F.2d 8 (2d Cir. 1968), where an alien was convicted of knowingly making false statements under oath in a visa application to a U.S. consul in Canada. The fact that the accused ultimately entered the United States was not an element of the offense. The court was careful to point out that the violation of 18 U.S.C. Section 1546 took place entirely in Canada. Hence, no material element of the crime took place on U.S. territory. No physical or material effect occurred on U.S. territory. On the other hand, the crime's effect on U.S. sovereignty supported jurisdiction on this theory. The Second Circuit defined the protective principle very aptly as, "[the authority to] prescribe a rule of law attaching legal consequences to conduct outside [the state's] territory that *threatens* its security as a state or the operation of its governmental functions, provided the conduct is generally recognized as a crime under the law of states that have reasonably developed legal systems." Lying to a consular officer in Canada constituted "an affront to the very sovereignty of the United States [and had] a deleterious influence on valid governmental interests." If lying to a consular officer is within the protective principle, then, for instance, attacking U.S. officials working internationally certainly would also be within the jurisdiction of U.S. courts.

The **universality theory** allows jurisdiction in any forum that obtains jurisdiction over the person of the perpetrator of certain offenses, which are considered to be particularly heinous or harmful to humans generally. Universal jurisdiction applies where the alleged perpetrator's conduct violates a universally recognized proscription, sometimes called a *jus cogens* offense. Genocide is a clear example of a *jus cogens*, universal offense. The universality theory allows any forum to assert jurisdiction over particular universally condemned acts, when no other state has a prior interest in asserting jurisdiction. Nations have an obligation either to prosecute or to extradite perpetrators of these crimes.

These theories of jurisdiction form the foundation for conceptualizing how nations, domestically and incident to international law, have applied their law to extraterritorial criminal conduct. Terrorism, for example, planned in one state, perpetrated on a vessel or airliner, prompts both objective and subjective territoriality as well as the protective principle, nationality, the passive personality theory, and perhaps even universality jurisdiction. Extraterritorial application of a criminal law may be justified by any one of the five principles of extraterritorial authority.

The United States and other national courts have expanded the traditional bases of extraterritorial jurisdiction, responding largely to a perceived burgeoning of transnational and international crime. The Congress and U.S. courts in the "war on drugs," for example, have sought to deter narcotics importation by asserting jurisdiction over thwarted extraterritorial conspiracies and, in the "war on terror," have asserted jurisdiction over alleged terrorists who have committed their violence outside U.S. territory. Cooperation among governments in investigation and extradition is of paramount importance to combating international and transnational crime. Hence, a state requesting assistance in criminal matters must conform to any and all limitations and requirements made by the requested state and those of international law. Any disparagement of a nation's sovereignty, international law, treaty formulations, or agreements to extradite or otherwise cooperate will ultimately harm the effectiveness of international crime prevention and criminal justice.

Although expanding jurisdiction might help by broadening enforcement, expansion also should be based on consistency in theory and application. There is presently an ongoing debate whether there is a coherent theory of jurisdiction and a coherent policy basis for expanding extraterritorial jurisdiction. You should keep these issues in mind as you work with the chapters on transnational crime and terrorism.

D. PLAYERS IN INTERNATIONAL CRIMINAL LAW: STATES, INDIVIDUALS, TRIBUNALS, AND OTHER ENTITIES AS "SUBJECTS" OF INTERNATIONAL LAW[5]

1. States as the Focal Point of International Law

Subjects of domestic law include individual human beings and legal persons. Domestic law provides a set of rules that govern these subjects. As for legal persons, such as corporations, domestic law even has a clear, explicitly-defined legal process for determining the legally required facts that establish the legal entity. A corporation can be defined as an entity that has been created by compliance with that prescribed process. In contrast to domestic legal systems, no such legal process exists in the case of the formation of the traditional subjects of international law—the entities called states. Moreover, the question of what other entities might be subjects of international law is in a state of evolution. Whether natural persons are subjects of international law has been an issue for some time and is extremely important to international criminal law.

In the international legal system the terms "nations," "peoples," "states," and "nation-states" are used interchangeably and somewhat imprecisely, from a socio-anthropological standpoint, to

---

5. Parts of this section are adapted with permission from CHRISTOPHER L. BLAKESLEY, EDWIN B. FIRMAGE, RICHARD F. SCOTT AND SHARON A. WILLIAMS, THE INTERNATIONAL LEGAL SYSTEM: CASES AND MATERIALS, Ch.2 (5th ed. 2001).

refer to the legally-organized political power-structures that are the highest authority in a country, i.e., states. The state (or nation-state) is the term used for these entities, which have long been, and still are, the major structural units of the legal-political order of the planet. Historically, the imprecision noted above goes back to ancient usages, to the times when emperors and kings really ruled their peoples, or nations. States inherited the aura of sovereignty from them. Sovereignty has been the sine qua non of statehood— traditionally there has been no higher earthly authority. States have been the recognized actors in the international legal system, since the end of the Thirty Years War through the treaties made at Westphalia in 1648 (when sovereign equality moved from a few key monarchies, such as the Holy Roman Empire and the Holy See, to a number of newly-independent states). States are legally endowed with independence, equality, and the capacity to deal with other states, whether in war or peace, and have had a virtually exclusive role in the evolution of the international legal system. In classical theory, states are the "subjects" of "inter-state" law that they make for themselves, either by accepted custom or by specific agreements. We still call it "inter*national* law," and it is too late to change that; but most states rule over more than one race, ethnic group, people, or nationality.

Section 201 of the Restatement (Third) of the Foreign Relations Law of the United States (1987) defines a state as "an entity which has a defined territory and permanent population, under the control of its own government, and which engages in, or has the capacity to engage in, formal relations with other such entities." For centuries since the Peace of Westphalia, human beings as such had no standing, except through their states. On the other hand, more recently, individuals have developed some significant standing in the arenas of international criminal law and human rights law. Today, however, civilization is moving into an era in which states are not the only subjects of international law and are no longer entirely sovereign. Nonetheless, statehood is still the essential part of the international legal system. The role of states is manifest in important legal instruments of international law, such as the United Nations Charter.

2. International Humanitarian Law and Individual Culpability

We have noted that individuals were seen as subjects of their state, with only derivative rights and obligations. The state has been obliged to protect and represent its subjects, but the individual had no independent rights or interests. With the rise of the human rights movement and international humanitarian law (international criminal law), however, individuals have gained at least part of the status of being subjects of international law, with their own, independent rights, obligations, and standing.

International humanitarian law implicates criminal liability for individuals. The catalog of abuses to which human beings have subjected each other is one of unrelieved horror, which, in turn, has led to the individual perpetrator being the subject of international prosecution and punishment. Abuses range from murder, physical and mental torture, to the slaughter and rape of religious, racial and ethnic masses. They also include slavery, mass rape, sex-slavery, traffic in women and children, forced labor, mass disloca-tions, and deprivations of liberty of movement. The freedom to speak, to practice one's religion, to select one's own occupation, and to marry whom one pleases are repressed. Terrorism, arbitrary arrest, imprisonment without trial, unfair trials, torture, and de-grading punishments are not uncommon.

Many of these abuses to the human personality are common crimes—matters of domestic criminal law. Others are perpetrated by individuals acting in some official capacity for the state. Still others are committed by violent opponents of states or groups of people claiming to promote some cause. Protections against these abuses are frequently afforded by the internal laws of the state. Domestic laws are designed not only to deter private individuals from harming their fellows but also, as in the case of the U.S. Constitution, to protect the individual from abuses by the state. But what protects people when the machinery of domestic law fails or even violates their rights? Does the international legal system offer protection? The traditional rule, until a generation ago, was chilling: a state could treat its own citizens "according to discre-tion." I OPPENHEIM, INTERNATIONAL LAW 682 (Lauterpacht 8th ed. 1955). Is this still true today? What substantive legal norms have been developed in the international system for the protection of the individual? Are they effective? Are citizens and aliens equally protected? By what processes and in what institutions are those norms applied and protections afforded both internationally and domestically? Some of these issues will be considered in the chap-ters on terrorism and genocide.

As the nation-state became the organizing unit of the Europe-an peoples an early, if halting, recognition developed that, in some circumstances, a state might be circumscribed in the way it treated its nationals. Doctrines of natural law furnished a major impetus. DeVisscher noted: "[T]he treaties by which States bound them-selves to treat their own nationals in a certain way appear only as isolated phenomena inspired first by political interest and later by considerations of humanity. The series of particular agreements inaugurated in 1660 by the Treaty of Oliva after a century and a half of religious commotions bore this aspect. In these, states receiving cessions of territory guaranteed to the ceding states the continuance and protection of the religion existing in the ceded territories. This protection, granted first to individuals, was gradually extended to minority groups, to religious minorities first and afterwards ethnic or national minorities." DEVISSCHER, THEORY AND REALITY IN PUBLIC INTERNATIONAL LAW 126 (Corbett trans., 1968).

3. The Development of International Criminal Tribunals

During the twentieth century there has been an increasing recognition by the international community that individuals may be prosecuted and found liable for international criminal acts, particularly crimes against peace, war crimes, crimes against humanity, genocide, and terrorism. These offenses may be classified as crimes against the peace and security of humanity. We will explore several of them. The most poignant examples of a finding of such liability up until the present time were the war crimes trials undertaken by the specially created International Military Tribunals at Nuremberg and Tokyo as well as some national court cases following atrocities committed in the Second World War, and a few from the Vietnam War. More recently the Ad Hoc Tribunals for the former Yugoslavia and Rwanda were created and the permanent International Criminal Court, established in Rome in 1998, is beginning to operate. Other tribunals include a mixed tribunal (with domestic and international judges), such as those created for Cambodia and Sierra Leone.

Individual criminal responsibility is the cornerstone of any international war crimes tribunal. *Nuremberg Principle I* provides that "[a]ny person who commits an act which constitutes a crime under international law is responsible therefor and liable to punishment." *Nazi Conspiracy and Aggression Opinion and Judgment, Nuremberg, 30 September 1945*, reprinted in 41 AM. J. INT'L L. 186 (1947). Acts by heads of state or other government officials, even if committed in an official capacity, may not provide an immunity defense or mitigate criminality. These officials, therefore, could also be held responsible for offenses committed pursuant to their orders. The development of international criminal tribunals has, however, been a halting process.

Efforts to establish an international criminal tribunal are not new, although they have intensified recently. It is a history of many attempts and few successes. Professor Cherif Bassiouni notes that "the first prosecution for initiating an unjust war is reported to have been in Naples, in 1268, when Conradin von Hohenstaufen was executed for that offense." *See* M. Cherif Bassiouni, *Interna-*

tional Law and the Holocaust, 9 CAL. W. INT'L L.J. 201, 206 (1979); ERNST KANTOROWICZ, FREDERICK THE SECOND (1194–1250) 673–677 (1957) (discussing the execution and the end of the Hohenstaufen reign). The "modern" idea of establishing an international criminal court could be said to have been launched in 1899 with the Hague Convention for the Pacific Settlement of International Disputes.

The 1919 Versailles Treaty was another early step toward establishing a war crimes court. The face of the treaty provided for the prosecution of Kaiser Wilhelm II for a supreme offense against the "international morality and the sanctity of treaties" and for war crimes charged against German officers and soldiers. Also in 1919, the Allies established a special commission to investigate the responsibility "for acts of war" and crimes against "the laws of humanity." The Report of the Commission contained the following conclusion: "All persons . . . who have been guilty of offenses against the laws and customs of war or the laws of humanity, are liable to criminal prosecution." This provision was developed in response to the killing of an estimated one million Armenians by Turkish authorities and the Turkish people, supported or abetted by the state's public policy. There can be no doubt that those who committed such atrocities knew they were committing "crimes against humanity." U.S. opposition, however, prevented the Commission's report from including this type of conduct among the offenses that an international criminal court would prosecute. Subsequently, the Treaty of Sèvres, Treaty of Peace Between the Allied and Associated Powers and Turkey Aug. 10, 1920, reprinted in 15 AM. J. INTL. L. 179, 231 (Supp. 1921), provided for the surrender by Turkey of such persons as might be accused of crimes against "the laws of humanity," but in 1923, the Treaty of Lausanne gave them amnesty. *See* Treaty of Peace Between the Allied Powers and Turkey (Treaty of Lausanne), July 24, 1923, 28 L.N.T.S. 11, 18 AM. J. INT'L L. 1 (Supp. 1924).

Between the two world wars, a wave of terror swept Europe, mostly in connection with nationalist claims in the Balkans. In 1936, Adolf Hitler exploited the international community's inability to prosecute or sanction crimes against humanity stating, "And who now remembers the Armenians?" Indeed, it is particularly revealing that he would preface his policy of exterminating the Jewish people, the Roma, and Slavs, among others, by revealing the absence of interest by the world community to prosecute such conduct. That failure and the inability to create efficient international structures to enforce this proscription, gave Hitler the comfort of knowing that he might succeed in genocide, as others had in the past. In 1937, the League of Nations adopted a Convention Against Terrorism; an annexed Protocol provided for the establishment of a special international criminal court to prosecute such crimes. India was the only country to ratify the Convention. It never entered into force.

After World War II, it became obvious that crimes against peace, war crimes, and what became known, with the London Charter, as "crimes against humanity" had been committed. The London Charter established the International Military Tribunal (IMT) at Nuremberg, which was designed to prosecute major war criminals in the European theater. In 1946, a similar international military tribunal was established in Tokyo to prosecute major Japanese war criminals.

Despite the precedent of Nuremberg and Tokyo, no international criminal tribunal was created for the next 50 years. Although the General Assembly of the United Nations urged consideration of the establishment of an international criminal court in 1989 and the International Law Commission (ILC) proposed the creation of an international criminal court in 1990, the first international criminal tribunal to come into existence since World War II was the International Criminal Tribunal for the former Yugoslavia (ICTY). Security Council Resolution 808, paragraph 1, provides: "An international tribunal shall be established for the prosecution of persons responsible for serious violations of international humanitarian law committed in the territory of the former Yugoslavia since 1991." The Secretary–General's Report relating to the atrocities in the former Yugoslavia noted that the creation of the Tribunal for the prosecution of the alleged breaches of international humanitarian law will apply existing law, including the Geneva Conventions of 1949, and that the Security Council would not be creating law or purporting to legislate. One year after the ICTY was established, the International Criminal Tribunal for Rwanda (ICTR) was created, also through action by the Security Council.

The next major development was the establishment of the International Criminal Court. This time the tribunal was created through a treaty. Consider the commentary on the ICC by Professor, and former ICTY Ad Litem Judge, Sharon Williams:

> The International Criminal Court (ICC) was established on 17 July 1998 in Rome by the United Nations Diplomatic Conference. * * * It [has] jurisdiction over some of the most serious international crimes. Its value is not only in prosecuting and punishing the alleged perpetrators of the listed crimes, genocide, war crimes, crimes against humanity and potentially aggression, but also in its capacity for deterrence. An impartial international criminal court with an independent prosecutor's office must discourage those who seek to instigate and perpetrate barbarous atrocities in violation of customary international and treaty law. The major challenge for the international

community is to make it truly effective and not merely symbolic. * * *

The world community must be prepared to act. Should deterrence fail it must be ready, willing and able to bring to justice those accused, demonstrating that such conduct will not go unchallenged. It is not a question of high-minded revenge, of the victors dictating their terms to the vanquished, but rather a deep-rooted imperative to advance the rule of law and to enhance the quality of human behaviour at the national and international levels. The world community now knows that it is not sufficient to act on an *ad hoc* basis. To do so requires the selective political consent of the . . . Security Council, acting under Chapter VII of the *Charter* * * * and there is a possibility that one of the five permanent members will veto the action. * * * The ICC is fundamental to international peace and security and the protection of human rights and dignity * * * .

The philosophical and practical underpinnings for the ICC are threefold * * * deterrence, prosecution of alleged perpetrators, and justice for victims. The critical factor in the establishment of the court is the capacity to enforce. The goal is to replace impunity with accountability. * * * [In the final plenary the United States requested an unrecorded vote. The Statute was adopted by 120 in favour, 7 against and 21 abstentions.]

It would be naive to suggest that there are not certain weaknesses in the statute. There are. Certain states and most NGOs pressed for the ICC to have universal jurisdiction or a variant thereof, over the listed crimes, but the result at the end of the day was restrictive preconditions in the final text of article 12. In fact, until the proverbial eleventh hour in Rome, article 12 was a make or break provision, and it still today retains its notoriety.

Sharon A. Williams, *The Rome Statute on the International Criminal Court: From 1947–2000 and Beyond*, 38 OSGOODE HALL L.J 298 (2000).

The Rome Statute has long since received the 60 required ratifications to enter into force.[6] Although in Rome some delegations wanted the list to be broader and to include international terrorism and drug trafficking, at the end of the day article 5 was restricted largely to cover only those crimes that were covered by customary international law. However, there were departures such as the inclusion of offences against humanitarian and UN person-

---

6. As of November, 2006, 102 nations have ratified the treaty establishing the Court.

nel and the prohibition on conscription or enlisting children under fifteen.

E. THE SOURCES OF INTERNATIONAL CRIMINAL LAW*

The substantive sources of international law are identified in the Statute of the International Court of Justice [I.C.J.], article 38(1), The I.C.J., also known as the World Court, is the judicial organ of the United Nations. The statute of the ICJ is particularly influential because the Court has subject-matter jurisdiction as to issues concerning many international agreements.

Article 38(1) was incorporated virtually verbatim from the League of Nations Statute of the Permanent Court of International Justice, and provides:

> 1. The Court, whose function is to decide in accordance with international law such disputes as are submitted to it, shall apply:
>
>> a. international conventions, whether general or particular, establishing rules expressly recognized by the contesting states;
>>
>> b. international custom, as evidence of a general practice accepted as law;
>>
>> c. the general principles of law recognized by civilized nations;
>>
>> d. ... judicial decisions and the teachings of the most highly qualified publicists of the various nations, as subsidiary means for the determination of the law.

This hierarchy of legal authority is *"civilian"* or derived largely from Roman law influence as established on the European continent and other areas that have been influenced by that model. Note that judicial decisions, like scholarly doctrine, are not binding, but subsidiary .. These two persuasive sources are to be used to prove and to interpret the meaning of the binding sources—treaties, custom, and general principles. International conventions (like legislation or codes in civil law jurisdictions), international custom, and general principles of law, are all binding or primary authority.

One of the distinguishing features of the civil law is the hierarchy of authoritative and persuasive sources. Civilian doctrine and law provide that legislation and custom are authoritative or primary sources of law. They are contrasted with persuasive or

* Adapted with permission from CHRISTOPHER L. BLAKESLEY, EDWIN B. FIRMAGE, RICHARD F. SCOTT, AND SHARON WILLIAMS, THE INTERNATIONAL LEGAL SYSTEM: CASES AND MATERIALS 3–4 (Foundation Press 5th ed. 2001).

secondary sources of law, such as jurisprudence (case law), doctrine, conventional usages—what common law states call practice or usage—and equity, that may guide the court in reaching a decision in the absence of legislation and custom. Equity is not a separate body of rules, as in common law systems, but is deemed to permeate all aspects of the law and should be part of every decision. Custom results from practice repeated for a long time and generally accepted as having acquired the force of law. This vision of authoritative or primary sources and its definition were adopted by public international law.

Thus, the authority articulated in I.C.J. Statute, article 38(1) and its hierarchy represent the basic legal sources of international law. Recognizing this derivation and discipline from the "civil law tradition," is necessary for one to understand international law properly, to be able to negotiate, litigate, or even to communicate effectively in the arena of international law. An international lawyer cannot be competent without understand the civilian philosophical context and mindset of many of its practitioners . Viewing international through a purely common law prism causes confusion, misinterpretation, and failure. To practice international law well, one should also be a comparativist.

First in the list of sources is "**[i]nternational conventions**, whether general or particular, establishing rules expressly recognized by the contesting states...." **Treaties** are denominated many ways: conventions, *modii vivendi*, concordats, charters, articles of agreement, pacts, protocols, and accords, agreements, memoranda of understanding, among others. On the other hand, differences are important between multilateral and bilateral treaties and other agreements in which reservations or other special rules are allowed. Not only are treaties a basic source of international law, they are *the* key vehicle by which the international system changes most rapidly. Treaties are a most vital part of international law—they provide for cooperation in criminal law matters, common defense, the promotion of friendship, and cooperation in all areas of international intercourse, such as protecting the environment and protecting the rights and interests of individuals. They are the *modii vivendi* of states; they provide the mechanism for the various subjects of international law to arrange their relations, indeed, to make their own law. This aspect of treaties is really not too different from citizens of states in their contractual relationships, except that treaties may reflect or create customary international law, discussed *infra*.

The modern international practitioner, or any practitioner (including those who practice criminal law) who has a client with a problem that transcends national borders, must of necessity work with international agreements and the international law of treaties.

Treaties lag behind developing needs within the international community and lack specificity due to the technologically complicated and politically sophisticated situations that they address. On the other hand, they are still the *modus vivendi*, because nations have a constant need to reach specific accord upon areas of common concern. Undertakings among states are major tools of operation in the international legal system. Other mechanisms, such as rules of customary law, derived from the usual modes of conduct of international relations, reason, judicial decisions, general principles of law common to the world's major legal systems and the like are also important and provide for evolution.

The second source of authority for international law indicated in ICJ Statute article 38(1) is **customary international law**. Custom is binding authority, although some argue that treaties are higher in the hierarchy. Customary international law also impacts the meaning of treaty terms. Certainly, subsequent practice of states parties to treaties, even relating to non-states-parties may create customary rules that impact interpretation of treaty terms. On the other hand, negative conduct may prove their validity and continued legality, through negative implication. Customary international law is viewed as law that is promulgated (and there is a process of promulgation) on the basis of general or consistent state practice (or the material element) and *opinio juris* (the subjective or psychological element). *Opinio juris* is established when it is proved that a state acts or fails to act in a certain way, because it considers itself legally bound so to act or not to act. Even negative conduct (or violations of a customary rule of international law) may actually promote the rule or it may create new customary international law, especially when the violator tries to hide the violation or makes excuses for it. On the other hand, widespread negative conduct may erode custom, general principles, or the intended meaning of a provision of a treaty.

It may be impossible to find a national legal system which arbitrarily refuses to apply rules of customary international law not in conflict with domestic law. In common law states, courts usually justify their application of customary international law by stating that international law is part of the law of the land. The simplicity of the proposition is deceptive, for if it were accepted as literally true, courts would need only to determine whether there was an applicable rule of customary international law and apply it so long as they found an applicable rule not in conflict with domestic law.

National constitutions may provide a specific legal basis for the application of rules of customary international law. Among those a number of modest formulations provide (or contain language to the effect) that "The State shall endeavour to ... foster respect for international law and treaty obligations in the dealings of organized peoples with one another." Article 51(c), the 1950 Constitution of India. Comparable provisions are found in the constitutions of a number of countries, including Bulgaria Article 24(1), Nepal Article 26(15), Namibia Article 96(d), the Netherlands Article 90, and Romania, Article 10.

Some constitutions provide a basis for courts to apply rules of customary international law by declaring specifically that international law is part of the law of the land, including the following examples. The Austrian Constitution of 1928 states in Article 9(1): "[t]he generally recognized principles of International Law are integral parts of the Federal Law." Article 2(2) of the 1987 Philippine Constitution states: "The Philippines ... adopts the generally accepted principles of international law as part of the law of the land." Article 15 of the Russian Constitution of 1993 states that: "[T]he commonly recognized principles and norms of international law and the international treaties of the Russian Federation shall be a component part of its legal system." Article 25 of the 1949 German Constitution, as amended, provides: "The general rules of public international law constitute an integral part of federal law. They take precedence over statutes and directly create rights and duties for the inhabitants of the federal territory." Article 10 of the Italian Constitution states: "Italy's legal system conforms with the generally recognized principles of international law." *See Re Martinez*, Italy, Court of Cassation, 1959, 28 INT'L L. REP. 170 (1963) (Conformity between the two means that rules of municipal law which are contrary to customary international law *"must be eliminated."*). Article 28(1) of the Greek Constitution of 1975 declares that "the generally recognized rules of international law ... shall be an integral part of domestic Greek law and shall prevail over any contrary provision of law" The Constitution of Slovenia in 1997 provided in Article 8, that "Statutes and other legislative measures shall comply with generally accepted principles of international law ...." One question that arises is whether any of these provisions mean that custom is automatically integrated or whether something further must be done to integrate it.

Stronger terms of acceptance of international law are found in other national constitutions, including Article 29(3) of the Constitution of Ireland (text of 1990), which provides that: "Ireland accepts the generally recognized principles of international law as its rule of conduct in its relations with other States." Article 98(2) of the Japanese Constitution of 1946 provides that "the ... established laws of nations shall be faithfully observed". The Hungarian Constitution of 1949, as amended in 1997, is exceptional in providing, in Ch. 1, sec. 7, that: "[t]he legal system of the Republic of Hungary accepts the generally recognized principles of international law, and shall harmonize the country's domestic law with the obligations assumed under international law."

Article 38(1)(c) provides the third authoritative source of international law. "**General principles of law** recognized by civilized nations" relate to principles that arise from the domestic law of the nations of the world. For example, "Thou Shalt Not Steal," is found in the domestic law of virtually all nations, so it is binding authority. In addition, some general principles have the aura of a universal, moral or natural law principle. These general principles are rules of the highest order in international law, sometimes called *jus cogens* principles. These seem to be a mixture of super custom and super general principle. The core crimes in international humanitarian law have this character. These are non-derogable by legislation, judicial decision, or treaty. There is little dispute over the extent of the authoritative character of general principles, which we will consider in more detail in the terrorism and genocide modules.

International law is evolving in many ways. The number and types of players, even subjects, is expanding. States continue to be the primary subjects of international law, of course, but both natural persons and legal persons, are gaining standing and more of the attributes of subjects. In addition, international organizations have developed many attributes of subjects. The international criminal tribunals from Nuremberg to the International Criminal Court, including the ad hoc tribunals for the former Yugoslavia and Rwanda and the mixed tribunals for Cambodia, Sierra Leone, and other places have made a tremendous impact on substantive international criminal law. These tribunals apply the legal sources that we have presented above: treaties, customary international law, and general principles to render their judgments. The attorneys establish the meaning of treaty terms, the nature and impact of custom and general principles with persuasive sources, such as jurisprudence (case-law) and doctrine (the writings of eminent scholars). International criminal law, transnational criminal law, and comparative criminal law have become necessary tools of lawyers, including those who practice criminal law.

Chapter II

TRANSNATIONAL CRIMES

A. INTRODUCTION

Most crimes are local in nature, involving a single or small number of victims in a particular locale. As the economy has globalized and security threats abound throughout the world, the number of cross-border crimes has grown exponentially. The sale of heroin and cocaine often involves the importation of the drugs from outside the United States, and large scale drug organizations—often called cartels—will launder the profits of the drug trade through accounts and businesses in a number of nations. An international sex trade has developed in which citizens of one country travel to another to purchase sex acts that would be illegal in the home country, and likely violate the laws of the host country, although local law enforcement may be lax due to bribery or a lack of resources. Computer crimes can involve the release of an e-mail worm from anywhere in the world that destroys files on hundreds of thousands of computers, spreading in a matter of days, if not hours. Terrorism knows no borders, and the financing of terrorist organizations involves the use of networks that span the globe to transfer cash and goods. International criminal syndicates have a hand in a large number of illegal enterprises, from knock-off luxury goods to selling weapons.

Nations are now confronting what has come to be known as "transnational crime" in which criminal conduct impacts a number of nations while the particular acts might occur in only one country, or even outside any nation, for example on the high seas. As Bruce Zagaris, a lawyer who practices extensively in the area, has noted, "[T]he new transnational crimes take advantage of globalization, trade liberalization and exploding new technologies to perpetrate diverse crimes and to move money, goods, services and people instantaneously for purposes of perpetrating violence for

22

political ends." Bruce Zagaris, *Revisiting Novel Approaches to Combating the Financing of Crime: A Brave New World Revisited*, 50 VILL. L. REV. 509 (2005).

As the criminal law develops to deal with crimes that can take place in a number of locations and may involve multiple victims scattered across continents, issues arise regarding the *definition* of the criminal offense, and the basis on which a country, or in some instances an international tribunal, asserts *jurisdiction* to put the alleged perpetrators on trial and seek a punishment. The definition of a criminal offense and a judicial system's jurisdiction over the offense are related concepts. The definition of criminal offenses involves the legislature enacting a statute that establishes the elements of the offense, such as the intent for the crime and the acts that must be proven for liability. In addition to defining the crime, the law can establish the requirements for the nation's or international body's judicial authority to enforce its laws against individual defendants. Based on the statute, the court determines whether it can exercise its authority to try and, upon conviction, punish the defendant, or whether the person falls outside its jurisdiction. For transnational crimes, jurisdiction is often a key issue that requires courts to interpret the scope of the legislative enactment.

One description of transnational criminal law is "the indirect suppression by international law through domestic penal law of criminal activities that have actual or potential trans-boundary effects." Neil Boister, *"Transnational Criminal Law"?*, 14 EUR. J. INT'L L. 953, 955 (2003). Unlike more traditional international law, which looks to international organizations to define crimes, transnational criminal law involves the application of laws adopted by the nation's legislature to define criminal conduct that may occur outside the country, at least in part.

Not all transnational crimes arise solely from conduct occurring outside the country seeking to prosecution. Some may involve issues related to acts that include one aspect within the country that is part of a much broader international criminal offense. In these instances, the conduct that occurs within the country exercising jurisdiction may not necessarily be criminal in itself, but when included with the foreign acts constitutes a criminal offense. For example, United States law now makes it a crime for a person who obtained funds in a foreign country through bribery to transmit or transfer the money through a United States financial institution. A foreign official can be prosecuted in the United States for money laundering based on dealings in the United States that are not illegal and in fact involve quite common financial transactions, but because the funds are traceable to corruption the official can be prosecuted in the United States. In countries with a written constitution, such as the United States, there is an important question whether the national government has the authority to enact legislation that permits its courts to be used to prosecute transnational crimes that may involve few if any criminal acts within its borders.

This Chapter considers issues related to transnational crime as one aspect of the broader category of criminal law. The issues here are different than what is encountered in other areas of the criminal law because the focus is less on whether the conduct constitutes conduct that is (or should be) punishable, and more on whether the government seeking the conviction is the appropriate forum for a criminal prosecution.

B. TRANSNATIONAL PROBLEM

Sophie Lorn operates an investment fund in Florence, Italy, for wealthy investors. She has clients from a number of countries, including the United States, although the fund does not have any operations outside Italy. One day, Sophie receives information from Bridget Barbeau, an old friend who lives is France, that Bridget's employer, Crédit Internationale S.A. (CI), will soon launch a hostile tender offer for Hague Bank, a Dutch bank with operations in Europe and the Middle East. CI's headquarters is in Bern, Switzerland, and it has a United States subsidiary incorporated in Delaware. Based on Bridget's information, Sophie purchases 50,000 shares of Hague Bank for the investment fund and 10,000 shares for her personal account through the Rome office of Credit Suisse, an international stock brokerage firm with offices in the United States. A few days later, CI announces the hostile offer for Hague Bank, and the stock price of Hague Bank increases significantly. Sophie sells all the shares she purchased, realizing $2 million in total profits on the transactions. A short time later, the U.S. Securities & Exchange Commission (SEC) begins an investigation of suspicious trading in Hague Bank stock, which is traded on both the London Stock Exchange and the New York Stock Exchange (NYSE). The SEC identifies the trades by Sophie as suspicious, and a review of the trading records shows that a block of 30,000 shares of Hague Bank that were part of Sophie's order were purchased on the NYSE on behalf of Credit Suisse, which is a "member" (i.e. has the right to purchase and sell shares directly on the floor of the exchange) of the NYSE. Bridget informs officers of CI that she tipped a number of friends, including Sophie, about Hague Bank's hostile offer, information that CI passes on to the SEC.

The SEC and the United States Attorney's Office meet to discuss bringing criminal charges and a civil enforcement action against Sophie for insider trading in violation of rules promulgated by the SEC. The relevant statute is 15 U.S.C. § 78o(b), which states as follows:

> It shall be unlawful for any person, directly or indirectly, by the use of any means or instrumentality of interstate commerce or of the mails, or of any facility of any national securities exchange—
>
> (b) To use or employ, in connection with the purchase or sale of any security registered on a national securities exchange or any security not so registered ... any manipulative or deceptive device or contrivance in contravention of such rules and regulations as the Commission may prescribe as necessary or appropriate in the public interest or for the protection of investors.

Can Sophie be charged in the United States with a violation of this statute? What basis for jurisdiction over Sophie's conduct best fits this scenario? Does the securities fraud statute apply to extraterritorial conduct, and does Congress have the power to reach defendants who have never conducted a transaction in the United States? Should it?

C. CONSTITUTIONAL POWER TO REACH FOREIGN CONDUCT

Jurisdictional issues can be quite complex because they involve questions about the authority of the nation to enact criminal laws and use its judicial system to punish conduct that may have little direct impact on its residents. The term jurisdiction is often used imprecisely. Effective analysis requires a sharp distinction between rulemaking and rule-enforcing jurisdiction. There are three forms of jurisdiction: prescriptive (also called legislative); adjudicative; and enforcement. The first question is whether the scope of the prescriptive jurisdiction is valid, which for a federal law in the United States often involves an analysis of Congress's constitutional authority to enact the legislation. If prescriptive jurisdiction is valid, then the next question is whether adjudicative or enforcement jurisdiction are appropriate. Adjudicative and enforcement jurisdiction are dependent on prescriptive jurisdiction; if the legislative authority is not broad enough to cover the proscribed conduct, obviously, no adjudication or enforcement is appropriate. A state first prescribes a rule, which is to say that either by act of the legislature, decree of the executive, administrative regulation, or decision of a court, it declares a principle or legal norm. Second, the state enforces the rule. That is, it arrests, subpoenas witnesses and documents, extradites, tries, or punishes a person for violation of the rule. A court enters a judgment vindicating the rule. Jurisdiction to adjudicate, where the judiciary decides questions of law and fact and metes out the punishment or remedy, is sometimes carved out of enforcement jurisdiction as a separate category. Jurisdiction to enforce or to adjudicate is dependant on jurisdiction to prescribe. See CHRISTOPHER L. BLAKESLEY, EDWIN B. FIRMAGE, RICHARD C. SCOTT & SHARON A. WILLIAMS, THE INTERNATIONAL LEGAL SYSTEM: CASES AND MATERIALS ch. 3 (5th ed. 2001).

Defendants have challenged statutes adopted by Congress that reach foreign conduct on the ground that the Commerce Clause does not authorize the application of U.S. law to activities wholly outside the country. For example, in *United States v. Cummings*, 281 F.3d 1046 (9th Cir. 2002), the defendant challenged his conviction under the International Parental Kidnapping Crime Act (IPK-CA), 18 U.S.C. § 1204, that makes it a crime to retain a child outside the United States contrary to the parental rights of another. The defendant argued that Congress does not have the power to criminalize the retention of an American child in another country when there is no further travel in foreign commerce after the removal of the child from the United States. The Ninth Circuit rejected that argument in analyzing the scope of the foreign commerce power:

> Congress's Commerce Clause authority is broad enough to stretch beyond the simple regulation of commercial goods traveling in interstate and foreign commerce to include regulation of non-economic activities—such as racial discrimination or growing wheat for personal consumption—that affect, impede, or utilize the channels of commerce. See, e.g., *Heart of Atlanta Motel, Inc. v. United States*, 379 U.S. 241 (1964) (upholding Title II of the Civil Rights Act because racial discrimination "impede[d] interstate travel" through the channels of commerce); *Wickard v. Filburn*, 317 U.S. 111 (1942) (upholding government's fine of a farmer for growing wheat for personal consumption in excess of his set quota because Congress sought to control wheat shortages and surpluses).

> Thus, so long as § 1204(a) falls into one of the delineated "categories of activity that Congress may regulate under its commerce power," its reach need not be confined to commercial goods to be constitutional. *United States v. Lopez*, 514 U.S. 549 (1995). The Supreme Court has identified three such categories: (1) regulating the use of the channels of commerce; (2) regulating and protecting the instrumentalities of commerce or persons in interstate commerce, even though the threat may come only from intrastate activities; and (3) regulating activities that have a substantial effect on commerce.
> * * *

Here, the wrongfully-removed children traveled in the channels of foreign commerce to reach Germany, where they were wrongfully retained.

Cummings argues that these principles do not speak to the constitutionality of the retention portion of § 1204(a) because they target conduct directly involved in the movement of people or things in commerce. He argues that once the movement ceases, the channels of commerce are no longer affected. Here, of course, § 1204(a) targets activity (i.e., retention) after movement has ceased.

We are unpersuaded. The cessation of movement does not preclude Congress's reach if the person or goods traveled in the channels of foreign commerce. In *United States v. Rambo*, 74 F.3d 948 (9th Cir. 1996), we upheld 18 U.S.C. § 922(*o*)'s prohibition on machinegun possession because the statute was "an attempt to prohibit the interstate transportation of a commodity through the channels of commerce." Section 922(*o*) permissibly proscribes possession after the items' movement through the channels of commerce ceases because, we noted, "there [could] be no unlawful possession under section 922(*o*) without an unlawful transfer." We concluded that "[b]y regulating the market in machineguns, including regulating intrastate machinegun possession, Congress has effectively regulated the interstate trafficking in machineguns."

Likewise, § 1204(a) reaches conduct once the unlawful foreign transportation has ended. See also *United States v. Jones*, 231 F.3d 508 (9th Cir. 2000) (upholding a federal statute that prohibited felons from possessing firearms that were previously shipped in or otherwise affected interstate commerce). We are satisfied that Congress can act to prohibit the transportation of specified classes of persons in foreign commerce and thus proscribe conduct such as retention of those persons, even though transportation is complete.

Not only does § 1204(a) target activity after the use of channels of foreign commerce is complete, but it also removes an impediment to the use of those channels. If a child is wrongfully retained in a foreign country, he or she cannot freely use the channels of commerce to return. Congress has authority to prevent individuals from impeding commerce, see *Heart of Atlanta Motel*; *United States v. Green*, 350 U.S. 415 (1956) (upholding Hobbs Act, which made it a crime to "obstruct[ ], delay[ ], or affect[ ] commerce or the movement of any article or commodity in commerce, by robbery or extortion"); and, as to those who "retain" children outside the United States, to prevent them from traveling back to this country via the channels of commerce. Thus, by wrongfully retaining his children in Germany, Cummings is interfering with the use of the channels of foreign commerce; IPKCA removes an impediment to travel and makes possible unrestricted use of the channels of commerce.

D. JURISDICTION

If a statute is silent on whether extraterritorial criminal conduct is prosecutable, a determination of the legislature's intent must be made. The application of international law principles can play a role in ascertaining whether a nation can exercise extraterritorial jurisdiction over a person for acts outside of that nation. There are five general principles used to determine whether a criminal statute can be applied to extraterritorial conduct, as summarized in *Chua Han Mow v. United States*, 730 F.2d 1308 (9th Cir. 1984):

> International law recognizes five general principles whereby a sovereign may exercise this prescriptive jurisdiction: (1) territorial, wherein jurisdiction is based on the place where the offense is committed; (2) national, wherein jurisdiction is based on the nationality or national character of the offender; (3) protective, wherein jurisdiction is based on whether the national interest is injured; (4) universal, which amounts to physical custody of the offender; and (5) passive personal, wherein jurisdiction is based on the nationality or national character of the victim. *United States v. Smith,* 680 F.2d 255, 257 (1st Cir.1982) (footnote omitted). Many cases involve the prosecution of United States citizens for acts committed abroad, but extraterritorial authority is not limited to cases involving the nationality principle. Extraterritorial application of penal laws may be justified under any one of the five principles of extraterritorial authority.

The Supreme Court explained the process of statutory interpretation for determining whether a statute can be applied to extraterritorial conduct in *United States v. Bowman*, 260 U.S. 94, 43 S.Ct. 39, 67 L.Ed. 149 (1922), where it considered the application of the federal conspiracy law to conduct that occurred on the high seas and in a foreign country:

> We have in this case a question of statutory construction. The necessary locus, when not specially defined, depends upon the purpose of Congress as evinced by the description and nature of the crime and upon the territorial limitations upon the power and jurisdiction of a government to punish crime under the law of nations. Crimes against private individuals or

their property, like assaults, murder, burglary, larceny, robbery, arson, embezzlement, and frauds of all kinds, which affect the peace and good order of the community must, of course, be committed within the territorial jurisdiction of the government where it may properly exercise it. If punishment of them is to be extended to include those committed out side of the strict territorial jurisdiction, it is natural for Congress to say so in the statute, and failure to do so will negative the purpose of Congress in this regard. We have an example of this in the attempted application of the prohibitions of the antitrust law to acts done by citizens of the United States against other such citizens in a foreign country. *American Banana Co. v. United Fruit Co.*, 213 U.S. 347 (1909). That was a civil case, but as the statute is criminal as well as civil, it appears an analogy.

But the same rule of interpretation should not be applied to criminal statutes which are, as a class, not logically dependent on their locality for the government's jurisdiction, but are enacted because of the right of the government to defend itself against obstruction, or fraud wherever perpetrated, especially if committed by its own citizens, officers, or agents. Some such offenses can only be committed within the territorial jurisdiction diction of the government because of the local acts required to constitute them. Others are such that to limit their locus to the strictly territorial jurisdiction would be greatly to curtail the scope and usefulness of the statute and leave open a large immunity for frauds as easily committed by citizens on the high seas and in foreign countries as at home. In such cases, Congress has not thought it necessary to make specific provision in the law that the locus shall include the high seas and foreign countries, but allows it to be inferred from the nature of the offense.

UNITED STATES v. LARSEN

952 F.2d 1099 (9th Cir. 1991)

T.G. NELSON, CIRCUIT JUDGE:

Charles Edward Larsen was convicted for his involvement in an international marijuana smuggling operation * * *. Larsen challenges the legality of his conviction on numerous grounds, including the court's extraterritorial application of 21 U.S.C. § 841(a)(1). We affirm.

Larsen's conviction was based on evidence which established that he, along with codefendants and numerous other individuals, conspired to import shipments of Southeast Asian marijuana into the United States from 1985 to 1987, and to distribute the marijuana in the United States. The profits from these ventures were concealed by a fictitious partnership created by the defendant and others. This partnership was used to purchase the shipping vessel intended to transport the marijuana. During some of the smuggling operations, Larsen served as captain of the vessel.

Under Count Eight, Larsen was convicted of aiding and abetting codefendant Walter Ulrich in the crime of knowing and intentional possession with intent to distribute marijuana in violation of 21 U.S.C. § 841(a)(1). The marijuana was seized by customs inspectors from a ship on the high seas outside of Singapore. Larsen claims that the district court erred when it denied his motion to dismiss Count Eight because 21 U.S.C. § 841(a)(1) does not have extraterritorial jurisdiction. A district court's jurisdiction is a matter of law, and reviewed de novo.

Congress is empowered to attach extraterritorial effect to its penal statutes so long as the statute does not violate the due process clause of the Fifth Amendment. There is a presumption against extraterritorial application when a statute is silent on the matter. However, this court has given extraterritorial effect to penal statutes when congressional intent to do so is clear. Since 21 U.S.C. § 841(a)(1) is silent about its extraterritorial application, we are "faced with finding the construction that Congress intended."*

The Supreme Court has explained that to limit the locus of some offenses "to the strictly territorial jurisdiction would be greatly to curtail the scope and usefulness of the statute and leave open a large immunity for frauds as easily committed by citizens on the high seas and in foreign countries as at home." *United States v. Bowman*, 260 U.S. 94 (1922). Congressional intent to attach extraterritorial application "may be inferred from the nature of the offenses and Congress' other legislative efforts to eliminate the type of crime involved." *United States v. Thomas*, 893 F.2d 1066 (9th Cir. 1990).

Until now, the Ninth Circuit has not applied this "intent of congress/nature of the offense test" to 21 U.S.C. § 841(a)(1); however, four other circuits have. They all held that Congress did intend the statute to have extraterritorial effect.

---

* 21 U.S.C. § 841(a) provides:
Except as authorized by this subchapter, it shall be unlawful for any person knowingly or intentionally—

(1) to manufacture, distribute, or dispense, or possess with intent to manufacture, distribute, or dispense, a controlled substance; or

(2) to create, distribute, or dispense, or possess with intent to distribute or dispense, a counterfeit substance.

Eds.

The Fifth Circuit held that Congress intended that 841(a)(1) have extraterritorial effect because it was a part of the Comprehensive Drug Abuse Prevention and Control Act of 1970, and the power to control illegal drug trafficking on the high seas was an essential incident to Congress' intent to halt drug abuse in the United States. *United States v. Baker,* 609 F.2d [134 (5th Cir. 1980)].

The Third Circuit held that Congressional intent to apply 841(a)(1) extraterritorially could be implied because "Congress undoubtedly intended to prohibit conspiracies to [distribute] controlled substances into the United States ... as part of its continuing effort to contain the evils caused on American soil by foreign as well as domestic suppliers of illegal narcotics.... To deny such use of the criminal provisions 'would be greatly to curtail the scope and usefulness of the statute[ ].' " *United States v. Wright–Barker,* 784 F.2d 161 (3d Cir. 1986) (quoting *Bowman*).

The First Circuit concluded that the district court had jurisdiction over a crime committed on the high seas in violation of 841(a)(1) because "[a] sovereign may exercise jurisdiction over acts done outside its geographical jurisdiction which are intended to produce detrimental effects within it." *United States v. Arra,* 630 F.2d 836, 840 (1st Cir.1980).

The Second Circuit similarly held that "because section 841(a)(1) properly applies to schemes to distribute controlled substances within the United States," its extraterritorial application was proper. *United States v. Orozco–Prada,* 732 F.2d 1076 (1984).

Extraterritorial application of a drug possession/distribution statute comports with the reasoning behind the Supreme Court's *Bowman* decision, since such a statute is "not logically dependent on [its] locality for the Government's jurisdiction, but [was] enacted because of the right of the government to defend itself against obstruction, or fraud wherever perpetrated" and "[i]t would be going too far to say that because Congress does not fix any locus it intended to exclude the high seas in respect of this crime."

Defendant claims that Congress intended to limit section 841(a)(1) to only territorial crimes, as demonstrated by its later enactment of 21 U.S.C. § 955c, *recodified at* 46 U.S.C.App. § 1903, which expressly confers jurisdiction over the high seas in cases dealing with controlled substance possession and distribution. Defendant implies that in providing a separate statute which expressly governs the high seas, Congress acknowledged that the former statute did not.

If the two statutes had precisely the same provisions, beyond the extraterritoriality issue, defendant's argument might have some merit. However, there are other differences between the statutes that can explain Congress' intent in enacting § 1903. For example,

§ 1903 does not require intent to distribute, as does § 841(a)(1). Recognizing this, the Second Circuit held that Congress did not enact § 1903 to fill a void left by the silence in § 841(a)(1) as to its extraterritorial effect but, rather, to extend drug possession/distribution laws to those cases where it was not possible to show intent to distribute. *Orozco-Prada*; see also *United States v. Cruz–Valdez*, 743 F.2d 1547 (11th Cir. 1985) ("a review of the legislative history accompanying [1903] reveals no intention by Congress to make [it] the sole statute for prosecution within the customs waters or to curb the use of § 841 ... in those circumstances" since "[d]ifferences in the statutes and their interpretation might lead the government to apply the statutes differently.")

Furthermore, as the Eleventh Circuit pointed out in a case dealing with a related matter, there is an enhanced penalty available for crimes charged under § 841(a)(1) which is not available under § 1903.[2]

Larsen cites to a passing reference in *Hayes* which stated that Congress accepted the views of representatives from the Department of Justice and the DEA who testified that the Comprehensive Drug Abuse Prevention and Control Act of 1970 did not apply to American ships on the high seas. While the *Hayes* court acknowledged that some might conclude that § 841(a)(1) does not apply extraterritorially because of this Congressional testimony, the court nevertheless held that § 841(a)(1) did have extraterritorial application.

In affirming Larsen's conviction, we now join the First, Second, Third, and Fifth Circuit Courts in finding that 21 U.S.C. § 841(a)(1) has extraterritorial jurisdiction. We hold that Congress' intent can be implied because illegal drug trafficking, which the statute is designed to prevent, regularly involves importation of drugs from international sources.

UNITED STATES v. MARTINELLI

62 M.J. 52 (C.A.A.F. 2005)

JUDGE ERDMANN delivered the opinion of the court.

This case presents yet another issue arising from the prosecution of servicemembers for violating federal criminal statutes relating to child pornography * * *. Specialist Christopher Martinelli's convictions are based upon violations of the Child Pornography Prevention Act of 1996 (CPPA), 18 U.S.C. § 2252A, the same

---

2. The difference is fifteen years, rather than five, in cases involving a quantity of marijuana exceeding 1000 pounds. 21 U.S.C. § 841(b)(6).

statute that we addressed in *United States v. O'Connor*, 58 M.J. 450 (C.A.A.F. 2003), and in *United States v. Mason*, 60 M.J. 15 (C.A.A.F 2004).

Unlike the circumstances in *O'Connor* and *Mason*, however, the conduct underlying Martinelli's conviction occurred outside the United States—specifically in Darmstadt, Germany. We granted review of this case to examine the question of whether the CPPA applies to conduct engaged in outside the territorial boundaries of the United States when charged under clause 3 of Article 134, Uniform Code of Military Justice (UCMJ), 10 U.S.C. § 934 (2000).

We hold that the CPPA does not have extraterritorial application and therefore does not extend to Martinelli's conduct in Germany. * * *

Martinelli's CPPA convictions are grounded in four discrete actions that he took with respect to images of "child pornography." Beginning in January 1999 and continuing through January 2000, Martinelli downloaded images of child pornography from the Internet using computers located at the off-post Netzwork Internet Cafe in Darmstadt, Germany. He would search Internet websites and log into Internet chat rooms in order to communicate with individuals willing to send him images. He would ultimately secure the images through one of two distinct routes: (1) he would receive materials via electronic mail (e-mail) sent by other individuals to e-mail accounts that he maintained with either Yahoo! or Hotmail or (2) he would be directed by individuals to their respective web pages, from which Martinelli would secure the images directly. Under either scenario, he would download the images from the e-mail attachments or web page contents to the hard drive of a computer at the Netzwork Cafe. Martinelli received at least sixty-four images of child pornography in this fashion.

After receiving the images, Martinelli would copy them in order to distribute them to other individuals in the form of attachments to e-mail transmissions. He transmitted some of these images to other individuals via his Yahoo! and Hotmail accounts, sending approximately twenty such messages over the relevant time period.

Martinelli also copied the images from the hard drives of the computers at the Netzwork Cafe to a separate disk, which he then took back to his barracks at the Cambrai Fritsch Kaserne, a United States Army installation in Darmstadt, Germany. At the barracks he would either keep the images on the disk or load them onto the hard drive of his computer.

Martinelli was charged with the following violations of the CPPA under clause 3 of Article 134:

Specification 1: knowingly mailing, transporting or shipping child pornography in interstate or foreign commerce (by computer) in violation of § 2252A(a)(1) (specifically, sending images over the Internet from the Netzwork Internet Cafe in Darmstadt, Germany);

Specification 2: knowingly receiving child pornography that has been mailed, shipped or transported in interstate or foreign commerce (by computer) in violation of § 2252A(a)(2)(A) (specifically, downloading images from the Internet in the Netzwork Internet Cafe in Darmstadt, Germany);

Specification 3: knowingly reproducing child pornography for distribution through the mails, or in interstate or foreign commerce (by computer) in violation of § 2252A(a)(3) (specifically, downloading images from the Internet; copying them to hard drive and transmitting the copied files to approximately twenty individuals over the Internet in the Netzwork Internet Cafe in Darmstadt, Germany);

Specification 4: knowingly possessing child pornography on land and in a building used by and under the control of the United States Government in violation of § 2252A(a)(5)(A) (specifically, possessing approximately fifty diskettes containing child pornography in buildings at the Cambrai Fritsch Kaserne).

* * * Whether Congress intended the CPPA to have extraterritorial application is a question of statutory interpretation. Interpretation of a statute and its legislative history are questions of law that we review de novo. * * *

The question we address today is not the jurisdiction of the UCMJ itself, but rather whether the CPPA has extraterritorial application under clause 3 of Article 134.[4] * * *

The extraterritorial application of Federal statutes does not involve any question as to Congress' authority to enforce its criminal laws beyond the territorial boundaries of the United States— Congress clearly has that authority. *United States v. Bowman*, 260 U.S. 94 (1922). Rather, the question here is whether Congress has in fact exercised that authority, which is a matter of statutory construction. *Equal Employment Opportunity Commission v. Arabian American Oil Co. (Aramco)*, 499 U.S. 244 (1991).

The Supreme Court has recognized as a longstanding principle of American law "that legislation of Congress, unless a contrary

---

4. The question of the extraterritorial application of federal statutes has nothing to do with the jurisdiction of the federal courts. It is a question of substantive law, which turns on the intent of Congress that a particular statute have extraterritorial application. See *Hartford Fire Ins. Co. v. California*, 509 U.S. 764 (1993) (Scalia, J., dissenting).

intent appears, is meant to apply only within the territorial jurisdiction of the United States." We must assume that Congress legislates against the backdrop of the presumption against extraterritoriality. Unless the "affirmative intention" of Congress to give extraterritorial effect to a statute is "clearly expressed," it is presumed that the statute is "primarily concerned with domestic conditions."

The presumption against extraterritoriality has been recognized in the specific context of criminal statutes, with an "exception" for a certain class of offenses:

> Crimes against private individuals or their property, like assaults, murder, burglary, larceny, robbery, arson, embezzlement, and fraud of all kinds, which affect the peace and good order of the community, must of course, be committed within the territorial jurisdiction of the government where it may properly exercise it. If punishment of them is to be extended to include those committed outside of the strict territorial jurisdiction, it is natural for Congress to say so in the statute, and failure to do so will negative the purpose of Congress in this regard....

> But the same rule of interpretation should not be applied to criminal statutes which are, as a class, not logically dependent on their locality for the Government's jurisdiction, but are enacted because of the right of the Government to defend itself against obstruction, or fraud wherever perpetrated, especially if committed by its own citizens, officer or agents. Some such offenses can only be committed within the territorial jurisdiction of the Government because of the local acts required to constitute them. Others are such that to limit their locus to the strictly territorial jurisdiction would be greatly to curtail the scope and usefulness of the statute and leave open a large immunity for frauds as easily committed by citizens on the high seas and in foreign countries as at home. In such cases, Congress has not thought it necessary to make specific provision in the law that the locus shall include the high seas and foreign countries, but allows it to be inferred from the nature of the offense.

Bowman. We have previously characterized *Bowman* as drawing a distinction between:

> (1) statutes punishing crimes against the peace and good order of the community (which apply only to [acts] committed within the territorial jurisdiction of the United States unless Congress had specifically directed otherwise); and (2) statutes punishing fraud or obstructions against the United States Government

(which include by implication acts which were committed in foreign countries).

United States v. Gladue, 4 M.J. 1 (C.M.A. 1977).

The principles articulated by the Supreme Court in *Aramco* and *Bowman* can be harmonized to provide the following analytical framework for assessing whether the CPPA was intended to have extraterritorial effect: Unless the CPPA can be viewed as falling within the second category described in *Bowman* ("criminal statutes which are, as a class, ... enacted because of the right of the government to defend itself against obstruction, or fraud wherever perpetrated," the statute is subject to the presumption against extraterritoriality recognized in both *Bowman* and *Aramco*).

We do not believe that the CPPA can be viewed as a "second category" offense under Bowman and thus exempt from application of the presumption against extraterritoriality. The ultimate objective behind the criminal proscription of activities pertaining to child pornography is to protect children from abuse. While few crimes are more serious or morally repugnant, child abuse does not involve "fraud" or "obstruction" against the United States Government. Rather, child abuse epitomizes that class of "[c]rimes against private individuals [including children]" that "affect the peace and good order of the community" described in the first category of *Bowman*.

We are aware of the body of law, primarily from the Ninth Circuit, that does not read the second category in Bowman as limited to crimes against the Government. Those cases all trace their roots, in one fashion or another, back to *United States v. Baker*, 609 F.2d 134 (5th Cir. 1980), where the Fifth Circuit read *Bowman* as allowing a court, in the absence of any expression of congressional intent, to "infer" Congress' intent to provide for extraterritorial application "from the nature of the offenses and Congress' other legislative efforts to eliminate the type of crime involved." The *Baker* court concluded that a federal statute prohibiting drug possession with intent to distribute fell within "the second category described in Bowman" and thus was intended to apply extraterritorially.

The holding in *Baker* has been subsequently used to support the "inference" of a congressional intent for extraterritorial application in several circumstances that do not involve crimes against the Government, including child pornography–related offenses. See, e.g., *United States v. Harvey,* 2 F.3d 1318 (3d Cir. 1993)(sentencing guidelines for child pornography offenses). We disagree, however, with *Baker*'s expanded view of the "second category" offenses in *Bowman*. The phrase "inferred from the nature of the offense" in *Bowman* was clearly cast in reference to the "class" of criminal statutes involving fraud or obstruction against the Government and is not a free standing principle of statutory construction:

But the same rule of interpretation should not be applied to criminal statutes which are, as a class, not logically dependent on their locality for the Government's jurisdiction, but are enacted because of the right of the Government to defend itself against obstruction, or fraud wherever perpetrated, especially if committed by its own citizens, officers or agents.... In such cases, Congress has not thought it necessary to make specific provision in the law that the locus shall include the high seas and foreign countries, but allows it to be inferred from the nature of the offense.[6]

Accordingly, we adhere to the view we originally expressed in *Gladue*. The only category of offenses exempt under the language of *Bowman* from any presumption against extraterritoriality and for which a congressional intent for extraterritorial application can be "inferred from the nature of the offense" are those involving "obstructions" and "frauds" against the Government.

Our conclusion that the CPPA is subject to a presumption against extraterritoriality under *Aramco* and *Bowman* does not end our inquiry into its applicability. We now "look to see whether language in the [relevant statute] gives any indication of a congressional purpose to extend its coverage beyond places over which the United States has sovereignty or has some measure of legislative control." *Aramco*. In searching for the clear expression of congressional intent required by *Aramco*, we are not limited to the text of the statute and can "consider all available evidence about the meaning of the statute, including its text, structure, and legislative history."

Our reading of the CPPA does not find any indication in the text and structure of the statute of a congressional purpose to extend its coverage. The text and structure of the statute prohibits five categories of conduct:

- mailing, transporting or shipping child pornography in interstate or foreign commerce by any means, including by computer (18 U.S.C. § 2252A(a)(1));

- receipt or distribution of child pornography that has been mailed, shipped or transported in interstate or foreign commerce by any means, including by computer (18 U.S.C. § 2252A(a)(2)(A), (B));

---

6. We also note that the *Baker* concept of "inferring" extraterritorial intent based on the nature of the offense and Congress' other efforts to eliminate the type of crime involved could apply to almost any crime committed anywhere in the world. This would turn the presumption against extraterritorial application on its head where criminal statutes are involved.

- reproduction of child pornography for distribution by mail or interstate or foreign commerce, including by computer (18 U.S.C. § 2252A(a)(3)(A));

- sale or possession with intent to sell of (1) child pornography that has moved in interstate or foreign commerce by any means, including by computer or was produced using materials that have moved in commerce or (2) any child pornography "in the special maritime and territorial jurisdiction of the United States, or on any land or building owned by, leased to, or otherwise used by or under the control of the United States Government, or in the Indian country (as defined in section 1151)...." (18 U.S.C. § 2252A(a)(4)(A), (B)); and

- possession of (1) child pornography that has moved in interstate or foreign commerce by any means, including by computer or was produced using materials that have moved in commerce or (2) any child pornography "in the special maritime and territorial jurisdiction of the United States, or on any land or building owned by, leased to, or otherwise used by or under the control of the United States Government, or in the Indian country (as defined in section 1151)...." (18 U.S.C. § 2252A(a)(5)(A), (B)).

The criminal acts in the first three subsections all refer to the movement of child pornography "in interstate or foreign commerce," whether it be the act of moving the material itself (§ 2252A(a)(1)) or the acts of receiving, distributing or reproducing for distribution materials that have moved in that fashion (§ 2252A(a)(2)–(3)).

The criminal acts in the final two subsections are sale, possession with intent to sell, and simple possession. Under these subsections, criminal liability can attach under either of two separate circumstances. The first involves the same "interstate or foreign commerce" context attendant to the offenses in § 2252A(a)(1)–(3). The second circumstance is purely dependent on physical location or the "situs" of the defendant—if the requisite act occurs "in the special maritime and territorial jurisdiction of the United States, or on any land or building owned by, leased to or otherwise used by or under the control of the United States Government," it does not matter whether the child pornography ever moved in commerce. See § 2252A(a)(4)(A), (5)(A).

There are two aspects of the statutory language in § 2252A(a)(1)–(a)(5) that could possibly be read as expressing congressional intention as to extraterritorial effect—(1) the references to "interstate or foreign commerce" and (2) the situs language in § 2252A(a)(4)(A), (a)(5)(A). In terms of the former, they are not, in and of themselves, a "clear expression" of any congressional intention that the acts proscribed by the statute constitute a federal crime no matter where in the world they occur. Rather, we view them as a straightforward reference to the source authority of Congress for proscribing these acts as criminal in the first instance, i.e., the Commerce Clause of the United States Constitution * * * .

Many Acts of Congress are based on the authority of that body to regulate commerce among the several States, and the parts of these Acts setting forth the basis for legislative jurisdiction will obviously refer to such commerce in one way or another. If we were to permit possible, or even plausible, interpretations of language such as that involved here to override the presumption against extraterritorial application, there would be little left of the presumption. The use of the term "foreign commerce" in addition to "interstate commerce" does not alter that conclusion, as the Supreme Court "has repeatedly held" that even statutes that expressly refer to "foreign commerce" do not apply abroad.

That leaves the situs language in §§ 2252A(a)(4)(A) and 2252A(a)(5)(A) as a possible basis for overcoming the presumption against extraterritoriality. There are three alternative locations referenced in the statute:

- "the special maritime and territorial jurisdiction of the United States"; or

- "any land or building owned by, leased to, or otherwise used by or under the control of the United States Government"; or

- "the Indian country" (as defined in 18 U.S.C. § 1151).

The reference to Indian country reflects a congressional focus on complex jurisdictional issues that flow from the unique, and inherently domestic, relationship between the United States Government and American Indians. It certainly does not reflect any clear legislative concern for matters arising outside the territorial boundaries of the United States.

The term "special maritime and territorial jurisdiction of the United States" is, like "Indian country," a term of art that carries its own distinct definition. See 18 U.S.C. § 7. That term of art has been the subject of different interpretations as to its extraterritorial reach, particularly whether it extends to lands within the territory of a sovereign foreign nation. * * *

The remaining situs language refers to conduct occurring "on any land or building owned by, leased to, or otherwise used by or under the control of the United States Government." That language undoubtedly reflects a congressional intent to criminally proscribe conduct in physical locations where the United States

Government enjoys some type of proprietary control over the location. The language, however, does not provide clear evidence of a congressional intent that the statute should apply outside the boundaries of the United States. That language could just as easily apply only to land and buildings located within the territorial United States such as national parks, federal office buildings and domestic military installations.

We also note that the language concerning "land or building" does not stand alone, but is instead bracketed by language dealing with the "special maritime and territorial jurisdiction of the United States" and "the Indian country (as defined in section 1151)." Under the canon of statutory construction noscitur a sociis (a word is known by the company it keeps), it is reasonable to conclude that Congress intended the "land or building" language to have the same domestic application as evidenced in the surrounding language. See *Amgen Inc. v. Smith*, 357 F.3d 103 (D.C.Cir. 2004) (applying the canon of noscitur a sociis to support consistent interpretation of separate phrases within a statutory section); *In re Application of the United States for an Order Authorizing the Roving Interception of Oral Communications*, 349 F.3d 1132 (9th Cir. 2003) (using the canon of noscitur a sociis to interpret a section of the federal wiretapping statute).

We do not view the statutory phrases discussed above, either individually or collectively, as the type of "clear expression" of congressional intention required by *Aramco*. The analysis dictated by *Bowman* and *Aramco* requires that the statutory text reflect a clear expression of Congress' intent that the statute have extraterritorial reach. The language must be clear enough to overcome a presumption that it was intended to apply domestically, not simply lend itself to a plausible argument that it applies overseas. Mere plausibility is not sufficient to overcome the presumption. In the context of that presumption, we do not view the "any land or building" language of §§ 2252A(a)(4)(A) and 2252A(a)(5)(A) as a "clear expression" by Congress that it have extraterritorial application.

Having concluded that the text and structure of the CPPA do not express any clear intent by Congress that the statute apply extraterritorially, we reach the same conclusion with respect to its legislative history. The clear focus of that legislative history is on the patent evils of child pornography and the new dimension that computer technology adds to those evils. Although the history contains extensive discussion of those issues, it is devoid of any reference to issues of extraterritoriality, much less any clear expression of congressional intent in that regard.

Our conclusion regarding the absence of any clearly expressed intent by Congress that the CPPA apply extraterritorially is bolstered by the numerous instances where such intent has been clearly expressed. Even in the specific context of child pornography, Congress knows how to makes its intention clear that a particular criminal statute extend to conduct engaged in outside the United States. See, e.g., 18 U.S.C. § 2260(b)("a person who, outside the United States, knowingly receives, transports, . . . any visual depiction of a minor engaging in sexually explicit conduct . . . intending that the visual depiction will be imported into the United States"); 18 U.S.C. § 2251(c)(1)("[a]ny person who . . . employs, uses, . . . any minor to engage in, or who has a minor assist any other person to engage in, any sexually explicit conduct outside of the United States").

Congress has clearly expressed its intent in other criminal statutes as well: the Biological Weapons Anti–Terrorism Act of 1989 provides, "There is extraterritorial federal jurisdiction over an offense under this section committed by or against a national of the United States," 18 U.S.C. § 175(a); the Maritime Drug Law Enforcement Act provides, "This section is intended to reach acts of possession, manufacture, or distribution committed outside the territorial jurisdiction of the United States." 46 U.S.C. app. § 1903(h).

Congress also amended 18 U.S.C. § 7 (2000), which defines the "special maritime and territorial jurisdiction" of the United States, as part of the Uniting and Strengthening America by Providing Appropriate Tools Required to Intercept and Obstruct Terrorism Act of 2001 (USA PATRIOT Act). The USA PATRIOT Act amendments inserted a new provision that, with respect to "offenses committed by or against a national of the United States," extends the special maritime and territorial jurisdiction of the United States under 18 U.S.C. § 7 to the "premises of . . . diplomatic, consular, military or other . . . missions . . . in foreign States. . . ." USA PATRIOT Act § 804 (codified at 18 U.S.C. § 7(9)(A)). This is a clear expression of congressional intent that a crime committed in "the special maritime and territorial jurisdiction" now includes conduct that may in some instances have occurred inside the boundaries of a foreign nation.

Finally, we note Congress' ability to make its intentions in this regard clear with respect to a broad range of criminal acts rather than a single crime. In legislation proscribing "[a]cts of terrorism transcending national boundaries," Congress has provided that the statute extends to "conduct occurring outside of the United States in addition to conduct occurring inside of the United States" and that "[t]here is extraterritorial Federal jurisdiction" over the wide range of offenses described in the statute. See 18 U.S.C. § 2332(e), (g)(1). These examples of express congressional intent constitute various indicia, none of which are present with respect to the CPPA.

To reach the conclusion urged by the Government, that Congress intended the CPPA to criminalize conduct inside the boundaries of sovereign foreign countries, we would have to disregard the *Bowman* and *Aramco* presumption and the absence of these indicia. The rules of statutory construction laid down by the Supreme Court simply do not support that conclusion.

Accordingly, we cannot view the CPPA as overcoming the presumption against extraterritorial application dictated by *Bowman* and *Aramco*. The charges against Martinelli fall squarely within the example the President described in the Manual for Courts–Martial, i.e., "a person may not be punished under clause 3 of Article 134 when the act occurred in a foreign country merely because that act would have been an offense under the United States Code had the act occurred in the United States." As a result, there is a substantial basis in law and fact for viewing Martinelli's guilty pleas to the CPPA-based clause 3 offenses under Article 134 for conduct occurring in Germany as improvident. * * *

GIRKE, CHIEF JUDGE, CONCURRING IN PART AND DISSENTING IN PART.

* * * I cannot agree that the CPPA does not have extraterritorial application. * * *

The Supreme Court explained the presumption against extraterritoriality in *Equal Employment Opportunity Commission v. Arabian American Oil Company (Aramco)*. *Aramco* was a civil case that involved racial discrimination in employment practices by United States companies who employ United States citizens abroad. The Supreme Court thus applied the presumption against extraterritoriality to employment practices abroad—which is exactly the kind of domestic concern to which the presumption should apply. In doing so, the Supreme Court made clear that the presumption applies unless the "language in the [relevant statute] gives any indication of a congressional purpose to extend its coverage beyond places over which the United States has sovereignty or some measure of legislative control."

In *United States v. Bowman*, the Supreme Court was confronted with a jurisdictional issue in a case involving three American citizens and one British citizen who planned to defraud a corporation in which the United States was a stockholder. The statute under which the defendants were to be prosecuted contained no explicit grant of extraterritorial jurisdiction to try the offenders on the high seas, where the crime took place. In response to the absence of an explicit statement of extraterritorial application in that particular criminal statute, the Supreme Court applied and clarified the exception to the presumption against extraterritoriality.

The Supreme Court delineated two types of criminal offenses in *Bowman*. The nature of some criminal offenses, such as those crimes against private individuals or their property which "affect the peace and good order of the community," is such that the acts that constitute the offenses occur locally. But other criminal offenses "are such that to limit their locus to the strictly territorial jurisdiction would be greatly to curtail the scope and usefulness of the statute...." Thus, when Congress does not explicitly state in the plain language of a particular criminal statute that it intends for that statute to apply extraterritorially, courts can infer such intent "from the nature of the offenses and Congress' other legislative efforts to eliminate the type of crime involved." [*United States v. Vasquez–Velasco*, 15 F.3d 833 (9th Cir. 1994).]

I interpret the *Bowman* language as drawing a dividing line between those criminal offenses that are "domestic" in nature and those whose nature "warrant[s] a broad sweep of power." For example, a U.S. citizen's assault on his next-door neighbor would affect the "peace and good order of the community" in his neighborhood and is a domestic crime. The nature of this offense does not warrant a sweep of power any broader than that provided to the local police force to arrest him. However, if a U.S. citizen commits a criminal offense whose effects are not confined to one particular situs—for example, smuggling illegal drugs between countries or trafficking in child pornography over the Internet—then, the nature of that offense warrants a broader sweep of power.

The majority reads the language in *Aramco* and *Bowman* to allow an exception to the presumption only for certain types of criminal statutes—those enacted so that the Government can defend itself against obstruction or fraud. However, I do not read this language as narrowly as the majority. Notably, Bowman was a case about fraud against the Government and, thus, the limiting language on which the majority relies directly applies to the circumstances of that case. * * *

Child pornography, particularly over the Internet, is just the type of offense that falls squarely within the *Bowman* criminal statute exception to the presumption against extraterritoriality. Child pornography is not an "inherently domestic" crime because it can be received from and sent to the United States by a few simple key strokes on the computer. Images of minors engaging in sexually explicit conduct proscribed by the CPPA can travel through the Internet easily, providing ready access to pedophiles.

Therefore, the first underlying reason for the presumption against extraterritoriality—that Congress legislates with domestic concerns in mind—is inapplicable to offenses related to trafficking child pornography. Concluding that the Congress did not intend to reach those individuals who can simply download pornographic images to a website from another country and e-mail them through servers that are located in the United States is inconsistent with Congress' goal of eradicating child pornography. The majority's holding "greatly . . . curtail[s] the scope and usefulness" of the CPPA by concluding that § 2252A does not apply extraterritorially.

Furthermore, the other underlying reason given for the presumption against extraterritoriality—to avoid unintended clashes with the governments of foreign countries—is also inapplicable to offenses targeted by the CPPA. It is well settled that the United States can assert jurisdiction over offenses that occur outside the territorial jurisdiction of the United States, but that affect the United States. And the United States Government is not invading some right or taking away some interest of a foreign government by prosecuting those individuals who send child pornography into the United States from that foreign country or who receive child pornography that has been sent through the United States. * * *

Of course the question in this case is whether Germany would protest U.S. jurisdiction over Appellant. And the answer is certainly no. Because of the Status of Forces Agreement that exists between the United States and Germany, Germany agreed that the United States would have the right to exercise jurisdiction over all military servicemembers that the U.S. sends to Germany. * * *

I disagree * * * with the majority's determination that the CPPA does not apply extraterritorially to reach Appellant's offenses. I believe the Bowman exception to the presumption against extraterritoriality applies in this case based on the nature of the offenses which the CPPA targets and because to deny application of the exception would greatly curtail the scope and usefulness of the CPPA. Congressional intent for a statute to apply extraterritorially can be inferred in criminal statutes, even in the absence of an explicit statement, based on the text of the entire statute, its legislative history and structure. A reading of the CPPA, together with the comprehensive scheme of the Act and repeated efforts by Congress to eradicate child exploitation and expand federal jurisdiction over these types of offenses, shows a clear congressional intent for the CPPA to apply extraterritorially to Appellant's acts in this case. Therefore, I must respectfully dissent * * *.

Notes and Questions

1. Locality. *Larsen* shows that the courts of appeals take a fairly lenient approach in finding extraterritorial jurisdiction for the application of drug statutes, while *Martinelli* shows the court looking for greater clarity from Congress. Is narcotics distribution the type of crime that is "not logically dependent on their locality for the Government's jurisdiction," as stated in *Bowman*? If so, why is the transmission of child pornography over the internet closer to a crime dependent on locality? Isn't the internet the quintessential medium that is not dependent in the least on national borders?

2. Other Statutes. Should it matter in interpreting a statute that there are other provisions that explicitly apply to extraterritorial conduct? For example, 21 U.S.C. § 952(a), which was also charged in *Larsen*, provides: "It shall be unlawful to import into the customs territory of the United States from any place outside thereof (but within the United States), or to import into the United States from any place outside thereof, any controlled substance in schedule I or II of subchapter I of this chapter, or any narcotic drug in schedule III, IV, or V of subchapter I of this chapter. . . ." Should this statute be used as an interpretive guide in determining Congressional intent in adopting 21 U.S.C. § 841(a)? As the cases acknowledge, Congress can easily expand the scope of the statutory prohibition to include extraterritorial conduct by making it clear in the language. Does that argue in favor of a narrower interpretation when there is not an explicit extension of jurisdiction to conduct outside the United States?

3. Another View of the CPPA. Consider the following analysis of the CPPA that argues in favor of extraterritorial jurisdiction over an offense such as the one rejected in *Martinelli*:

> With the recent technological advances in communication, child exploitation has become an international problem. There can be no doubt that the Internet makes children targets for pedophiles around the globe. "As an international system, the Internet . . . is considered the absolute best hunting ground (for a) pedophile, and the most efficient pornography distribution engine ever conceived." [Lesli C. Esposito, *Regulating the Internet: The New Battle Against Child Pornography*, 30 CASE W. RES. J. INT'L L. 541 (1998)] According to Interpol, an international police organization, the Internet was the genesis of child pornography rings in Europe involving over 30,000 pedophiles. Given the fact that the Internet allows pedophiles from any country to target children, neither 18 U.S.C. § 1470 nor 18 U.S.C. § 2422 can be logically dependant on locality or territoriality for the jurisdiction. Rather, these statutes were enacted based on Congress's sense that it needed to protect the state and the people against such social harm "wherever perpetrated, especially if committed by its own citizens, officers, or agents."

Christopher L. Blakesley & Dan Stigall, *Wings for Talons: The Case for the Extraterritorial Jurisdiction over Sexual Exploitation of Children Through Cyberspace*, 50 WAYNE L. REV. 109 (2004). Professor Blakesley and Mr. Stigall criticized the majority in *Martinelli* for misinterpreting the statute. They argue: "Given the unique, international nature of the

Internet, and the Congressional intent to combat sexual exploitation of children over the Internet, 18 U.S.C. § 2252A is clearly part of a legislative scheme that would be greatly curtailed if not given extraterritorial application. Accordingly, the CAAF and all federal courts should infer from the legislative history, the type of crime in question, and the impact on the relevant legislative scheme, that 18 U.S.C. § 2252A applies extraterritorially." Christopher L. Blakesley & Dan Stigall, *The Myopia of* U.S. v. Martinelli: *Extraterritorial Jurisdiction in the 21st Century*, 38 Geo. Wash. Int'l L. Rev. ___ (2006).

4. Extending Jurisdiction to Foreign Travel. Congress enacted legislation to combat foreign sex tourism, in which Americans would travel abroad to engage in sex acts with underage minors. In some countries, there is little enforcement of local laws prohibiting such acts, and so the United States has tried to curtail such conduct by its citizens and residents by expanding federal jurisdiction to cover conduct while a person is traveling in "foreign commerce." 18 U.S.C. § 2423 provides in relevant part:

(b) Travel with intent to engage in illicit sexual conduct.—A person who travels in interstate commerce or travels into the United States, or a United States citizen or an alien admitted for permanent residence in the United States who travels in foreign commerce, for the purpose of engaging in any illicit sexual conduct with another person shall be fined under this title or imprisoned not more than 30 years, or both.

(c) Engaging in illicit sexual conduct in foreign places.—Any United States citizen or alien admitted for permanent residence who travels in foreign commerce, and engages in any illicit sexual conduct with another person shall be fined under this title or imprisoned not more than 30 years, or both.

(d) Ancillary offenses.—Whoever, for the purpose of commercial advantage or private financial gain, arranges, induces, procures, or facilitates the travel of a person knowing that such a person is traveling in interstate commerce or foreign commerce for the purpose of engaging in illicit sexual conduct shall be fined under this title, imprisoned not more than 30 years, or both.

(f) Definition.—As used in this section, the term "illicit sexual conduct" means (1) a sexual act (as defined in section 2246) with a person under 18 years of age that would be in violation of chapter 109A if the sexual act occurred in the special maritime and territorial jurisdiction of the United States; or (2) any commercial sex act (as defined in section 1591) with a person under 18 years of age.

Note that § 2423(c) reaches any foreign travel in which illicit sexual conduct occurs, which covers more than just persons who travel for the purpose of engaging in such acts. Consider the following factual scenario:

Bredimus, a United States citizen, left his residence in Texas to travel to Bangkok, Thailand to meet with suppliers for his manufacturing company. After attending scheduled business meetings, Bredimus had a two-day break before his scheduled flight back to the United States. After his last business meeting, Bredimus contacted Suhongsaha, and hired her to accompany him to Chiang Rai Province in Northern Thailand as a procurer and interpreter. Bredimus and Suhongsaha traveled to the city of Mai Sao and rented two rooms at the Srisamoot Hotel. Bredimus asked Suhongsa to find young boys or girls who would come to the hotel to meet him. That same day, Bredimus videotaped himself engaged in a sex act with a thirteen-year old Thai boy at the hotel. Upon his arrival back in the United States, an Immigraiton and Customs Enforcement (ICE) agent searched Bredimus's luggage and seized the videotape. After it was viewed by ICE agents, Bredimus admitted that he was the adult in the video and gave a complete statement, including information about Suhongsaha's assistance. He said it was the first time he had ever done such a thing. Federal prosecutors consider charging Bredimus with violating § 2423.

What provisions of § 2423, if any, can Bredimus be indicted for violating? Are there any constitutional arguments he can raise regarding the power of Congress to reach his conduct? Should prosecutors charge Suhongsaha with violating United States law? Would she have a stronger constitutional argument than Bredimus?

5. Human Trafficking. A significant problem that has not been adequately addressed is the international human trafficking, especially of women and children, many of whom are forced into virtual slave labor, sometimes involving the sex trade. While there are international conventions addressing the issue, it is only recently that Congress and a few states have passed legislation specifically targeting trafficking. The Trafficking Victims protection Act of 2000, 18 U.S.C. §§ 1581 *et seq*, criminalizes trafficking for purposes of sexual services of women or children, peonage, slavery, and involuntary servitude. A few states also now have statutes that criminalize trafficking as its own crime, separate from kidnapping, murder, or other related crimes. One of the federal criminal provisions reads:

> Whoever knowingly recruits, harbors, transports, provides, or obtains by any means, any person for labor or services in violation of this chapter shall be fined under this title or imprisoned not more than 20 years, or both. If death results from the violation of this section, or if the violation includes kidnapping or an attempt to kidnap, aggravated sexual abuse, or the attempt to commit aggravated sexual abuse, or an attempt to kill, the defendant shall be fined under this title or imprisoned for any term of years or life, or both.

What is the *mens rea* of the trafficking crime? What does the *mens rea* modify? Which part, or parts, of the crime might occur outside the territory of the United States? What advantages, if any, do you see for specifically criminalizing trafficking, rather than relying on kidnapping, sexual assault, or murder statutes?

E. INVESTIGATING AND PROSECUTING VIOLATIONS OF FOREIGN LAW

1. Investigative Requests From Foreign Governments

Transnational crimes are difficult to prosecute in part because gathering evidence across borders can be cumbersome and time-consuming. The traditional method for compelling a person in another country to produce evidence was by means of "letters rogatory," which are letters of request from the judicial authority of one country to the courts of the recipient country requesting assistance from those judicial authorities to obtain evidence. These letters are based on principles of international comity and not any specific treaty or other enforceable obligation. In the United States, 18 U.S.C. § 1782(a) governs the conduct of the courts in responding to letters rogatory from foreign courts or international tribunals:

> (a) The district court of the district in which a person resides or is found may order him to give his testimony or statement or to produce a document or other thing for use in a proceeding in a foreign or international tribunal, including criminal investigations conducted before formal accusation. The order may be made pursuant to a letter rogatory issued, or request made, by a foreign or international tribunal or upon the application of any interested person and may direct that the testimony or statement be given, or the document or other thing be produced, before a person appointed by the court. By virtue of his appointment, the person appointed has power to administer any necessary oath and take the testimony or statement. The order may prescribe the practice and procedure, which may be in whole or part the practice and procedure of the foreign country or the international tribunal, for taking the testimony or statement or producing the document or other thing. To the extent that the order does not prescribe otherwise, the testimony or statement shall be taken, and the document or other thing produced, in accordance with the Federal Rules of Civil Procedure.

> A person may not be compelled to give his testimony or statement or to produce a document or other thing in violation of any legally applicable privilege.

In civil matters, The Hague Convention on the Taking of Evidence Abroad in Civil and Commercial Matters can provide another procedure for discovering and gathering evidence that avoids having to resort to the courts or diplomatic channels. The Securities & Exchange Commission (SEC) has entered into a number of Memoranda of Understanding (MOU) with regulatory counterparts in other nations that permit information sharing and, in some instances, the use of one regulator's compulsory authority to gather evidence for use by the requesting regulator. Regulators of the largest securities markets have signed MOUs with the SEC, including the European Union, United Kingdom, Canada, Mexico, Japan, Germany, France, and Russia.

In the criminal arena, the United States has negotiated a number of Mutual Legal Assistance Treaties (MLATs) that provide for specified procedures in criminal cases for obtaining testimony and documents. As the targets of a criminal investigation, those who may be compelled to produce evidence can seek to resist by invoking any protections in the treaty or arguing that the request does not come within its terms. In *In re Commissioner's Subpoenas*, 325 F.3d 1287 (11th Cir. 2003), the court explained why MLATs are the preferred method for obtaining evidence in criminal investigations:

> Traditionally, evidence sought by a foreign government had to be obtained through a process whereby a written request known as a "letter rogatory" was sent from the court of one country to the court of another asking the receiving court to provide the assistance. A federal statute authorizes federal district courts in this country to entertain such requests and provides that "[t]he district court of the district in which a person resides or is found may order him to give his testimony or statement or to produce a document or other thing for use in a proceeding in a foreign or international tribunal, including criminal investigations conducted before formal accusation." 28 U.S.C. § 1782. Not only can a foreign tribunal bring a request in the form of a "letter rogatory," but section 1782 has been amended to also allow similar requests for assistance to be brought by "interested persons" including foreign governments in foreign investigations or proceedings and private litigants of a foreign proceeding. Requests for assistance initiated directly by an interested person rather than a foreign court are often referred to as "letters of request." Despite the apparent versatility of 28 U.S.C. § 1782, law enforcement authorities found the statute to be an unattractive option in practice because it provided wide discretion in the district court to refuse the request and did not obligate other nations to return the favor that it grants. MLATs, on the other hand, have the desired quality of compulsion as they contractually obligate the two countries to provide to each other evidence and other forms of

assistance needed in criminal cases while streamlining and enhancing the effectiveness of the process for obtaining needed evidence.

2. Domestic Conduct Affecting Other Nations

With the advent of the global economy, in which conduct in one nation can touch other nations, the scope of the criminal law has broadened. In the United States, the Foreign Corrupt Practices Act, 15 U.S.C. §§ 78dd–1 et seq., makes it a crime for a United States person or company to pay a bribe to a foreign official or political party to assist in securing or retaining business in the official's country. The law does not permit the prosecution of the foreign official, but it does allow for charges against "non-U.S. nationals" for any conduct involved in the bribery that takes place in the United States. Moreover, United States citizens and residents can be charged for their conduct anywhere in the world. In *Pasquantino v. United States*, 544 U.S. 349, 125 S.Ct. 1766, 161 L.Ed.2d 619 (2005), the Supreme Court considered whether conduct in the United States that is directed at avoiding the tax laws of Canada could constitute a violation of a domestic federal criminal statute.

PASQUANTINO v. UNITED STATES
544 U.S. 349, 125 S.Ct. 1766, 161 L.Ed.2d 619 (2005)

JUSTICE THOMAS delivered the opinion of the Court.

At common law, the revenue rule generally barred courts from enforcing the tax laws of foreign sovereigns. The question presented in this case is whether a plot to defraud a foreign government of tax revenue violates the federal wire fraud statute, 18 U.S.C. § 1343. Because the plain terms of § 1343 criminalize such a scheme, and because this construction of the wire fraud statute does not derogate from the common-law revenue rule, we hold that it does.

Petitioners Carl J. Pasquantino, David B. Pasquantino, and Arthur Hilts were indicted for and convicted of federal wire fraud for carrying out a scheme to smuggle large quantities of liquor into Canada from the United States. According to the evidence presented at trial, the Pasquantinos, while in New York, ordered liquor over the telephone from discount package stores in Maryland. They employed Hilts and others to drive the liquor over the Canadian border, without paying the required excise taxes. The drivers avoided paying taxes by hiding the liquor in their vehicles and failing to declare the goods to Canadian customs officials. During the time of petitioners' smuggling operation, between 1996 and 2000, Canada heavily taxed the importation of alcoholic beverages. Uncontested evidence at trial showed that Canadian taxes then due on alcohol purchased in the United States and transported to Canada were approximately double the liquor's purchase price. [The jury convicted the defendants of wire fraud.]

* * * We granted certiorari to resolve a conflict in the Courts of Appeals over whether a scheme to defraud a foreign government of tax revenue violates the wire fraud statute. Compare *United States v. Boots*, 80 F.3d 580 (1st Cir. 1996) (holding that a scheme to defraud a foreign nation of tax revenue does not violate the wire fraud statute), with *United States v. Trapilo*, 130 F.3d 547 (2d Cir. 1997) (holding that a scheme to defraud a foreign nation of tax revenue violates the wire fraud statute). * * * [1]

We first consider whether petitioners' conduct falls within the literal terms of the wire fraud statute. The statute prohibits using interstate wires to effect "any scheme or artifice to defraud, or for obtaining money or property by means of false or fraudulent pretenses, representations, or promises." 18 U.S.C. § 1343. Two elements of this crime, and the only two that petitioners dispute here, are that the defendant engage in a "scheme or artifice to defraud," and that the "object of the fraud ... be '[money or] property' in the victim's hands," *Cleveland v. United States*, 531 U.S. 12 (2000).

Taking the latter element first, Canada's right to uncollected excise taxes on the liquor petitioners imported into Canada is "property" in its hands. This right is an entitlement to collect money from petitioners, the possession of which is "something of value" to the Government of Canada. *McNally v. United States*, 483 U.S. 350 (1987). Valuable entitlements like these are "property" as that term ordinarily is employed. Had petitioners complied with this legal obligation, they would have paid money to Canada. Petitioners' tax evasion deprived Canada of that money, inflicting an economic injury no less than had they embezzled funds from the Canadian treasury. The object of petitioners' scheme was to deprive Canada of money legally due, and their scheme thereby had as its object the deprivation of Canada's "property."

* * * Our conclusion that the right to tax revenue is property in Canada's hands, contrary to petitioners' contentions, is consistent with *Cleveland*. In that case, the defendant, *Cleveland*, had

---

1. We express no view on the related question whether a foreign government, based on wire or mail fraud predicate offenses, may bring a civil action under the Racketeer Influenced and Corrupt Organizations Act for a scheme to defraud it of taxes. See Attorney General of Canada v. R.J. Reynolds Tobacco Holdings, Inc., 268 F.3d 103 (2d Cir. 2001) (holding that the Government of Canada cannot bring a civil RICO suit to recover for a scheme to defraud it of taxes); Republic of Honduras v. Philip Morris Cos., 341 F.3d 1253 (11th Cir. 2003) (same with respect to other foreign governments).

obtained a video poker license by making false statements on his license application. We held that a State's interest in an unissued video poker license was not "property," because the interest in choosing particular licensees was " 'purely regulatory' " and "[could not] be economic." We also noted that "the Government nowhere allege[d] that Cleveland defrauded the State of any money to which the State was entitled by law."

Cleveland is different from this case. Unlike a State's interest in allocating a video poker license to particular applicants, Canada's entitlement to tax revenue is a straightforward "economic" interest. There was no suggestion in *Cleveland* that the defendant aimed at depriving the State of any money due under the license; quite the opposite, there was "no dispute that [the defendant's partnership] paid the State of Louisiana its proper share of revenue" due. Here, by contrast, the Government alleged and proved that petitioners' scheme aimed at depriving Canada of money to which it was entitled by law. Canada could hardly have a more "economic" interest than in the receipt of tax revenue. Cleveland is therefore consistent with our conclusion that Canada's entitlement is "property" as that word is used in the wire fraud statute.

Turning to the second element at issue here, petitioners' plot was a "scheme or artifice to defraud" Canada of its valuable entitlement to tax revenue. The evidence showed that petitioners routinely concealed imported liquor from Canadian officials and failed to declare those goods on customs forms. By this conduct, they represented to Canadian customs officials that their drivers had no goods to declare. This, then, was a scheme "designed to defraud by representations," *Durland v. United States*, 161 U.S. 306 (1896), and therefore a "scheme or artifice to defraud" Canada of taxes due on the smuggled goods.

Neither the antismuggling statute, 18 U.S.C. § 546,[3] nor U.S. tax treaties convince us that petitioners' scheme falls outside the terms of the wire fraud statute.[4] Unlike the treaties and the

---

3. Section 546 provides: "Any person owning in whole or in part any vessel of the United States who employs, or participates in, or allows the employment of, such vessel for the purpose of smuggling, or attempting to smuggle, or assisting in smuggling, any merchandise into the territory of any foreign government in violation of the laws there in force, if under the laws of such foreign government any penalty or forfeiture is provided for violation of the laws of the United States respecting the customs revenue, and any citizen of, or person domiciled in, or any corporation incorpo- rated in, the United States, controlling or substantially participating in the control of any such vessel, directly or indirectly, whether through ownership of corporate shares or otherwise, and allowing the employment of said vessel for any such purpose, and any person found, or discovered to have been, on board of any such vessel so employed and participating or assisting in any such purpose, shall be fined under this title or imprisoned not more than two years, or both."

4. Any overlap between the antismuggling statute and the wire fraud statute is beside the point. The Federal

antismuggling statute, the wire fraud statute punishes fraudulent use of domestic wires, whether or not such conduct constitutes smuggling, occurs aboard a vessel, or evades foreign taxes. Petitioners would be equally liable if they had used interstate wires to defraud Canada not of taxes due, but of money from the Canadian treasury. The wire fraud statute "applies without differentiation" to these two categories of fraud. *Clark v. Martinez*, 543 U.S. 371 (2005). "To give these same words a different meaning for each category would be to invent a statute rather than interpret one." We therefore decline to "interpret [this] criminal statute more narrowly than it is written." *Brogan v. United States*, 522 U.S. 398 (1998).

We next consider petitioners' revenue rule argument. Petitioners argue that, to avoid reading § 1343 to derogate from the common-law revenue rule, we should construe the otherwise— applicable language of the wire fraud statute to except frauds directed at evading foreign taxes. Their argument relies on the canon of construction that "[s]tatutes which invade the common law . . . are to be read with a presumption favoring the retention of long-established and familiar principles, except where a statutory purpose to the contrary is evident." *United States v. Texas*, 507 U.S. 529 (1993). This presumption is, however, no bar to a construction that conflicts with a common-law rule if the statute " 'speak[s] directly' to the question addressed by the common law."

Whether the wire fraud statute derogates from the common-law revenue rule depends, in turn, on whether reading § 1343 to reach this prosecution conflicts with a well-established revenue rule principle. We clarified this constraint on the application of the nonderogation canon in *United States v. Craft*, 535 U.S. 274 (2002). The issue in *Craft* was whether the property interest of a tenant by the entirety was exempt from a federal tax lien. We construed the federal tax lien statute to reach such a property interest, despite the tension between that construction and the common-law rule that entireties property enjoys immunity from liens, because this "common-law rule was not so well established with respect to the application of a federal tax lien that we must assume that Congress considered the impact of its enactment on the question now before us." So too here, before we may conclude that Congress intended to exempt the present prosecution from the broad reach of the wire fraud statute, we must find that the common-law revenue rule clearly barred such a prosecution. We examine the state of the common law as of 1952, the year Congress enacted the wire fraud statute.

Criminal Code is replete with provisions that criminalize overlapping conduct. The mere fact that two federal criminal statutes criminalize similar conduct says little about the scope of either.

The wire fraud statute derogates from no well-established revenue rule principle. We are aware of no common-law revenue rule case decided as of 1952 that held or clearly implied that the revenue rule barred the United States from prosecuting a fraudulent scheme to evade foreign taxes. The traditional rationales for the revenue rule, moreover, do not plainly suggest that it swept so broadly. We consider these two points in turn.

We first consider common-law revenue rule jurisprudence as it existed in 1952, the year Congress enacted § 1343. Since the late 19th and early 20th century, courts have treated the common-law revenue rule as a corollary of the rule that, as Chief Justice Marshall put it, "[t]he Courts of no country execute the penal laws of another." *The Antelope*, 10 Wheat. 66 (1825). The rule against the enforcement of foreign penal statutes, in turn, tracked the common-law principle that crimes could only be prosecuted in the country in which they were committed. See, e.g., J. Story, COMMENTARIES ON THE CONFLICT OF LAWS § 620, p. 840 (M. Bigelow ed. 8th ed. 1883). The basis for inferring the revenue rule from the rule against foreign penal enforcement was an analogy between foreign revenue laws and penal laws.

Courts first drew that inference in a line of cases prohibiting the enforcement of tax liabilities of one sovereign in the courts of another sovereign, such as a suit to enforce a tax judgment. The revenue rule's grounding in these cases shows that, at its core, it prohibited the collection of tax obligations of foreign nations. Unsurprisingly, then, the revenue rule is often stated as prohibiting the collection of foreign tax claims.

The present prosecution is unlike these classic examples of actions traditionally barred by the revenue rule. It is not a suit that recovers a foreign tax liability, like a suit to enforce a judgment. This is a criminal prosecution brought by the United States in its sovereign capacity to punish domestic criminal conduct. Petitioners nevertheless argue that common-law revenue rule jurisprudence as of 1952 prohibited such prosecutions. Revenue rule cases, however, do not establish that proposition, much less clearly so. * * *

Having concluded that revenue rule jurisprudence is no clear bar to this prosecution, we next turn to whether the purposes of the revenue rule, as articulated in the relevant authorities, suggest differently. They do not.

First, this prosecution poses little risk of causing the principal evil against which the revenue rule was traditionally thought to guard: judicial evaluation of the policy-laden enactments of other sovereigns. See, e.g., *Moore v. Mitchell*, 30 F.2d 600 (2d Cir. 1929) (L. Hand, J., concurring). As Judge Hand put it, allowing courts to enforce another country's revenue laws was thought to be a delicate inquiry

> when it concerns the relations between the foreign state and its own citizens.... To pass upon the provisions for the public order of another state is, or at any rate should be, beyond the powers of a court; it involves the relations between the states themselves, with which courts are incompetent to deal, and which are intrusted to other authorities.

The present prosecution creates little risk of causing international friction through judicial evaluation of the policies of foreign sovereigns. This action was brought by the Executive to enforce a statute passed by Congress. In our system of government, the Executive is "the sole organ of the federal government in the field of international relations," *United States v. Curtiss–Wright Export Corp.*, 299 U.S. 304 (1936), and has ample authority and competence to manage "the relations between the foreign state and its own citizens" and to avoid "embarass[ing] its neighbor[s]," *Moore* (L.Hand, J., concurring). True, a prosecution like this one requires a court to recognize foreign law to determine whether the defendant violated U.S. law. But we may assume that by electing to bring this prosecution, the Executive has assessed this prosecution's impact on this Nation's relationship with Canada, and concluded that it poses little danger of causing international friction. We know of no common-law court that has applied the revenue rule to bar an action accompanied by such a safeguard, and neither petitioners nor the dissent directs us to any. The greater danger, in fact, would lie in our judging this prosecution barred based on the foreign policy concerns animating the revenue rule, concerns that we have "neither aptitude, facilities nor responsibility" to evaluate.

More broadly, petitioners argue that the revenue rule avoids giving domestic effect to politically sensitive and controversial policy decisions embodied in foreign revenue laws, regardless of whether courts need pass judgment on such laws. This worries us little here. The present prosecution, if authorized by the wire fraud statute, embodies the policy choice of the two political branches of our Government—Congress and the Executive—to free the interstate wires from fraudulent use, irrespective of the object of the fraud. Such a reading of the wire fraud statute gives effect to that considered policy choice. It therefore poses no risk of advancing the policies of Canada illegitimately.

Still a final revenue rule rationale petitioners urge is the concern that courts lack the competence to examine the validity of unfamiliar foreign tax schemes. Foreign law, of course, posed no unmanageable complexity in this case. The District Court had before it uncontroverted testimony of a Government witness that petitioners' scheme aimed at violating Canadian tax law.

Nevertheless, Federal Rule of Criminal Procedure 26.1 addresses petitioners' concern by setting forth a procedure for interpreting foreign law that improves on those available at common law. Specifically, it permits a court, in deciding issues of foreign law, to consider "any relevant material or source—including testimony—without regard to the Federal Rules of Evidence." By contrast, common-law procedures for dealing with foreign law—those available to the courts that formulated the revenue rule—were more cumbersome. Rule 26.1 gives federal courts sufficient means to resolve the incidental foreign law issues they may encounter in wire fraud prosecutions.

Finally, our interpretation of the wire fraud statute does not give it "extraterritorial effect." Petitioners used U.S. interstate wires to execute a scheme to defraud a foreign sovereign of tax revenue. Their offense was complete the moment they executed the scheme inside the United States; "[t]he wire fraud statute punishes the scheme, not its success." *United States v. Pierce*, 224 F.3d 158 (2d Cir. 2000) This domestic element of petitioners' conduct is what the Government is punishing in this prosecution, no less than when it prosecutes a scheme to defraud a foreign individual or corporation, or a foreign government acting as a market participant. In any event, the wire fraud statute punishes frauds executed "in interstate or foreign commerce," so this is surely not a statute in which Congress had only "domestic concerns in mind." *Small v. United States*,125 S.Ct. 1752 (2005).

* * *

It may seem an odd use of the Federal Government's resources to prosecute a U.S. citizen for smuggling cheap liquor into Canada. But the broad language of the wire fraud statute authorizes it to do so and no canon of statutory construction permits us to read the statute more narrowly. * * *

JUSTICE GINSBURG DISSENTING.

This case concerns extension of the "wire fraud" statute, 18 U.S.C. § 1343 to a scenario extraterritorial in significant part: The Government invoked the statute to reach a scheme to smuggle liquor from the United States into Canada and thereby deprive Canada of revenues due under that nation's customs and tax laws. Silent on its application to activity culminating beyond our borders, the statute prohibits "any scheme" to defraud that employs in its execution communication through interstate or international wires. A relevant background norm, known as the common-law revenue rule, bars suit in one country to enforce another country's tax laws.

* * * The Court today reads the wire fraud statute to draw into our courts, at the prosecutor's option, charges that another nation's revenue laws have been evaded. The common-law revenue rule does not stand in the way, the Court instructs, for that rule has no application to criminal prosecutions under the wire fraud statute.

As I see it, * * * the Court has ascribed an exorbitant scope to the wire fraud statute, in disregard of our repeated recognition that "Congress legislates against the backdrop of the presumption against extraterritoriality." See *EEOC v. Arabian American Oil Co.*, 499 U.S. 244 (1991); *Small v. United States*, 544 U.S. 385 (2005) (The Court has "adopt[ed] the legal presumption that Congress ordinarily intends its statutes to have domestic, not extraterritorial, application."). Notably, when Congress explicitly addressed international smuggling, see 18 U.S.C. § 546, it provided for criminal enforcement of the customs laws of a foreign nation only when that nation has a reciprocal law criminalizing smuggling into the United States. Currently, Canada has no such reciprocal law.

Of overriding importance in this regard, tax collection internationally is an area in which treaties hold sway. There is a treaty between the United States and Canada regarding the collection of taxes, but that accord requires certification by the taxing nation that the taxes owed have been "finally determined." See Protocol Amending Convention with Respect to Taxes on Income and on Capital, September 26, 1980, S. Treaty Doc. No. 104–4, 2030 U.N.T.S. 236, Art. 15, ¶ 2. Moreover, the treaty is inapplicable to persons, like petitioners in this case, who are United States citizens at the time that the tax liability is incurred.

Today's novel decision is all the more troubling for its failure to take account of Canada's primary interest in the matter at stake. United States citizens who have committed criminal violations of Canadian tax law can be extradited to stand trial in Canada.[3] Canadian courts are best positioned to decide "whether, and to what extent, the defendants have defrauded the governments of Canada and Ontario out of tax revenues owed pursuant to their own, sovereign, excise laws."

The Government's prosecution of David Pasquantino, Carl Pasquantino, and Arthur Hilts for wire fraud was grounded in Canadian customs and tax laws. The wire fraud statute, 18 U.S.C. § 1343, required the Government to allege and prove that the defendants engaged in a scheme to defraud a victim—here, the

---

3. Indeed, the defendants have all been indicted in Canada for failing to report excise taxes and possession of un- lawfully imported spirits, but Canada has not requested their extradition.

Canadian Government—of money or property. To establish the fraudulent nature of the defendants' scheme and the Canadian Government's entitlement to the money withheld by the defendants, the United States offered proof at trial that Canada imposes import duties on liquor, and that the defendants intended to evade those duties. The defendants' convictions for wire fraud therefore resulted from, and could not have been obtained without proof of, their intent to violate Canadian revenue laws.

* * * Expansively interpreting the text of the wire fraud statute, which prohibits "any scheme or artifice to defraud, or for obtaining money or property by means of ... fraudulent pretenses," the Court today upholds the Government's deployment of § 1343 essentially to enforce foreign tax law. This Court has several times observed that the wire fraud statute has a long arm, extending to "everything designed to defraud by representations as to the past or present, or suggestions and promises as to the future." *Durland v. United States*, 161 U.S. 306 (1896). But the Court has also recognized that incautious reading of the statute could dramatically expand the reach of federal criminal law, and we have refused to apply the proscription exorbitantly. See *McNally v. United States*, 483 U.S. 350 (1987) (refusing to construe 18 U.S.C. § 1341, the mail fraud statute, to reach corruption in local government, stating: "[W]e read § 1341 as limited in scope to the protection of property rights. If Congress desires to go further, it must speak more clearly than it has."); see also *Cleveland v. United States*, 531 U.S. 12 (2000) (holding that § 1341 does not reach schemes to make false statements on a state license application, in part based on reluctance to "approve a sweeping expansion of federal criminal jurisdiction in the absence of a clear statement by Congress").[6]

Construing § 1343 to encompass violations of foreign revenue laws, the Court ignores the absence of anything signaling Congress' intent to give the statute such an extraordinary extraterritorial effect.[7] "It is a longstanding principle of American law," *Aramco*, that Congress, in most of its legislative endeavors, "is primarily concerned with domestic conditions."

Section 1343, which contains no reference to foreign law as an element of the domestic crime of wire fraud, contrasts with federal

---

6. I note that, on the Court's interpretation, federal prosecutors could resort to the wire and mail fraud statutes to reach schemes to evade not only foreign taxes, but state and local taxes as well.

7. I do not read into § 1343's coverage of frauds executed "in interstate or foreign commerce," ante, at 1781, congressional intent to give § 1343 extraterritorial effect. A statute's express application to acts committed in foreign commerce, the Court has repeatedly held, does not in itself indicate a congressional design to give the statute extraterritorial effect.

criminal statutes that chart the courts' course in this regard. See, e.g., 18 U.S.C. § 1956(c)(1) (defendant must know that transaction involved the proceeds of activity "that constitutes a felony under State, Federal, or foreign law"); 16 U.S.C. § 3372(a)(2)(A) (banning importation of wildlife that has been "taken, possessed, transported, or sold in violation of any ... foreign law"). These statutes indicate that Congress, which has the sole authority to determine the extraterritorial reach of domestic laws, is fully capable of conveying its policy choice to the Executive and the courts. I would not assume from legislative silence that Congress left the matter to Executive discretion.[8]

The presumption against extraterritoriality, which guides courts in the absence of congressional direction, provides ample cause to conclude that § 1343 does not extend to the instant scheme. Moreover, as to foreign customs and tax laws, there is scant room for doubt about Congress' general perspective: Congress has actively indicated, through both domestic legislation and treaties, that it intends "strictly [to] limit the parameters of any assistance given" to foreign nations. *Attorney General of Canada v. R.J. Reynolds Tobacco Holdings, Inc.*

First, Congress has enacted a specific statute criminalizing offenses of the genre committed by the defendants here: 18 U.S.C. § 546 prohibits transporting goods "into the territory of any foreign government in violation of the laws there in force." Section 546's application, however, is expressly conditioned on the foreign government's enactment of reciprocal legislation prohibiting smuggling into the United States. The reciprocity limitation reflects a legislative determination that this country should not provide other nations with greater enforcement assistance than they give to the United States. The limitation also cabins the Government's discretion as to which nation's customs laws to enforce, thereby avoiding the appearance of prosecutorial overreaching. Significantly, Canada has no statute criminalizing smuggling into the United States, rendering § 546 inapplicable to schemes resembling the one at issue here.[9]

Second, the United States and Canada have negotiated, and the Senate has ratified, a comprehensive tax treaty, in which both

---

8. The application of 18 U.S.C. § 1343 (2000 ed., Supp. II), to schemes to defraud a foreign individual or corporation, or even a foreign governmental entity acting as a market participant, is of a different order, and does not necessarily depend on any determination of foreign law. As the Court of Appeals observed in *United States v. Boots*, 80 F.3d 580 (1st Cir.1996), upholding a defendant's wire fraud conviction in a case like the one here presented "would amount functionally to penal enforcement of Canadian customs and tax laws."

9. Section 546's requirement that a vessel have been used to transport the goods to the foreign country would render § 546 inapplicable to these defendants' conduct in any event.

nations have committed to providing collection assistance with respect to each other's tax claims. Significantly, the Protocol does not call upon either nation to interpret or calculate liability under the other's tax statutes; it applies only to tax claims that have been fully and finally adjudicated under the law of the requesting nation. Further, the Protocol bars assistance in collecting any claim against a citizen or corporation of "the requested State." These provisions would preclude Canada from obtaining United States assistance in enforcing its claims against the Pasquantinos and Hilts. I would not assume that Congress understood § 1343 to provide the assistance that the United States, in the considered foreign policy judgment of both political branches, has specifically declined to promise.

Complementing the principle that courts ordinarily should await congressional instruction before giving our laws extraterritorial thrust, the common-law revenue rule holds that one nation generally does not enforce another's tax laws. The Government argues, and the Court accepts, that domestic wire fraud prosecutions premised on violations of foreign tax law do not implicate the revenue rule because the court, while it must "recognize foreign [revenue] law to determine whether the defendant violated U.S. law," need only "enforce" foreign law "in an attenuated sense." As discussed above, however, the defendants' conduct arguably fell within the scope of § 1343 only because of their purpose to evade Canadian customs and tax laws; shorn of that purpose, no other aspect of their conduct was criminal in this country. It seems to me unavoidably obvious, therefore, that this prosecution directly implicates the revenue rule. It is equally plain that Congress did not endeavor, by enacting § 1343, to displace that rule.

Finally, the rule of lenity counsels against adopting the Court's interpretation of § 1343. It is a "close question" whether the wire fraud statute's prohibition of "any scheme ... to defraud" includes schemes directed solely at defrauding foreign governments of tax revenues. We have long held that, when confronted with "two rational readings of a criminal statute, one harsher than the other, we are to choose the harsher only when Congress has spoken in clear and definite language." *McNally.*

* * * For the reasons stated, I would hold that § 1343 does not extend to schemes to evade foreign tax and customs laws.

3. The Application of Foreign Convictions in the United States

In *Small v. United States,* 544 U.S. 385, 125 S.Ct. 1752, 161 L.Ed.2d 651 (2005), the Supreme Court considered the corollary issue of whether a foreign conviction would be counted for violating a provision of United States law that prohibits possession of a firearm by a person who was convicted of a crime "in any court" that was punishable by imprisonment for over one year. Small had been convicted in Japan of illegally smuggling weapons into that country and was sentenced to five years in prison. After serving his sentence and returning home, he purchased a gun and was charged with unlawful possession of a firearm. In holding that the foreign conviction did not meet the previous conviction requirement, the Court analyzed the Congressional intent behind the phrase "in any court" to determine whether extraterritorial convictions—not conduct—qualified:

> In determining the scope of the statutory phrase we find help in the "commonsense notion that Congress generally legislates with domestic concerns in mind." *Smith v. United States*, 507 U.S. 197 (1993). This notion has led the Court to adopt the legal presumption that Congress ordinarily intends its statutes to have domestic, not extraterritorial, application. See *Foley Bros., Inc. v. Filardo*, 336 U.S. 281 (1949). That presumption would apply, for example, were we to consider whether this statute prohibits unlawful gun possession abroad as well as domestically. And, although the presumption against extraterritorial application does not apply directly to this case, we believe a similar assumption is appropriate when we consider the scope of the phrase "convicted in any court" here.

> For one thing, the phrase describes one necessary portion of the "gun possession" activity that is prohibited as a matter of domestic law. For another, considered as a group, foreign convictions differ from domestic convictions in important ways. Past foreign convictions for crimes punishable by more than one year's imprisonment may include a conviction for conduct that domestic laws would permit, for example, for engaging in economic conduct that our society might encourage. See, e.g., Art. 153 of the Criminal Code of the Russian Soviet Federated Socialist Republic, in Soviet Criminal Law and Procedure 171 (criminalizing "Private Entrepreneurial Activity"); Art. 153 (criminalizing "Speculation," which is defined as "the buying up and reselling of goods or any other articles for the purpose of making a profit"); cf. e.g., Gaceta Oficial de la Republica de Cuba, ch. II, Art. 103, p. 68 (Dec. 30, 1987) (forbidding propaganda that incites against the social order, international solidarity, or the Communist State). They would include a conviction from a legal system that is inconsistent with an American understanding of fairness. And they would include a conviction for conduct that domestic law punishes far less severely. See, e.g., Singapore Vandalism Act, ch. 108, §§ 2, 3, III Statutes of

Republic of Singapore p. 258 (imprisonment for up to three years for an act of vandalism). Thus, the key statutory phrase "convicted in any court of, a crime punishable by imprisonment for a term exceeding one year" somewhat less reliably identifies dangerous individuals for the purposes of U.S. law where foreign convictions, rather than domestic convictions, are at issue.

In addition, it is difficult to read the statute as asking judges or prosecutors to refine its definitional distinctions where foreign convictions are at issue. To somehow weed out inappropriate foreign convictions that meet the statutory definition is not consistent with the statute's language; it is not easy for those not versed in foreign laws to accomplish; and it would leave those previously convicted in a foreign court (say of economic crimes) uncertain about their legal obligations.

4. Should the United States Help Enforce Foreign Laws?

The United States plays a central role in the global financial system. Many significant bank transactions occur through American banks for branches of foreign institutions in the United States. Many of the largest players in the global securities markets are either headquartered in the United States or have a substantial presence in the American market, including extensive brokerage operations. Particularly in less stable economies, the United States can be a safe haven for assets, even in the face of restrictions imposed on the transfer of funds or currency exchanges. Consider the following hypothetical, and determine whether the United States should become involved in prosecuting for a violation of domestic law.

Crédit Internationale S.A. (CI) is a Swiss bank that has subsidiaries operating as securities dealers in a number of countries, including the United States (where it is properly licensed by the Securities & Exchange Commission as a broker-dealer). The firm caters to high net-worth individuals and private companies investing in global markets. CI develops a program called "Safety Accounts" that it markets to clients in the Middle East, Latin America, and Southeast Asia, as a means to keep funds "safe" from confiscation by governments. The accounts are in the name of a trust created in the Carribean nation of the Turks and Caicos Islands, which does not impose taxes on trusts, and the funds are held in the CI branch in the Bahamas, which does not require account holders to be identified by name. When a customer requests a payment from a "Safety Account," that request is routed from the local office through CI's headquarters in Bern, Switzerland, to the Bahamas office. Some electronic messages pass through a telephone switching station in South Florida on their way to the Bahamas. Once the sale of securities in the account takes place, the funds are wired through CI's correspondent bank account with Citigroup in New York City to the bank of the account owner. CI has over 5,000 Safety Accounts, with assets of approximately $900 million, and it executes approximately 100 transactions a month through Citigroup's New York office. The U.S. Department of Justice receives a Request for Assistance from the Government of Mexico stating that a number of wealthy Mexican citizens have accounts with CI that are being used to avoid paying income and capital gains taxes in Mexico. According to the Request, under applicable Mexican law, any account owned by a citizen must be disclosed to the government, with the income and capital gains reported annually and subject to a 50% tax. The U.S. Attorney's Office for the Southern District of New York initiates an investigation of CI and its Mexican customers for violating 18 U.S.C. § 1343, the wire fraud statute, for engaging in a scheme to defraud the Mexican government of taxes.

Can the United States successfully prosecute CI for its conduct? Can it successfully prosecute the Mexican citizens who have CI accounts (assuming they do not pay taxes to Mexico on the income and capital gains in their accounts)?

F. EXTRADITION

1. Principles of Extradition

Extradition is the most common method by which one country can secure the custody of a person it wants to prosecute from another country. This is not a modern creation of international law, and its roots can be traced back over three thousand years. In *Quinn v. Robinson*, 783 F.2d 776 (9th Cir. 1986) the court noted, "The first-known extradition treaty was negotiated between an Egyptian Pharaoh and a Hittite King in the Thirteenth Century B.C." United States citizens can be extradited to a foreign country to faces charges there, as provided by 18 U.S.C. § 3190. The procedures related to extradition are much less than those provided in a full-scale criminal proceeding, as described by Professor Parry:

> [T]he defenses available to the fugitive are extremely limited: he cannot, for example, introduce evidence which contradicts the demanding country's proof; evidence to establish alibi;

evidence of insanity; or evidence that the statute of limitations has run. Fourth, the actual guilt of the fugitive does not have to be established, but instead the demanding country need show only probable cause that he is guilty. The accused has the opportunity to contend that she has been accused of a political offense, such as treason, spying, or possibly common crimes committed for political purposes. On the other hand, judges will not inquire into the fairness of the proceedings that await the accused in the requesting country. In other words, the accused has little ability to challenge the evidence or present her side of the story, and the evidentiary threshold is sufficiently low that her chance of victory is small.

John T. Parry, *The Lost History of International Extradition Litigation*, 43 Va. J. Int'l L. 93 (2002).

Another means to gain custody over a person is by using extralegal means, such as kidnapping. Jurisdiction can be a matter of having control of the person so that he or she can be brought before a nation's courts for an adjudication of guilt. Needless to say, many nations object to the use of force or threats in taking a person into custody to be tried in another country without their explicit permission. Yet, the law has never expressly forbidden such "self-help" in seeking to remove person into a nation so that he can be tried by its courts. Whether this is consistent with international law is a different question from whether jurisdiction exists to try a person who has been removed to a country in other ways not treated explicitly by an extradition treaty.

2. Political Offense Exception

The modern world involves a number of situations in which one group, frequently based on ethnic or racial characteristics, or religious affiliation, is fighting against a government or competing group. Often, these conflicts involve substantial violence, which can occur in a civil war or insurgency, or through the use of terror tactics. Most treaties recognize a "Political Offense" exception to extradition that permits a nation to refuse to return a person because the conduct relates to political activism, and extraditing a person who has failed in obtaining political change will condemn the person to an almost automatic conviction and, perhaps, death. At the same time, a political *motive* for conduct can be easily asserted for almost any crime, so that a generous application of the Political Offense exception would undermine extradition.

In *Barapind v. Enomoto*, 400 F.3d 744 (9th Cir.2005) the Ninth Circuit, sitting *en banc*, considered a defendant's assertion of the

Political Offense exception under the Treaty for the Mutual Extradition of Criminals Between the United States of America and Great Britain, 47 Stat. 2122, which was applicable to India, and the Treaty bars extradition for crimes "of a political character." Barapind, a citizen of India, had been a leader of the All India Sikh Student Federation in the 1980s before illegally entering the United States, and he was charged with a number of murders there related to activities involving the Sikh insurgency against the Indian government. One of the crimes involved the murder of three purported police collaborators and the wife of one, Kulwant Kaur. In analyzing Barapind's claim that the alleged crimes came within the Political Offense exception to the Treaty, the Ninth Circuit applied the test it adopted in the seminal decision in *Quinn v. Robinson*, 783 F.2d 776 (9th Cir. 1986). The court rejected Barapind's claim under *Quinn*:

> To determine whether the political offense doctrine bars extradition, we apply a two-prong "incidence test." For a crime to qualify as "one of a political character," Treaty art. 6, there must be: "(1) the occurrence of an uprising or other violent political disturbance at the time of the charged offense, and (2) a charged offense that is 'incidental to' 'in the course of,' or 'in furtherance of' the uprising," *Quinn*.

> There is no real doubt that the crimes Barapind is accused of committing occurred during a time of violent political disturbance in India. As the extradition court noted, "[t]ens of thousands of deaths and casualties" resulted between the mid–1980s and early 1990s as Sikh nationalists clashed with government officers and sympathizers in Punjab. Substantial violence was taking place, and the persons engaged in the violence were pursuing specific political objectives. The dispute between the parties concerns the "incidental to" prong, which asks whether Barapind's crimes were "causally or ideologically related" to the political uprising. In *Quinn*, we discussed the "incidental to" analysis in depth, stating that extradition courts should focus not on the types of acts alleged, but rather on the motivation for those acts.

> * * * Barapind failed to demonstrate that Kulwant's murder was a political offense. * * * [T]he court properly concluded that Barapind's proffered evidence would not satisfy the *Quinn* formulation. Under *Quinn*, a court may not rely on a fugitive's mere assurance that a crime had some political purpose. Rather, the fugitive has the burden of showing a factual nexus between the crime and the political goal. In this case, all we know about Kulwant is: (1) she was the wife of a suspected police collaborator; and (2) Barapind's crew did not intend to kill her based on any of her political beliefs or affiliations. But we do not know why Barapind's accomplices

did, in fact, kill Kulwant. Was it an accident? Was it because she attempted to interfere with the murder of her husband? Or were the men attempting to eliminate witnesses who could later identify them—and, if so, why didn't they also kill Sohan and his wife?

Barapind has not answered any of these questions. As the extradition court noted, he has provided no evidence at all to explain the motive for Kulwant's murder. Without such evidence, there is no basis for finding that the murder was a political offense under *Quinn*. Because Barapind failed to prove that his charge fell under the political offense exception, the extradition court properly certified his extraditability for Kulwant's murder.

In an opinion dissenting from the majority's decision to apply *Quinn* rather than reconsider that precedent, Circuit Judge Rymer wrote:

> * * * I believe we must overrule *Quinn*, because indiscriminate violence against innocent persons should not qualify for the political offense exception to extradition, even if politically motivated. Nor should the propriety of committing common crimes be left to the perpetrators' discretion. And civilians are different from the military. Overruling *Quinn* would realign us with the two circuits that have addressed attacks on non-combatant civilian targets and held them to be unprotected.

> I believe *Quinn* must be overruled for the additional reason that it tries to set the parameters of a "political offense" for all time and all places. Suffice it to say, as Justice Denman did in the leading English case *In re Castioni*, [1891] 1 Q.B. 149: "I do not think it is necessary or desirable that we should attempt to put into language in the shape of an exhaustive definition exactly the whole state of things, or every state of things which might bring a particular case within the description of an offence of a political character."

3. Extradition to the United States

The federal statute governing extradition of a defendant from a foreign country to the United States is 18 U.S.C. § 3184, which provides for the following procedures for initiating an extradition proceeding:

> Whenever there is a treaty or convention for extradition between the United States and any foreign government, or in cases arising under section 3181(b), any justice or judge of the United States, or any magistrate judge authorized so to do by a court of the United States, or any judge of a court of record of

general jurisdiction of any State, may, upon complaint made under oath, charging any person found within his jurisdiction, with having committed within the jurisdiction of any such foreign government any of the crimes provided for by such treaty or convention, or provided for under section 3181(b), issue his warrant for the apprehension of the person so charged, that he may be brought before such justice, judge, or magistrate judge, to the end that the evidence of criminality may be heard and considered. Such complaint may be filed before and such warrant may be issued by a judge or magistrate judge of the United States District Court for the District of Columbia if the whereabouts within the United States of the person charged are not known or, if there is reason to believe the person will shortly enter the United States. If, on such hearing, he deems the evidence sufficient to sustain the charge under the provisions of the proper treaty or convention, or under section 3181(b), he shall certify the same, together with a copy of all the testimony taken before him, to the Secretary of State, that a warrant may issue upon the requisition of the proper authorities of such foreign government, for the surrender of such person, according to the stipulations of the treaty or convention; and he shall issue his warrant for the commitment of the person so charged to the proper jail, there to remain until such surrender shall be made.

4. Principle of Specialty

Most extradition treaties contain a provision requiring the parties to prosecute a defendant only on the charges specified in the request for extradition. In applying for extradition, the nation seeking the defendant's return must include in its request all charges that will be prosecuted, and the extraditing country can limit the offenses for which the person can be prosecuted by allowing the extradition only for certain crimes. Therefore, new charges cannot be brought against the defendant after extradition in violation of the treaty, although some cases permit the addition of counts arising from the same set of facts that form the basis of the crime for which the person was extradited. For example, United States courts have permitted the addition of asset forfeiture counts because they deal with the disposition of the proceeds of the criminal conduct and do not charge a new offense.

An issue that has split the federal courts is whether a defendant has standing to seek the dismissal of charges that would violate the principle of specialty. A violation of the principle contravenes the treaty, so the only party directly aggrieved by the violation is the extraditing nation. In *Antwi v. United States*, 349

F.Supp.2d 663 (S.D.N.Y. 2004), the district court weighed the competing arguments regarding the right of the defendant to raise a specialty claim:

The international extradition law principle of specialty, which is incorporated into the treaty between Ghana and the United States, permits the requesting state to prosecute the extradited fugitive only for offenses that are enumerated in an extradition treaty and for which the fugitive's extradition was sought. For this reason, some courts have held that the rights created by an extradition treaty based on the rule of specialty belong only to the state parties to the treaty, and that consequently, "a defendant would not have standing to invoke the rule of specialty ... absent protest or objection by the offended sovereign." [*United States v.*] *Nosov*, 153 F.Supp.2d [477 (S.D.N.Y. 2001)].

The more persuasive analysis, however, finds that extradited parties do have standing. Although the Supreme Court has not expressly addressed the question of standing, the violation by the United States of the principle of specialty in an extradition has been actionable by the extradited defendant for over a century. See *United States v. Rauscher*, 119 U.S. 407 (1886). In *Rauscher*, Great Britain extradited the defendant to the United States to stand trial for murder, a crime in the relevant extradition treaty between Great Britain and the United States, but he was tried instead for "infliction of cruel and unusual punishment," a crime not present in the treaty. The defendant was permitted to raise this as a violation of the extradition treaty. As the Court noted more recently, "[i]n *Rauscher*, ... no importance was attached to whether or not Great Britain had protested the prosecution of Rauscher for the crime of cruel and unusual punishment as opposed to murder." *United States v. Alvarez–Machain*, 504 U.S. 655 (1992). The Court used *Rauscher* to reject the respondent's argument that the foreign government from which the defendant was brought to the United States would have to register a protest before the defendant could assert a right under an extradition treaty. The Supreme Court has observed that if an extradition treaty "has the force of law, ... it would appear that a court must enforce it on behalf of an individual regardless of the offensiveness of the practice of one nation to the other nation." Although extradited defendants are not parties to extradition treaties, they remain interested third parties. This means that extradition treaties still may "contain provisions which confer certain rights upon the citizens or subjects of one of the nations residing in the territorial limits of the other, which partake of the nature of municipal law, and which are capable of enforcement as between private parties in the courts of the country." *Rauscher*. The principle of specialty thus denotes a "right conferred upon persons brought from a foreign country into this [country] under such [extradition] proceedings."

There is a recognized limitation, however, on a defendant's right to object on the ground that his extradition has violated the doctrine of specialty. He may not raise such a claim if the state from which he is extradited explicitly waives any objection based on the rule of specialty. Such a waiver abrogates that portion of the treaty with respect to the defendant.

5. Dual Criminality Principle

Most extradition treaties contain a provision requiring that the crime for which extradition is sought be an offense under the law of the nation receiving the extradition request. A typical treaty provision provides, "Extradition shall be granted for conduct which constitutes an offense punishable by the laws of both Contracting Parties...." The principle does not require complete identity between the two crimes, and the analysis is a practical determination of the scope of the criminal laws of the two nations involved in the extradition request. The First Circuit explained the analysis in *United States v. Saccoccia*, 58 F.3d 754 (1st Cir. 1995):

> The principle of dual criminality does not demand that the laws of the surrendering and requesting states be carbon copies of one another. Thus, dual criminality will not be defeated by differences in the instrumentalities or in the stated purposes of the two nations' laws. By the same token, the counterpart crimes need not have identical elements. Instead, dual criminality is deemed to be satisfied when the two countries' laws are substantially analogous. Moreover, in mulling dual criminality concerns, courts are duty bound to defer to a surrendering sovereign's reasonable determination that the offense in question is extraditable. See *Casey v. Department of State*, 980 F.2d 1472 (D.C.Cir. 1992) (observing that an American court must give great deference to a foreign court's determination in extradition proceedings).

> Mechanically, then, the inquiry into dual criminality requires courts to compare the law of the surrendering state that purports to criminalize the charged conduct with the law of the requesting state that purports to accomplish the same result. If the same conduct is subject to criminal sanctions in both jurisdictions, no more is exigible.

6. Extraditing Citizens to Another Country

One of the most difficult cases is when a nation seeks to have another country deport one of its own citizens for a crime in the other nation. An interesting situation arises when the conduct occurs in both the country seeking to extradite the foreign national and that person's own country. Should the host nation be responsible for prosecuting the crime? Or, should a country extradite its citizen to face a charge that will require proof of conduct in the extraditing nation, even if there are concerns about the fairness of the trial that will take place? This situation arose in *The Queen on the Application of Bermingham & Others v. The Director of the Serious Fraud Office*, [2006] EWHC 200 (Admin), involving the prosecution of three British citizens for crimes related to transactions at Enron Corporation. The defendants were investment bankers indicted by a grand jury in Houston, Texas, for their role in transferring ownership of a business entity from their employer, Greenwich NatWest, to another entity in which they had an ownership interest for $1 million and promptly reselling it for more than $20 million. The three British bankers received approximately $7.3 million to divide among themselves, and the charges alleged that they defrauded their employer in the transaction that allowed two senior Enron financial executives to pocket the other $12.3 million from the deal. One meeting related to the transaction took place in Houston attended by the Greenwich NatWest bankers and Enron executives, which provided the basis for the federal charges. At all other times, particularly when the final transfer occurred, the three British defendants were resident in London.

In fighting their extradition, the defendants—dubbed the "NatWest Three"—argued that the Serious Fraud Office (SFO) in Great Britain should have investigated and prosecuted them, not federal authorities in Texas, making what the court called a *"forum conveniens"* argument. They argued that the SFO must act to protect their rights under the European Convention on Human Rights (ECHR) to prevent extradition to a jurisdiction that might not protect their rights under the ECHR. The defendants relied on § 1(3) of the 1987 Statute, the legislation creating the SFO, which states: "The Director may investigate any suspected offence which appears on reasonable grounds to involve serious or complex fraud." The British appellate court rejected that argument in upholding an extradition order to transfer the defendants to the United States:

> As I have said the Director [of the SFO] acknowledged a duty to take the ECHR into account in making any decision. To the extent that action taken by him might touch the Conven-

tion rights of any affected person—most obviously, anyone the subject of an investigation instituted by him—he was clearly right to do so. It is I suppose possible to envisage circumstances in which that would arise in practice, perhaps where the effects of an investigation upon an especially vulnerable person would be particularly severe. Indeed in such a case the Director's duty would not merely be to have regard to the ECHR but to take a decision which would vindicate the Convention right in question. I cannot, however, envisage any circumstances in which a decision not to investigate might offend the relevant person's Convention rights. At all events, given we are dealing only with investigation, I apprehend that cases in which the director's decision might touch Convention rights would be very rare, and exhibit very special facts. And this is not the basis of what is suggested here. My question can only be answered in the affirmative, and thus in the defendants' favour, if s.1(3) is construed so as to impose a positive obligation on the Director to embark upon an investigation so that he might pre-empt the potential trial venue in favour of this jurisdiction (by proceeding to prosecute here) if it appears that the Convention rights of a suspected person might be violated by trial elsewhere.

This would be an entirely fanciful construction of s.1(3). It obviously cannot be got out of the subsection's words, which only confer a power to investigate. More than this: it would usurp the role of the District Judge [in an extradition proceeding]. As I have shown those provisions impose on the judge an express obligation to decide whether the relevant person's extradition would be compatible with his Convention rights, and to order his discharge if he concludes that it would not. Thus Parliament has distinctly allocated the task of determining complaints under the ECHR to the courts. * * * [T]he defendants' argument, if correct, "would enable a request to be made . . . when the extradition process was well advanced, with a view to halting it or interrupting it with collateral challenges to the decisions of investigating or prosecuting bodies." In my judgment that would be a wholly unacceptable state of affairs.

The House of Lords refused to hear the appeal, and the defendants were extradited to the United States in July 2006. See Kristen Hays, *British Trio Appears in Houston Court on Enron Charges*, ASSOCIATED PRESS, July 14, 2006.

Chapter III

TERRORISM

A. INTRODUCTION AND CONCEPTUAL BACKGROUND

Both before and after September 11, 2001, terrorism has made headlines around the world. Terroristic acts know no borders, and terrorism has occurred on every continent. Preventing and punishing terrorism is truly a global issue. One part of this effort is the criminal prosecution of terroristic acts. However, terrorism presents interesting and troublesome issues for the criminal law. As a result, it is a good vehicle to study many concepts of criminal law, including which circumstances invoke or should invoke the criminal justice system. Addressing this issue sheds light on the nature and role of criminal law and the criminal justice system.

Most, if not all, individuals and groups consider violence committed against their own innocent compatriots to be criminal, regardless of whether the violence is committed by perpetrators within their nation, or group, or by outsiders. Notwithstanding, it is evident that attempts to suppress terrorism have proved far from satisfactory.

In one sense, terrorism is a significant harm to society that should be prosecuted as a crime. Legitimate prosecution requires extant legislation that is specific and concrete, so that the commission of the offense may be proved or disproved. In another sense, terrorism is a form of warfare, a tactic or strategy that may warrant legitimate self-defense. Terrorism, in each of these senses, requires a clear definition and concrete elements so that the term is not allowed to degenerate into an epithet, to be used as a propaganda buzz-word that enables unconstitutional prosecution, aggression, illegal acts of war, and illegitimate actions in self-defense. Too often, "terrorism" is used inappropriately in another sense: it is

72

used as a poor metaphor for war and as a means to invoke illegitimate acts of counter-terror, and to erode constitutional values and the rule of law.

Terrorist groups use epithets to demonize their "enemy" and to claim justification for killing innocents. Similarly, governments use the terms "terrorism" and "terrorist" equally as an epithet to justify going to war, to deny due process, to hold detainees secretly and indefinitely, and to abuse, or even torture and kill them, and sometimes even to kill innocents, thus committing terrorism in the guise of counter-terrorism. Most legislation from most states does not proscribe this form of terrorism, if "authorized" or "sanctioned" by government. This frequent appropriation of the term as a rhetorical device by governments and other groups is one difficulty in finding a useful definition of terrorism.

A clear definition of terrorism would help us to proscribe criminal conduct no matter who commits it. A coherent and neutral definition would also avoid the pitfalls and dangers to democracy caused by over-reaction to terrorism or perceived terrorist threats. Therefore, we must define terrorism carefully and well. On the other hand, academics, including philosophers, legal scholars, military scholars, anthropologists, political scientists, and historians have attempted to define terrorism. Consider the following definition offered by the philosopher David Rodin *Terrorism Without Intention*, 114 (no. 4) ETHICS 752, 755 (2004): "the deliberate, negligent, or reckless use of force against noncombatants, by state or nonstate actors for ideological ends and *in the absence of a substantively just legal process*" (emphasis added). Do you think that Rodin's definition is sufficient for criminal law purposes? What does "substantially just" mean? Consider this as you read our proposed definition of terrorism, *infra*.

Note that Rodin's definition seems to allow for justification of terrorism in some instances. Indeed, later in his article he argues just that. Can terrorism be justified? If so, what is the justification? This, of course, raises issues such as defenses, justifications or excuses for acts of terrorism. It also raises issues related to the motive or perhaps even intent or purpose of terrorist acts. Is the use of "shock and awe" in a war, such as recently promoted by the U.S. government in the Iraq war, a deliberate use of force against noncombatants for ideological ends? If so, is there a substantively just legal process? Does "shock and awe" make the conduct terrorism or might those elements be terror-producing conduct that plays a part in any war, as opposed to terrorism? If the latter is true, what elements would make the conduct terrorism? Does committing these acts for military ends justify it? Terrorism is *certainly undertaken for the purpose of obtaining a political, philosophical, or some other ideological end or advantage*, either with one's own, one's allies, or with "the enemy." If this latter point is correct, does the purpose of the conduct render it terrorism? Is motive a necessary element?

Some commentators see terrorism as nothing more than the lower end of the warfare spectrum, a form of low-intensity, unconventional aggression. For example, Walter Laquer defines terrorism as: "[t]he use or threat of violence, a method of combat or a strategy to achieve certain goals, that its aim is to induce a state of fear in the victim, that it is ruthless and does not conform to humanitarian norms and that publicity is an essential factor in terrorist strategy...." Walter Laquer, *Reflections on Terrorism*, 65 FOR. AFF. 86 (1986). Is this definition sufficient from a legal point of view? In what ways might the definition be described as over inclusive or underinclusive? Is the intent to cause fear a necessary element of the definition? Is it important to consider other purposes that may be at play in conduct deemed to be terrorism, such as coercion of a group of people, a government, or one's "enemy," as being an element of the offense? What about the intention to impress or influence one's own fighters or followers such as to indicate the leadership's prowess or skill, or to encourage enlistment in the "movement?"

Generally, for our purposes, terrorism is: the willful, wanton, or criminally reckless use of violence committed by any means against innocent individuals with the intent to cause death or great bodily harm or with wanton disregard for those consequences and for the purpose of causing fear, coercing or intimidating some specific group, or government, in order to gain some perceived political, military, religious, or other philosophical (including nihilistic) benefit. We use the term "reckless" here to mean the form of recklessness that is the equivalent of the mental state for depraved heart murder—where the perpetrator knows the significantly high risk to life and limb, but takes that risk anyway.

Regardless of whether terror violence occurs in a setting where it should be called a war crime, a crime against humanity, state or group terrorism, it may be proscribed violence. Here, we use the term "may" to distinguish the terror-violence that generally occurs in any war from "terrorism," which is the intentional or wanton use of extreme violence against innocents. Terrorism, from this point of view, is a form of especially violent crime, and so it has traditionally been considered by Anglo–American, Continental, Islamic, and other systems of jurisprudence. International law condemns this conduct and provides for universal jurisdiction to be asserted over each of these types of terrorism on the basis of at least three legal theories, discussed in the Introduction Chapter, the Genocide Chapter and *infra*, Section B.

This chapter considers several crimes related to terrorism. Not only is there no agreed upon definition of terrorism in international instruments or in the United States, there also are a multitude of actions that are criminalized as terrorism, including homicide, hijacking of airplanes, and financial or material support of terrorist organizations.

B. TERRORISM PROBLEM[1]

Monrad Reigelman is an American preacher and head of a large religious television company. His company purchases diamonds from a mining company in Sierra Leone that uses the receipts from the sales to fund a rebel organization responsible for the deaths of thousands of innocent people in Sierra Leone, Liberia, and Sudan. The rebel group in each country is part of an umbrella organization, named God's Own Will. This umbrella organization is a religious-based, loosely-knit network of cells organized to overthrow regimes controlled by governments hostile to God's Own Will and to the ethnic minorities that it represents in those countries. God's Own Will is well organized in rural areas, and it provides religious training, health care and support for families there. Reigelman had read media reports of connections between an armed faction of the group and its humanitarian side. When he donated money from his company to the headquarters of God's Own Will, Reigelman included a request that the funds be used only for humanitarian purposes. In fact, all funds from donors, including Reigelman's company, were used for some humanitarian work in rebel-controlled areas, but also for rebel military activity.

Reigelman and his company also own a large amount of stock in an air cargo company, Aeromignon, registered in Harare, Zimbabwe. Jelpi Perdue, a French national and a former special forces operative in the French Foreign Legion, began working in Sudan as a manager for Aeromignon. Arpad Viszla, a Hungarian citizen, is the founder and CEO of Aeromignon; he is also a former U.S. army officer. Oleg Rachmaninof, a Russian citizen, is a pilot for Aeromignon. Perdue is an undercover investigator for the United Nations Security Council. He had been sent to Sudan to investigate activities of another company that was believed to be trafficking in illicit weapons and diamonds, but he ended up reporting on Aeromignon's activities, which were found to be involved with the military arm of God's Own Will.

1. This problem was inspired by, adapted and made into a fully fictional story from the following article by Jon Swain, *Briton linked to Congo war crimes*, The Sunday Times (London), Sept. 10, 2006, http://www. timesonline. co.uk /article/ 0,,2087–2350645,00.html.

Aeromignon's role was set up to appear to be only logistical, but Perdue explained that he was put in charge of helicopter gunships and civilian aircraft that had been converted to drop bombs that were being flown by Aeromignon crews. Under a crewing agreement that Viszla had signed with Sudanese rebels, Aeromignon was to provide aircrews who would operate along and behind the government lines in support of ground troops fighting to end the oppression of their people in Sudan.

Perdue provided evidence that Ukrainian and Russian aircrews were recruited by Viszla for Aeromignon on behalf of the Sudanese rebels to fly blanket bombing raids from very high altitude over areas where the civilians supported the Government. Rachmaninof was a close friend of Viszla's and was the best pilot, so he flew several of these raids that killed and maimed civilians caught in the battle zones thousands of feet below. Rachnaninof had been in the room when the negotiations took place and the agreement was made between the rebels and Viszla for Aeromignon. The rebels also targeted United States Consular Offices in Sudan, killing the consul general. They also targeted workers for a human rights NGO, killing three United States citizens. According to Perdue, "Rudimentary bombs were made from industrial gas cylinders filled with TNT. These were rolled out of the backs of giant Antonov transport aircraft flown at high altitude in indiscriminate raids."

Perdue further stated that Aeromignon crews not only rolled crude bombs out of the backs of their aircraft, they also strafed civilians from an MI–24 helicopter gunship. Viszla was aware of these activities, although he did not fly any of the aircraft involved or otherwise participate in the missions. Perdue also explained that aviation-fuel bombs that are "very destructive" were dropped on villages. In all, thousands of innocent Sudanese, as well as the others already mentioned, were killed by the action of Aeromignon and its crews.

Assuming that all of the facts noted above were true, and that Rachmaninof, Reigelman, and Viszla were found and arrested in the United States, consider whether Rachmaninof, Viszla, and Reigelman may be prosecuted in federal court in the United States for violating the federal terrorism statutes, 18 U.S.C. §§ 2332 and 2339C, as shown below. Explain how the United States government will decide whether to commence a prosecution, and what issues would be decided by the jury. How is § 2331 relevant?

Also, could any of this conduct be prosecuted as a war crime or a crime against humanity, as presented in the Genocide Chapter? For this part of the question, assume that an international criminal tribunal exists with jurisdiction over the three defendants.

C. DEFINING AND PROSECUTING TERRORISM IN THE UNITED STATES

The first step in determining culpability for a crime is to analyze the definition and elements of the crime, which include prescriptive or legislative jurisdiction, as explained *infra* and in the Introduction Chapter. State or federal statutory schemes will often have different variations and degrees of a crime. For instance, in homicide, most states have murder in the first degree, murder in the second degree, voluntary manslaughter, and involuntary manslaughter, all of which are different forms of homicide. However, in general, there is only one statute in any one (US) state that defines "murder in the first degree" or "voluntary manslaughter." It is highly unlikely that there would be competing definitions of "murder" within any state's statutes. In contrast, "terrorism" tends to be defined in a multitude of ways. The multiplicity of definitions is compounded with terrorism because there are also international definitions derived from the United Nations, treaties, and foreign jurisdictions that affect prosecutions and enforcement strategies.

1. Federal Statutes

U.S. domestic law generally incorporates international treaties that call for prosecution (or extradition to a state that will prosecute) of specific terroristic conduct, including hijacking, sabotage, murder, and torture. The core attributes that appear in most, but not all, definitions of terrorism are 1) use of force or violence to instill fear in a civilian population or use of force or violence to influence or disrupt a government; and 2) a broadly defined political motivation. It is also important to identify whether the particular statute prohibits acts *within* the United States or acts that occur *outside* the United States. Crimes that primarily occur *within* the United States are referred to as "domestic terrorism," and those that primarily occur *outside* the United States are referred to as "international terrorism."

As examples of the core attributes, consider the F.B.I. and the State Department definitions of terrorism. The F.B.I. currently defines terrorism as "the unlawful use of force and violation against persons or property to intimidate or coerce government, the civilian population, or any segment thereof, in furtherance of political or social objectives." 28 C.F.R. § 0.85(*l*) (2004). The State Department defines terrorism as: "premeditated, politically motivated violence perpetrated against noncombatant targets by subnational groups or clandestine agents." 22 U.S.C. § 2656f(d)(2) (2005). The State Department, elaborates its definition of terrorist activity:

> Any activity which is unlawful under the laws of the place where it is committed (or which, if it had been committed in the United States, would be unlawful under the laws of the United States or any State) and which involves any of the following: (I) The highjacking or sabotage of any conveyance (including an aircraft, vessel, or vehicle); (II) The seizing or detaining, and threatening to kill, injure, or continue to detain, another individual in order to compel a third person (including a governmental organization) to do or abstain from doing any act as an explicit or implicit condition for the release of the individual seized or detained; (III) A violent attack upon an internationally protected person (as defined in Section 1116(b)(4) of Title 18) or upon the liberty of such a person; (IV) An assassination; (V) The use of any—(a) biological agent, chemical agent, or nuclear weapon or device, or (b) explosive, firearm, or other weapon or dangerous device (other than for mere personal monetary gain), with intent to endanger, directly or indirectly, the safety of one or more individuals or to cause substantial damage to property; (VI) A threat, attempt, or conspiracy to do any of the foregoing. 8 U.S.C. § 1182 (a)(3)(B)(iii) (2005).

The major federal antiterrorism legislation includes the Omnibus Antiterrorism Act of 1986, the Antiterrorism and Effective Death Penalty Act of 1996 (AEDPA), and, most recently, the USA Patriot Act of 2001. The crimes that were implemented to combat "terrorism" include direct acts and conspiracy to commit violence as well as supporting terrorism through financial contributions or other means.[2] The operative definition of "international terrorism" in the criminal statutes, 18 U.S.C. § 2331, provides:

> "(1) the term "international terrorism" means activities that—

> > (A) involve violent acts or acts dangerous to human life that are a violation of the criminal laws of the United States or of any State, or that would be a criminal violation if committed within the jurisdiction of the United States or of any State;

---

2. The crimes are both general, such as homicide, and specific. For example, there are crimes penalizing the use of weapons of mass destruction; damaging structures of the United States, both here and abroad; bombings of public and government facilities or transporta-tion systems; producing or using missile systems designed to destroy aircraft; harboring or concealing terrorists; and receiving military-type training from a foreign terrorist organization. *See* 18 U.S.C. §§ 2332–2339D.

(B) appear to be intended—

(i) to intimidate or coerce a civilian population;

(ii) to influence the policy of a government by intimidation or coercion; or

(iii) to affect the conduct of a government by mass destruction, assassination, or kidnapping; and

(C) occur primarily outside the territorial jurisdiction of the United States, or transcend national boundaries in terms of the means by which they are accomplished, the persons they appear intended to intimidate or coerce, or the locale in which their perpetrators operate or seek asylum;"

* * *

A similar definition in the statutes defines "domestic terrorism" for acts that occur primarily within the United States. Although the definitions are spelled out in § 2331, the crimes that follow in the next sections of the statutory scheme rarely use the terminology of "international terrorism" and "domestic terrorism." Instead, the crimes prohibit specific actions, such as murder, bombings, and providing material support or resources to a federally-identified terrorist organization. It would appear that the fact that these crimes are within the statutory provisions on domestic and international terrorism operates in a similar manner to a sentence enhancement with other crimes. Parallel legal concepts in U.S. state and federal law include "hate crimes" and aggravating circumstances in capital cases, which function to increase the possible punishment.

The core attribute of terrorism, having an intent to disrupt a government or instill fear in a civilian population, is reflected, however, in the "Limitation on Prosecution" provision in the following statute. Consider 18 U.S.C. § 2332, which reads, in pertinent part:

(a) Homicide.—Whoever kills a national of the United States, while such national is outside the United States, shall—

(1) if the killing is murder (as defined in section 1111(a)), be fined under this title, punished by death or imprisonment for any term of years or for life, or both;

(2) if the killing is a voluntary manslaughter as defined in section 1112(a) of this title, be fined under this title or imprisoned not more than ten years, or both; and

(3) if the killing is an involuntary manslaughter as defined in section 1112(a) of this title, be fined under this title or imprisoned not more than three years, or both.

[Subsection (b) provides for criminal penalties for attempt or conspiracy to commit the homicides listed in (a). Subsection (c) provides for criminal penalties for causing serious bodily injury.]

(d) Limitation on Prosecution.—No prosecution for any offense described in this section shall be undertaken by the United States except on written certification of the Attorney General or the highest ranking subordinate of the Attorney General with responsibility for criminal prosecutions that, in the judgment of the certifying official, *such offense was intended to coerce, intimidate, or retaliate against a government or a civilian population.* (Emphasis added)

How does § 2332 differ from the forms of homicide punished in other criminal statutes. What additional elements, if any, have to be established in order to prove "international terrorism" with a homicidal act? What is the function of the "Limitation on Prosecution" in § 2332? Is proving that the defendant had the requisite intent an element of the crime that the prosecution must prove? If not, what is the role of the certification by the Attorney General of the intent with which the crime was committed? Consider how the Second Circuit Court of Appeals decided the issue in *United States v. Yousef* in the next section. How would the limitation provision affect your analysis of the Problem in Section B?

Other provisions criminalize various methods of support for groups that the Department of State, in consultation with the Attorney General and the Secretary of the Treasury, has designated to be terrorist. *See* 8 U.S.C. 1189. The provisions of 18 U.S.C. 2339B, for example, impose imprisonment for those who provide material support or resources to an identified terrorist organization. This statute proscribes intended or knowing transfer of property to actual or intended terrorist activity.

Another similar provision is 18 U.S.C. § 2339C, which prohibits financing terrorism and provides for extraterritorial jurisdiction. Consider the applicability of this provision to the Problem in Section B:

(a) Offenses.—

(2) In general.—Whoever, in a circumstance described in subsection (b), by any means, directly or indirectly, unlawfully and willfully provides or collects funds with the intention that such funds be used, or with the knowledge that such funds are to be used, in full or in part, in order to carry out—

* * *

(B) any other act intended to cause death or serious bodily injury to a civilian, or to any other person not taking an active part in the hostilities in a situation of armed conflict, when the purpose of such act, by its nature or context, is to intimidate a population, or to compel a government or an international organization to do or to abstain from doing any act,

Shall be punished as prescribed in subsection (d) (1).

(3) Attempts and conspiracies.—Whoever attempts or conspires to commit an offense under paragraph (1) shall be punished as prescribed in subsection (d) (1).

(4) Relationship to predicate act [an act described in subsection (a) (1)].—For an act to constitute an offense set forth in this subsection, it shall not be necessary that the funds were actually used to carry out a predicate act.

(c) Jurisdiction.—There is jurisdiction over the offenses in subsection (a) in the following circumstances—

* * *

(2) the offense takes place outside the United States and—

(A) a perpetrator is a national of the United States...;

(B) a perpetrator is found in the United States; or

(C) was directed toward or resulted in the carrying out of a predicate act against—

(i) any property that is owned, leased, or used by the United States or by any department or agency of the United States, including an embassy or other diplomatic or consular premises of the United States; [or]

* * *

(iii) any national of the United States...

2. Judicial Interpretation of the Terrorism Statutes

In *Yousef*, the Second Circuit decided both statutory construction and constitutional issues arising in a prosecution under 18 U.S.C. § 2332.

UNITED STATES v. YOUSEF

327 F.3d 56 (2d Cir. 2003)

TERRORISM

Introduction

Defendants-appellants Ramzi Yousef, Eyad Ismoil, and Abdul Hakim Murad appeal from judgments of conviction entered in the United States District Court for the Southern District of New York (Kevin Thomas Duffy, *Judge*) on April 13, June 2, and June 15, 1998, respectively. Judge Duffy presided over two separate jury trials. In the first trial, Yousef, Murad, and Wali Khan Amin Shah were tried on charges relating to a conspiracy to bomb United States commercial airliners in Southeast Asia. In the second trial, Yousef and Ismoil were tried for their involvement in the February 1993 bombing of the World Trade Center in New York City.

I. World Trade Center Bombing

The conspiracy to bomb the World Trade Center began in the Spring of 1992, when Yousef met Ahmad Mohammad Ajaj at a terrorist training camp on the border of Afghanistan and Pakistan. After formulating their terrorist plot, Yousef and Ajaj traveled to New York together in September 1992. In Ajaj's luggage, he carried a "terrorist kit" that included, among other things, bomb-making manuals. After Yousef and Ajaj arrived at John F. Kennedy International Airport, inspectors of the Immigration and Naturalization Service ("INS") discovered the "terrorist kit" in Ajaj's luggage and arrested him. Although Yousef was also stopped, he and Ajaj did not disclose their connection to one another, and INS officials allowed Yousef to enter the United States. * * *

Once in New York, Yousef began to put together the manpower and the supplies that he would need to carry out his plan to bomb the World Trade Center. Yousef assembled a group of co-conspirators to execute his plan, including defendants Mohammad Salameh, Nidal Ayyad, Mahmud Abouhalima, and Abdul Rahman Yasin. Next, Yousef began accumulating the necessary ingredients for the bomb. He ordered the required chemicals, and his associates rented a shed in which to store them. Yousef and Salameh established their headquarters at an apartment they rented in Jersey City, New Jersey, an urban center located across the Hudson River from Manhattan. The apartment also functioned as their bomb-making factory.

In December 1992, Yousef contacted Ismoil, who was then living in Dallas, Texas. On February 22, 1993, Ismoil joined Yousef and the others in New York to help complete the bomb preparations.

On February 26, 1993, Yousef and Ismoil drove a bomb-laden van onto the B–2 level of the parking garage below the World Trade Center. They then set the bomb's timer to detonate minutes later. At approximately 12:18 p.m. that day, the bomb exploded, killing six people, injuring more than a thousand others, and causing widespread fear and more than $500 million in property damage.

Soon after the bombing, Yousef and Ismoil fled from the United States. Yousef and Ismoil were indicted for their participation in the bombing on March 31, 1993 and August 8, 1994, respectively. Yousef was captured in Pakistan nearly two years after the bombing, and Ismoil was arrested in Jordan a little over two years after the attack. Both were returned to the United States to answer the charges in the indictment.

II. Airline Bombing

A year and a half after the World Trade Center bombing, Yousef entered Manila, the capital of the Philippines, under an assumed name. By September 1994, Yousef had devised a plan to attack United States airliners. According to the plan, five individuals would place bombs aboard twelve United States-flag aircraft that served routes in Southeast Asia. The conspirators would board an airliner in Southeast Asia, assemble a bomb on the plane, and then exit the plane during its first layover. As the planes continued on toward their next destinations, the time-bombs would detonate. Eleven of the twelve flights targeted were ultimately destined for cities in the United States.

Yousef and his co-conspirators performed several tests in preparation for the airline bombings. In December 1994, Yousef and Wali Khan Amin Shah placed one of the bombs they had constructed in a Manila movie theater. The bomb exploded, injuring several patrons of the theater. Ten days later, Yousef planted another test bomb under a passenger's seat during the first leg of a Philippine Airlines flight from Manila to Japan. Yousef disembarked from the plane during the stopover and then made his way back to Manila. During the second leg of the flight, the bomb exploded, killing one passenger, a Japanese national, and injuring others.

The plot to bomb the United States-flag airliners was uncovered in January 1995, only two weeks before the conspirators intended to carry it out. * * * Yousef fled the country, but was captured in Pakistan the next month. * * *

In the trial of Yousef, Murad, and Shah on the airline bombing charges the jury found all three defendants guilty on all counts. Similarly, in Yousef and Ismoil's trial on charges relating to the

World Trade Center bombing ,the jury found both defendants guilty on all counts. * * *

BACKGROUND

Preparation for Airline Bombing Conspiracy

In August 1994, after the bombing of the World Trade Center, and his flight from the United States, Yousef traveled to Manila under an alias. By September, Yousef had developed an elaborate plan to bomb a dozen United States-flag aircraft and recorded that plan on his laptop computer. According to the plan, five individuals would plant bombs aboard twelve United States-flag aircraft operating on routes in Southeast Asia. Each conspirator would board an airliner in Southeast Asia, assemble a bomb on board the plane, and leave the aircraft at its first stop. The time-bombs would detonate during the second leg of each of the targeted flights. Eleven of the twelve flights were ultimately destined for cities in the United States. Each of the targeted aircraft was capable of carrying up to 280 people.

After Yousef had formulated his airline bombing plan, he began to acquire the information and the ingredients necessary to carry it out. Yousef compiled detailed flight data on the twelve aircraft, including their departing times, flight numbers, flight durations and aircraft types, and transferred this information to his laptop computer. In early November 1994, Yousef placed a large order for chemicals and equipment in Manila, and, during the next two months, he and his co-conspirators performed several tests in preparation for the aircraft bombings. On December 1, 1994, Yousef and Shah conducted a test by placing a bomb under a patron's seat at the Greenbelt movie theater in Manila. At 10:30 p.m., the bomb exploded, injuring several people. Ten days later, on December 11, Yousef planted another test bomb under the seat of a passenger on a Philippine Airlines jet flying from Manila to Cebu (another city in the Philippines) and then to Japan. Yousef disembarked from the plane in Cebu. Two hours after the aircraft departed from Cebu, the bomb exploded, killing one Japanese passenger and injuring others.

In late December, Murad traveled from the Middle East to the Philippines, and Shah, who had left the Philippines immediately after the movie theater bombing, returned to Manila under an assumed name. Thus, by January 1995, the conspirators were assembled in Manila and ready to carry out their attack on twelve United States flag aircraft. But for a fire in the defendants' apartment in Manila, the plan might have succeeded. * * *

. . .

III.   Arrests of Shah, Yousef, and Murad

On January 11, 1995, several days after their search of the Manila apartment, Manila police arrested Shah. Police apprehended Shah after they determined that a pager called by Yousef following Murad's arrest was registered in the name of Shah's girlfriend. Shah escaped from custody one week later, only to be recaptured on December 11, 1995 in Malaysia by Malaysian police. Shah was then delivered to the custody of the United States, where he agreed to speak to Federal Bureau of Investigation ("FBI") agents after he signed a written waiver of his *Miranda* rights. *See Miranda v. Arizona* (1966).

In early February 1995, the United States Embassy in Islamabad, Pakistan received a tip that Yousef was somewhere in Islamabad. On February 7, 1995, Pakistani officials, together with a special agent from the United States Department of State, arrested Yousef at a guest house in Islamabad. The next day, agents from the FBI and the United States Secret Service arrived from the United States, took Yousef into custody, and transported him back to the United States. On the plane, Yousef was informed of the charges against him pertaining to the World Trade Center bombing and advised of his rights. Without the use or need of an interpreter, he waived his *Miranda* rights and made an extensive confession about the World Trade Center bombing plot. . . .

Philippine authorities turned Murad over to FBI agents in Manila on April 12, 1995. During the plane ride to the United States, Murad was read his *Miranda* rights twice and given written copies of the waiver in both English and Arabic. Murad indicated that he understood his rights and waived them in writing. He then agreed to speak to the FBI agents on the airplane without an interpreter. Murad told the agents that his part in the aircraft bombing scheme was to board a United Airlines flight in Singapore with its first stop in Hong Kong and to plant a bomb onboard the plane. After arriving in Hong Kong, Murad was to take a different flight back to Singapore, planting a bomb aboard that plane as well. Murad told the agents that he expected the resulting explosion to tear a hole in the aircraft, causing it to crash in the Pacific Ocean. He also asserted his belief that co-conspirators would bomb other flights. Murad stated that the goal of the attacks was to "make the American people and the American government suffer for their support of Israel."

Murad described the explosive device components of the bombs, which matched items seized at the Manila apartment he shared with Yousef. Murad stated that he had been told that the Philippine Airlines bombing of December 11, 1994 was a test-run to ensure that the chemicals and timing device worked correctly.

[On February 21, 1996, a grand jury in the Southern District of New York indicted Yousef, Murad, and Shah for various crimes relating to their conspiracy to bomb United States airliners in Southeast Asia in 1994 and 1995.] * * *

In Count Fifteen, the defendants were charged with violating 18 U.S.C. § 2332(b) and (d) by conspiring to kill United States nationals while they were located outside of the United States. In Count Sixteen, the defendants were charged with violating 18 U.S.C. § 2332a by conspiring to use a weapon of mass destruction outside the United States against United States nationals. * * *

The trial of Yousef, Murad, and Shah on the airline bombing charges began on May 29, 1996 and ended on September 5, 1996, when the jury found all three defendants guilty on all counts. On appeal, defendants-appellants Yousef and Murad attack their convictions and sentences, raising a number of issues.

* * * Yousef argues that we should overturn his conviction on Count Fifteen because 18 U.S.C. § 2332 unconstitutionally delegates legislative power to the Attorney General of the United States. Alternatively, he contends that his conviction should be overturned because the District Court failed to charge the jury that it had to find intent to retaliate against the United States and its citizens as an element of the crime charged in Count Fifteen.

In Count Fifteen, Yousef and his co-defendants were charged with conspiring to kill United States nationals outside the United States in violation of 18 U.S.C. § 2332(b) and (d).

Under 18 U.S.C. § 2332(a) it is a crime to "kill[ ] a national of the United States, while such national is outside the United States." Section 2332(b) prohibits any person outside the United States from "engag[ing] in a conspiracy to kill[ ] a national of the United States." Section 2332(d) is entitled "Limitation on prosecution" and provides:

No prosecution for any offense described in this section shall be undertaken by the United States except on written certification of the Attorney General or the highest ranking subordinate of the Attorney General with responsibility for criminal prosecutions that, in the judgment of the certifying official, such offense was intended to coerce, intimidate, or retaliate against a government or a civilian population.

Prosecutorial Discretion Under Section 2332(d)

Yousef argues that § 2332 is an unconstitutional delegation of legislative authority, * * * because the statute authorizes the Attorney General to define what conduct constitutes an offense.

Section 2332 does not represent an unconstitutional delegation of power to the Attorney General. Indeed, § 2332(d) does not delegate any legislative power to the Attorney General. Rather, it merely sets limits on how the Attorney General can exercise his discretion to prosecute. * * * Section 2332(d) limits the Justice Department's prosecution of crimes under § 2332 to those crimes in which the defendant intended to target the Government or civilian population of the United States. Exercise of such prosecutorial discretion involves no rulemaking power on the part of the Executive Branch and, therefore, cannot constitute delegation of legislative power to the Attorney General—let alone an unlawful delegation of such power.

Even if § 2332(d) did represent a delegation of legislative power to the Attorney General, such a delegation would not be unconstitutional. It has long been the rule that Congress may delegate some of its legislative powers to the Executive Branch, so long as that delegation is made "under the limitation of a prescribed standard."

* * * Subsection (d) provides a clearly intelligible principle to which the Attorney General must adhere-namely, to prosecute only those cases where the intent of the offense was to coerce, intimidate, or retaliate against the Government or civilian population of the United States.

In sum, § 2332 does not unconstitutionally delegate legislative power to the Attorney General. * * *

Nor does § 2332 unconstitutionally remove an element of the offense from the jury. Although a criminal defendant has the right to a jury determination of every element of the crime, *see Apprendi v. New Jersey*, 530 U.S. 466 (2000), an analysis of the text and structure of § 2332 demonstrates that subsection (d) does not comprise an element of the offenses proscribed by § 2332. First, subsection (d) follows three self-contained subsections each of which defines the elements of a distinct offense. *See* 18 U.S.C. § 2332(a)–(d). In particular, each subsection of (a) through (c) imposes an attendant level of intent, and none of these subsections makes reference to § 2332(d). Second, subsection (d) is expressly designated as a "limit on prosecution" rather than as an element of the offenses set forth in § 2332. We conclude, therefore, that the District Court did not err by failing to charge an intent to retaliate against the United States Government or its citizens. Even if the Court had erred in this regard, any error would have been harmless, given the overwhelming evidence that the defendants specifically intended the aircraft bombings to serve as retaliation against the United States Government and its citizens for United States foreign policy.

———

Notes and Questions

1. What Is Terrorism? Do you agree with the Second Circuit's analysis of each part of the federal statutes? For example, why was this conduct considered terrorism under the statutes? Does 18 U.S.C. 2332 proscribe terrorism? Where is terrorism mentioned? How might terrorism be considered the offense? What role do you think terrorism plays in section 2332? Is it a substantive part of the offense(s)? If so, how is it defined and what are its elements? Is it just a penalty enhancer? Does it function somewhat like a "hate crime?" Do you agree with the court that the "certification" by the Attorney General is not a substantive element of the offense? What would be an argument that the certification is an element of the offense? If so, does it present constitutional issues?

2. Other Federal Prosecutions. The U.S. Department of Justice has published the following list of prosecutions for terrorism in *"Some Other Prosecutions and Convictions in the United States for 'Terrorism,' " from the U.S. Department of Justice, Examples of Terrorism Convictions Since Sept. 11, 2001,* June 23, 2006, *complete list available at* www.usdoj.gov.

> **Richard Reid (District of Massachusetts)**—British national Richard Reid was sentenced to life in prison following his guilty plea in January 2003 on charges of attempting to ignite a shoe bomb while on an airplane from Paris to Miami. Reid was subdued by passengers on the Dec. 22, 2001 American Airlines flight before he could ignite the explosives.
>
> **John Walker Lindh (Eastern District of Virginia)**—Lindh pleaded guilty in July 2002 to one count of supplying services to the Taliban and a charge that he carried weapons while fighting on the Taliban's front lines in Afghanistan against the Northern Alliance. Lindh was sentenced to 20 years in prison.
>
> **Lackawanna Six: Shafal Mosed, Yahya Goba, Sahim Alwan, Mukhtar Al–Bakri, Yasein Taher , Elbaneh Jaber (Western District of New York)**—Six defendants from the Lackawanna, New York area pleaded guilty to charges of providing material support to al Qaeda, based on their attendance at an al Qaeda terrorist training camp. The defendants were sentenced to terms ranging from seven years to 10 years in prison.
>
> **Portland Cell: Maher "Michael" Hawash, October Martinique Lewis, Habis Abdullah Al–Saoub, Patrice Lamumba Ford, Ahmed Ibrahim Bilal, Muhammad Ibrahim Bilal, Jeffrey Leon Battle (District of Oregon)**—The defendants in the so-called "Portland Cell" case pleaded guilty to criminal charges ranging from laundering money to conspiracy to supply goods to the Taliban, to seditious conspiracy. Ford and Battle were each

sentenced to 18 years in prison. The charges resulted from an investigation into the defendants' training for preparation to fight violent jihad in Afghanistan.

Earnest James Ujaama (Western District of Washington)— Pursuant to a cooperation agreement, Earnest James Ujaama was sentenced to two years in jail in February 2004 following his guilty plea on a charge of conspiring to supply goods and services to the Taliban in violation of the International Emergency Economic Powers Act.

Sayed Mustajab Shah, Ilyas Ali, Muhammed Abid Afridi (Southern District of California)—In April 2006, Muhammed Abid Afridi was sentenced to 57 months in prison on one count of conspiracy to distribute heroin and hashish and one count of providing material support to terrorists. Afridi was arrested in September 2002 and indicted by a federal grand jury in October 2002 along with co-defendants Sayed Mustajab Shah and Ilyas Ali for their involvement in an international drugs-for-weapons program. Shah's sentencing is scheduled for June 2006. Ali was sentenced to 57 months in prison.

Carlos Ali Romero Valera, Uwe Jensen, Edgar Fernando Blanco Puerta, Elkin Alberto Arroyave Ruiz, Carlos Adolfo Romero–Panchano, Fanny Cecilia Barrera De–Amaris, Adriana Gladys Mora (Southern District of Texas)—As part of Operation White Terror, Carlos Ali Romero Valera, Uwe Jensen, Edgar Fernando Blanco Puerta, and Elkin Alberto Arroyave Ruiz were convicted on charges of supplying material support to a terrorist organization (the United Self–Defense Forces (AUC) of Colombia) through a weapons-for-drugs deal. In December 2005, Fanny Cecilia Barrera de Amaris and Carlos Adolfo Romero–Panchano were convicted on charges of conspiracy to provide material support and resources to a foreign terrorist organization. Both were extradited in 2004 and pleaded guilty. Barrera de Amaris was sentenced to five years and one month in prison while Panchano was sentenced to three years. Adriana Gladys Mora was convicted in January 2004 of conspiring to provide material support to a terrorist organization and distributing cocaine.

Iyman Faris (Eastern District of Virginia)—In October 2003, Iyman Faris was sentenced to 20 years in prison for providing material support and resources to al Qaeda and conspiracy for providing the terrorist organization with information about possible U.S. targets for attack. Faris pleaded guilty in May 2003.
* * *

Lynne Stewart, Mohammed Yousry, Ahmed Abdel Sattar, (Southern District of New York)—In February 2005, a federal jury in Manhattan convicted attorney Lynne Stewart, Mohammed Yousry, and Ahmed Abdel Sattar on charges including providing, and concealing the provision of, material support or resources to terrorists. The defendants were associates of Sheikh Abdel–Rahman, leader of the terrorist organization Islamic Group (IG), who is serving a life sentence for his role in terrorist activity, including the 1993 bombing of the World Trade Center.

* * *

Zacarias Moussaoui (Eastern District of Virginia)—In April 2005, Zacarias Moussaoui pleaded guilty to six charges against him related to his participation in the September 11th conspiracy. In May 2006, Moussaoui was sentenced to life in prison.

Basman Elashi, Bayan Elashi, Ghassan Elashi, Hazim Elashi, Ihsan Elashi (Northern District of Texas)—In April 2005, a federal jury convicted Basman, Bayan and Ghassan Elashi, and the Infocom Corporation, on charges of conspiracy to deal in the property of a specially designated terrorist and money laundering. The activities were related to Infocom, an Internet Service provider believed to be a front for Hamas. Hazim and Ihsan Elashi were also convicted in the same case and were sentenced to 66 months and 72 months in prison, respectively.

Mark Robert Walker (Western District of Texas)—In April 2005, Walker was sentenced to two years in prison for aiding a terrorist organization. He was indicted in December 2004 and pleaded guilty to two counts of attempting to make a contribution of goods and services to a designated terrorist organization (Al-Ittihad Al–Isiami in Somalia).

Carlos Gamarra–Murillo (Middle District of Florida)—In August 2005, Gamarra–Murillo was sentenced to 25 years in prison for engaging in the business of brokering and exporting defense articles without a license and providing material support to a foreign terrorist organization (FARC). Gamarra–Murillo was charged in April 2004 and pleaded guilty in February 2005.

* * *

Hamid Hayat (Eastern District of California)—On April 25, 2006, a federal jury in Sacramento convicted Hamid Hayat of Lodi, California, of one count of providing material support or resources to terrorists and three counts of lying to the FBI in a terrorism investigation. The jury found that Hayat provided material support to terrorists by attending a jihad training camp overseas, and that he attempted to conceal his training from the FBI. Hayat faces up to 39 years in prison; sentencing is scheduled for July 2006.

D. INTERNATIONAL AND FOREIGN DEFINITIONS OF TERRORISM

1. The Role of the League of Nations and the United Nations

As early as 1937, the League of Nations attempted to define terrorism, even promulgating an anti-terrorism convention.[3] Al-

3. In 1937, the League of Nations adopted a Convention on the Preven-   tion and Punishment of Terrorism. This Convention, moribund at birth, defined

though these early efforts were unsuccessful, in recent years, the General Assembly of the United Nations has focused on terrorism, noting that it is never justified, and reiterating that terrorism is constituted by: "criminal acts intended or calculated to provoke a state of terror in the general public, a group of persons or particular persons for political purposes." In 1998, the U.N., in its Convention for the Suppression of Terrorist Bombings, provided that:

> Each State Party shall adopt such measures as may be necessary, including, where appropriate, domestic legislation to ensure that criminal acts within the scope of this Convention, in particular where they are intended or calculated to provoke a state of terror in the general public or in a group of persons or particular persons, are under no circumstances justifiable by considerations of a political, philosophical, ideological, racial, ethnic, religious or other similar nature and are punished by penalties consistent with their grave nature. . . .

The United Nations, however, has still not been able to arrive at any consensus on the definition of terrorism. United Nations Conventions have defined terrorism only very vaguely. For example, it was defined as violence which transcends national borders without military authority. The U.N. Sixth (Legal) Committee has been debating a Draft Comprehensive Convention on International Terrorism since 1997, but this has been bogged down. It, like earlier conventions on hijacking and financing terrorism and others, mainly calls upon nations to prosecute or to extradite alleged perpetrators if found in the country.

The Security Council, on September 12, 2001, unanimously approved Resolution 1368 (2001), stating that any act of international terrorism was a threat to international peace and security. While calling on all states to bring to justice "the perpetrators, organizers and sponsors" of these terrorist acts, it stressed that "those responsible for aiding, supporting or harboring them would be held accountable," and pointedly recognized the right to individual and collective self-defense under the Charter.

The United Nations has also focused on prohibiting the financial support of terrorism. The International Convention for the Suppression of the Financing of Terrorism[4] adopted by the General

---

terrorism to be: "[c]riminal acts directed against a State and intended to or calculated to create a state of terror in the minds of particular persons, or a group of persons or the general public." League of Nations Terrorism Convention, Annex to Convention for Prevention and Punishment of Terrorism, Nov. 16, 1937, League of Nations O.J.

No. 19, at 23, League of Nations Doc. C.546(1) M.383(1) 1937 V (1938) at art. 1(2). Even after the League of Nations Convention was formally dead, it did influence other attempts to promulgate treaties and rules to define and combat terrorism.

4. International Convention for the Suppression of the Financing of Terror-

Assembly in 1999. Security Council Resolution 1373 provides that the Security Council:

> 1.   Decides that all States shall:
>
>   (a) Prevent and suppress the financing of terrorist acts;
>
>   (b) Criminalize the wilful provision or collection, by any means, directly or indirectly, of funds by their nationals or in their territories with the intention that the funds should be used, or in the knowledge that they are to be used, in order to carry out terrorist acts;
>
>   (c) Freeze without delay funds and other financial assets or economic resources of persons who commit, or attempt to commit, terrorist acts or participate in or facilitate the commission of terrorist acts; of entities owned or controlled directly or indirectly by such persons; and of persons and entities acting on behalf of, or at the direction of such persons and entities, including funds derived or generated from property owned or controlled directly or indirectly by such persons and associated persons and entities;
>
>   (d) Prohibit their nationals or any persons and entities within their territories from making any funds, financial assets or economic resources or financial or other related services available, directly or indirectly, for the benefit of persons who commit or attempt to commit or facilitate or participate in the commission of terrorist acts, of entities owned or controlled, directly or indirectly, by such persons and of persons and entities acting on behalf of or at the direction of such persons...

Subsection (b) above requires States to criminalize certain acts of financing terrorism. How would you describe the *mens rea* identified in (b)? Does the federal statute that is described earlier conform to Security Council Resolution 1373?

Would it be constitutional or legal for the U.S. Congress to pass a law criminalizing *being* a member of a group? France has such a crime: *"association de malfaiteurs"* (association of wrongdoers) and Italy has the crime of being in a *"grupo di tipo Mafioso"* (group of the Mafioso type).

ism, Dec. 9, 1999, S. Treaty Doc. No. 106–49 (2000), 39 I.L.M. 270. *See also* Resolution 1373 of the United Nations

Security Council, S.C. Res. 1373, U.N. Doc. S/RES/1373 (Sept. 28, 2001).

2. Foreign Domestic Legislation

Because terrorism is likely to cross national borders, domestic legislation in other countries is important to the overall prosecution of terrorism-related crimes. Compare the following Belgian and French laws to the laws in the United States.

The Belgian *Code Pénal* article 137, reads:

> [Terrorism is conduct, which,] by its nature or context, may inflict severe damage on a country or international organization and is committed with the firm intention or the aim of gravely intimidating a nation or constraining or forcing the leadership or international organization to accomplish or refrain from accomplishing certain acts, or gravely destabilizing or destroying the fundamental political, economic or social structures of a country or international organization.

The French *Code Pénal* article 421–1, provides an extensive list of terrorist conduct:

> The following offences constitute acts of terrorism where they are committed intentionally in connection with an individual or collective undertaking the purpose of which is seriously to disturb the public order through intimidation or terror:
>
> > 1E willful attacks on life, willful attacks on the physical integrity of persons, abduction and unlawful detention and also as the hijacking of planes, vessels or any other means of transport, defined by Book II of the present Code;
> >
> > 2E theft, extortion, destruction, defacement and damage, and also computer offences, as defined under Book III of the present Code;
> >
> > 3E offences committed by combat organizations and disbanded movements as defined under articles 431–13 to 431–17, and the offences set out under articles 434–6, 441–2 to 441–5;
> >
> > 4E the production or keeping of machines, dangerous or explosive devices, set out under article 3 of the Act of 19th June 1871 which repealed the Decree of 4th September 1870 on the production of military grade weapons;
> >
> > > — the production, sale, import or export of explosive substances as defined by article 6 of the Act no. 70–575 of 3rd July 1970 amending the regulations governing explosive powders and substances;
> > >
> > > — the purchase, keeping, transport or unlawful carrying of explosive substances or of devices made with

such explosive substances, as defined by article 38 of the Ordinance of 18th April 1939 defining the regulations governing military equipment, weapons and ammunition;

— the detention, carrying, and transport of weapons and ammunition falling under the first and fourth categories defined by articles 4, 28, 31 and 32 of the aforementioned Ordinance;

— the offences defined by articles 1 and 4 of the Act no. 72–467 of 9th June 1972 forbidding the designing, production, keeping, stocking, purchase or sale of biological or toxin-based weapons;

— the offences referred to under articles 58 to 63 of the Act no. 98–467 of 17th June 1998 on the application of the Convention of the 13th January 1993 on the prohibition of developing, producing, stocking and use of chemical weapons and on their destruction;

5E receiving the product of one of the offences set out in paragraphs 1 to 4 above.

How do the Belgian and French provisions on terrorism compare with those in the federal statutes described earlier? Are any of the definitions of terrorism satisfactory? Are the domestic legislative definitions of terrorism, albeit not very coherent or clearly drafted, nevertheless generally helpful in coming up with a valid, neutral definition of terrorism? Is there a core set of concepts or principles common to all of the statutes?

E.   PUBLIC AUTHORITY DEFENSE

A soldier or government official may be ordered to engage in conduct that results in the loss of innocent life. For example, a group of soldiers may enter a village in Afghanistan searching for Taliban and take aggressive action against a position that is occupied by both militants and civilians. If civilians are killed, would the soldiers be charged with terrorism for those deaths? The criminal law recognizes a defense of public authority as a justification for homicide, for example, when the killer acts pursuant to and within the parameters of his or her proper legal authorization. Any breach of the legal parameters of the authority or any authorization that is actually unlawful will generally eliminate the justification. For example, a police officer is legally justified in using deadly force when it is necessary, reasonable, and proportionate to a threat to herself, to another person, or to the public at large. Killing, when these elements of justification are not evident to a reasonable person in the circumstances, is a criminal homicide. The rule in international law is similar. Deadly force or an armed attack is justified, if a nation is legally at war or is acting in legitimate self-defense. A combatant is authorized to use deadly force within the legal parameters of self-defense in international law and the laws of war.

The core concept of terrorism is the use of violence against innocents, so it is necessary to define the term innocent. The basic concept of "innocent" for terrorism is a *mélange* of the concepts in criminal law and international humanitarian law including terms such as "innocent civilians," non-combatants, or those *"hors du combat."* In general, willful, wanton, or criminally reckless violence against innocents to gain some military, political, religious, or philosophical (including nihilistic) advantage constitutes terrorism. We use the term "reckless" here to mean the form of recklessness that is the equivalent of the mental state for depraved heart murder—where the perpetrator knows the significantly high risk to life and limb, but takes that risk anyway. It is interesting to consider whether the standard criminal law affirmative defense of acting under public authority can apply to terrorism.

It may be helpful in understanding the complexity of acts of violence based on public authority, and when those acts constitute terrorism, by a hypothetical scenario. Suppose that the relevant military official, delegated to do so by the President of the United States, orders a civilian airliner to be shot down, because it has been hijacked to be flown into a major building, where thousands will be killed. Would the order be justified? If so, on what basis? Would the hijacking be an act of terrorism, giving rise to self-defense? The hijackers were attackers, who acted by using hostages and turning the plane (and the hostages) into missiles. Thus, the original deadly attack, the hijacking with intent to destroy a large number of people, justifies deadly force to be used to thwart the result. What about the fact that innocent passenger will be intentionally killed? This is not dissimilar to the use of force in a war against an attacking enemy, when some innocents will be killed incident to the defensive action. The unfortunate term, "collateral damage," is used to denote the justification in the killing, which may include innocents along with the perpetrators. If, on the other hand, the action were unnecessary and the order made recklessly (with a malignant heart—the mens rea for depraved heart murder or MPC "reckless murder"), the order would be criminal.

For example, recall the infamous "Robo Cruiser" incident, reported in Proceedings, the U.S. Naval Institute Magazine, by U.S. Naval Commander, David R. Carlson, Commander of the *U.S.S. Sides,* a frigate on the scene when the *U.S.S. Vincennes* (nicknamed "Robo Cruiser") shot down an Iranian Airbus killing the 290 innocent passengers aboard. Commander Carlson noted that the "Robo–Cruiser" had "no good reason" for downing the airbus, and that: "[t]he *Vincennes* saw an opportunity for action, and pressed hard for Commander Middle East Force to give permission to fire . . . The tragedy was avoidable, and we must learn from it . . . When the decision was made to shoot down the Airbus, the airliner was climbing, not diving; it was showing the proper identification friend or foe . . . The *Vincennes* was never under attack by the Iranian aircraft." B Brennan, *Iranian Air Tragedy Was Avoidable, Officer Says*, Baton Rouge Morning Advocate, Sept. 2, 1989, p. 9A, col. 1. Was the order to shoot down the Airbus legal? Was the downing of the civilian airliner terrorism?

F. INTERNATIONAL AND EXTRATERRITORIAL JURISDICTION OVER TERRORISM

The term *jurisdiction* is often used imprecisely. Effective analysis requires us to draw sharp distinctions between rule-making and rule-enforcing jurisdiction. Three forms of jurisdiction obtain: prescriptive; adjudicative; and enforcement. Enforcement and adjudicative jurisdiction are derivative of and dependant on prescriptive jurisdiction. Thus, the first question is whether the scope of the prescriptive (legislative) jurisdiction is valid. Domestic constitutional law, legislation, or judicial decisions may limit a state's authority to apply domestic law to events occurring outside that state's territory. International law does similarly, although international law is permissive as to a state's right to assert jurisdiction—a state may assert jurisdiction, unless an international rule prohibits it. This rule is based on the concept of sovereignty.

Adjudicative and enforcement jurisdiction are derived from and dependent on prescriptive or legislative jurisdiction—if the legislative scope is not broad enough to cover the conduct, obviously, no adjudication or enforcement is appropriate. Therefore, we must first ask whether prescriptive jurisdiction is valid, and then must ask whether adjudicative or enforcement jurisdiction are appropriate. A state first prescribes a rule, which is to say that either by act of the legislature, decree of the executive, administrative regulation, or decision of a court, it declares a principle or legal norm. Second, the state enforces the rule; it arrests, subpoenas witnesses and documents, extradites, tries, or punishes a person for violation of the rule. A court enters a judgment vindicating the rule. Where the judiciary decides questions of law and fact and metes out the punishment or remedy, jurisdiction to adjudicate is often carved out of enforcement jurisdiction as a separate category. When prescriptive jurisdiction obtains, often adjudicative and enforcement jurisdiction follow.

The U.S. Omnibus Diplomatic Security and Antiterrorism Act of 1986, as expanded by the USA Patriot Act, is an example of expanding jurisdiction. It provides jurisdiction to extradite or prosecute perpetrators of certain terror-violence. It allows domestic prosecution of those who commit terror-violence against American citizens abroad, if the offense is "intended to coerce, intimidate, or retaliate against a government or a civilian population." 18 U.S.C. § 2331(e) provides for fines and imprisonment for those who commit murder or manslaughter against American nationals abroad, and for those who attempt or conspire to do so.

Extraterritorial application of a criminal law may be justified by any one of the five principles of extraterritorial authority analyzed herein. In the following decision, the Second Circuit discusses customary international law and the bases of jurisdiction as applied to terrorism. Any of the five principles of extraterritorial authority analyzed here may justify Extraterritorial application of a criminal law, although the Court rejects universal jurisdiction in these circumstances.

UNITED STATES v. YOUSEF
327 F.3d 56 (2d Cir. 2003)

[The Second Circuit considers the jurisdictional basis for the prosecution for the acts described in the first part of the opinion on page 82 *supra*.]

Jurisdiction over Yousef on Counts Twelve through Nineteen was based on 18 U.S.C. § 32. Yousef argues that this statute cannot give rise to jurisdiction because his prosecution thereunder conflicts with established principles of customary international law. Yousef's argument fails because, while customary international law may inform the judgment of our courts in an appropriate case, it cannot alter or constrain the making of law by the political branches of the government as ordained by the Constitution.

Principles of customary international law reflect the practices and customs of States in the international arena that are applied in a consistent fashion and that are generally recognized by what used to be called "civilized states." That is, principles of customary international law consist of the *"settled* rule[s] of international law" as recognized through "the general assent of civilized nations. *The Paquete Habana,* 175 U.S. 677 (1900) (emphasis added). * * *

It has long been established that customary international law is part of the law of the United States to the limited extent that "where there is *no treaty,* and *any controlling executive or legisla-*

tive act or judicial decision, resort must be had to the customs and usages of civilized nations." *The Paquete Habana* (emphasis added).

While it is permissible for United States law to conflict with customary international law, where legislation is susceptible to multiple interpretations, the interpretation that does not conflict with "the law of nations" is preferred. *Murray v. Charming Betsy,* 6 U.S. (2 Cranch) 64 (1804). The *Charming Betsy* canon comes into play only where Congress's intent is ambiguous. *Attorney General of Canada v. R.J. Reynolds Tobacco Holdings, Inc.,* 268 F.3d 103 (2d Cir. 2001) (stating that United States courts " 'are not to read *general words* ... without regard to the limitations customarily observed by nations upon the exercise of their powers.' ") (quoting *United States v. Aluminum Co. of Am.,* 148 F.2d 416, 443 (2d Cir.1945) (emphasis added)).

If a statute makes plain Congress's intent (instead of employing ambiguous or "general" words), then Article III courts, which can overrule Congressional enactments only when such enactments conflict with the Constitution, *see, e.g., Sinclair Refining Co. v. Atkinson,* 370 U.S. 195 (1962) (stating that, "[I]n dealing with problems of interpretation and application of federal statutes, we have no power to change deliberate choices of legislative policy that Congress has made within its constitutional powers"), must enforce the intent of Congress irrespective of whether the statute conforms to customary international law. Thus the Supreme Court stated in *The Nereide,* 13 U.S. (9 Cranch) 388 (1815) (Marshall, C.J.), that while courts are "bound by the law of nations which is a part of the law of the land," Congress may "manifest [its] will" to apply a different rule "by passing an act for the purpose." The Court reaffirmed this principle in *McCulloch v. Sociedad Nacional de Marineros de Honduras,* 372 U.S. 10 (1963), stating that Congress may enact laws superseding "the law of nations" if "the affirmative intention of the Congress [is] clearly expressed." * * *

In the event that there is no "controlling executive or legislative act or judicial decision" that the court must apply, a court should identify the norms of customary international law by looking to "the general usage and practice of nations [,] or by [looking to] judicial decisions recognizing and enforcing that law ... [, or by] consulting the works of jurists writing professedly on public law," *United States v. Smith,* 18 U.S. (5 Wheat.) 153 (1820) (Story, J.).

* * * United States domestic law provides a complete basis for jurisdiction over the conduct charged in these counts, independent of customary international law. Nevertheless, contrary to Yousef's claims, jurisdiction is consistent with three of the five principles of

customary international law criminal jurisdiction—the objective, protective, and passive personality principles.

First, jurisdiction over Counts Twelve through Eighteen is consistent with the "passive personality principle" of customary international jurisdiction because each of these counts involved a plot to bomb United States-flag aircraft that would have been carrying United States citizens and crews and that were destined for cities in the United States. Moreover, assertion of jurisdiction is appropriate under the "objective territorial principle" because the purpose of the attack was to influence United States foreign policy and the defendants intended their actions to have an effect—in this case, a devastating effect—on and within the United States. Finally, there is no doubt that jurisdiction is proper under the "protective principle" because the planned attacks were intended to affect the United States and to alter its foreign policy. * * *

[The Second Circuit continues, discussing universal jurisdiction]: [T]he bombing of Philippine Airlines Flight 434, appears to present a less straight-forward jurisdictional issue because the airplane that was bombed was not a United States-flag aircraft, it was flying between two destinations outside of the United States, and there is no evidence that any United States citizens were aboard the flight or were targets of the bombing. The District Court nevertheless concluded that jurisdiction over Yousef for the offenses charged in [this count] was proper, *inter alia,* under the principle of "universal jurisdiction."

* * * Endorsing the exercise of universal jurisdiction in the prosecution of an aircraft-related crime, the [district] court stated that "aircraft hijacking may well be one of the few crimes so clearly condemned under the law of nations that states may assert universal jurisdiction to bring offenders to justice, even when the state has no territorial connection to the hijacking and its citizens are not involved."

The court in [*United States v.] Yunis*[, 924 F.2d 1086 (D.C. Cir. 1991)] cited to the Restatement (Third) of the Foreign Relations Law to support exercise of universal jurisdiction in a criminal prosecution related to crimes involving aircraft. Section 404 [of the Restatement (Third)] states, "[a] state has jurisdiction to define and prescribe punishment for certain offenses recognized by the community of nations as of universal concern, such as piracy, slave trade, attacks on or hijacking of aircraft, genocide, war crimes, and perhaps certain acts of terrorism, even where none of the other bases of jurisdiction indicated in § 402 is present." Restatement (Third) § 404 (1987).

The District Court then added: "The disregard for human life which would accompany the placing of a bomb aboard an airplane with the intent for that bomb to explode while the airplane is in flight and fully occupied with people, or otherwise sabotaging that plane, is at least as heinous a crime of international concern as hijacking a plane." * * *

[Later in its opinion, the Second Circuit explained the types of crimes that come within the scope this universality principle for jurisdiction]: The universality principle permits a State to prosecute an offender of any nationality for an offense committed outside of that State and without contacts to that State, but only for the few, near-unique offenses uniformly recognized by the "civilized nations" as an offense against the "Law of Nations." The strictly limited set of crimes subject to universal jurisdiction cannot be expanded by drawing an analogy between some new crime such as placing a bomb on board an airplane and universal jurisdiction's traditional subjects. * * *

The class of crimes subject to universal jurisdiction traditionally included only piracy. In modern times, the class of crimes over which States can exercise universal jurisdiction has been extended to include war crimes and acts identified after the Second World War as "crimes against humanity." See, e.g., *Demjanjuk v. Petrovsky*, 776 F.2d 571 (6th Cir. 1985).

The concept of universal jurisdiction has its origins in prosecutions of piracy, which States and legal scholars have acknowledged for at least 500 years as a crime against all nations both because of the threat that piracy poses to orderly transport and commerce between nations and because the crime occurs statelessly on the high seas. . . .

Notes and Questions

1. **The Expansion of Prescriptive Jurisdiction**. In *United States v. Yunis*, 924 F.2d 1086 (D.C. Cir.1991) the government prosecuted a defendant who hijacked a foreign airliner in Jordan on which there were four American citizens. The District of Columbia Circuit described the circumstances in which the United States obtained custody over Yunis, who was charged and convicted of hostage taking in violation of 18 U.S.C. § 1203, and air piracy in violation of 49 U.S.C. App. § 1472(n):

> On June 11, 1985, appellant and four other men boarded Royal Jordanian Airlines Flight 402 shortly before its scheduled departure from Beirut, Lebanon. They wore civilian clothes and carried military assault rifles, ammunition bandoleers, and hand grenades. Appellant took control of the cockpit and forced the pilot to take off immediately. The remaining hijackers tied up Jordanian air marshals assigned to the flight and held the civilian passengers, including two American citizens, captive in their seats. The hijack-

ers explained to the crew and passengers that they wanted the plane to fly to Tunis, where a conference of the Arab League was under way. The hijackers further explained that they wanted a meeting with delegates to the conference and that their ultimate goal was removal of all Palestinians from Lebanon.

After a refueling stop in Cyprus, the airplane headed for Tunis but turned away when authorities blocked the airport runway. Following a refueling stop at Palermo, Sicily, another attempt to land in Tunis, and a second stop in Cyprus, the plane returned to Beirut, where more hijackers came aboard. These reinforcements included an official of Lebanon's Amal Militia, the group at whose direction Yunis claims he acted. The plane then took off for Syria, but was turned away and went back to Beirut. There, the hijackers released the passengers, held a press conference reiterating their demand that Palestinians leave Lebanon, blew up the plane, and fled from the airport.

An American investigation identified Yunis as the probable leader of the hijackers and prompted U.S. civilian and military agencies, led by the Federal Bureau of Investigation (FBI), to plan Yunis' arrest. After obtaining an arrest warrant, the FBI put "Operation Goldenrod" into effect in September 1987. Undercover FBI agents lured Yunis onto a yacht in the eastern Mediterranean Sea with promises of a drug deal, and arrested him once the vessel entered international waters. The agents transferred Yunis to a United States Navy munitions ship and interrogated him for several days as the vessel steamed toward a second rendezvous, this time with a Navy aircraft carrier. Yunis was flown to Andrews Air Force Base from the aircraft carrier, and taken from there to Washington, D.C. In Washington, Yunis was arraigned on an original indictment charging him with conspiracy, hostage taking, and aircraft damage. A grand jury subsequently returned a superseding indictment adding additional aircraft damage counts and a charge of air piracy.

Yunis was abducted aboard a private foreign flagged yacht. If the yacht were in a Cyprus port, that fact would give Cyprus primary jurisdiction. If the yacht were on the High Seas, the flag state would have primary jurisdiction. The hijacking for which Yunis was arrested appeared to have been an Amal militia action aimed at intimidating or coercing Jordan, the PLO, and Lebanon. The D.C. Circuit held hijacking to be an international crime, based on relevant treaties and customary international law, which creates an obligation and a right to extradite or prosecute. Does it seem legal or appropriate to extend U.S. jurisdiction over fully foreign conduct of a foreign (here, Lebanese) national committed against a foreign (here Jordanian) airliner, over foreign territory and the high seas? If so, what would be the rationale and the jurisdictional theory?

The District of Columbia Circuit rejected Yunis's claim that the United States did not have jurisdiction over him, stating:

> Nor is jurisdiction precluded by norms of customary international law. The district court concluded that two jurisdictional theories of international law, the "universal principle" and the "passive personal principle," supported assertion of U.S. jurisdiction to prosecute Yunis on hijacking and hostage-taking charges. Under the universal principle, states may prescribe and prosecute "certain offenses recognized by the community of nations as of universal concern, such as piracy, slave trade, attacks on or hijacking of aircraft, genocide, war crimes, and perhaps certain acts of terrorism," even absent any special connection between the state and the offense. See *Restatement (Third) of the Foreign Relations Law of the United States* §§ 404, 423 (1987). Under the passive personal principle, a state may punish non-nationals for crimes committed against its nationals outside of its territory, at least where the state has a particularly strong interest in the crime.

> * * * Yunis argues that hostage taking has not been recognized as a universal crime and that the passive personal principle authorizes assertion of jurisdiction over alleged hostage takers only where the victims were seized because they were nationals of the prosecuting state. Whatever merit appellant's claims may have as a matter of international law, they cannot prevail before this court. Yunis seeks to portray international law as a self-executing code that trumps domestic law whenever the two conflict. That effort misconceives the role of judges as appliers of international law and as participants in the federal system. Our duty is to enforce the Constitution, laws, and treaties of the United States, not to conform the law of the land to norms of customary international law. As we said in *Committee of U.S. Citizens Living in Nicaragua v. Reagan*, 859 F.2d 929 (D.C.Cir. 1988): "Statutes inconsistent with principles of customary international law may well lead to international law violations. But within the domestic legal realm, that inconsistent statute simply modifies or supersedes customary international law to the extent of the inconsistency."

> To be sure, courts should hesitate to give penal statutes extraterritorial effect absent a clear congressional directive. See *Foley Bros. v. Filardo*, 336 U.S. 281 (1949); *United States v. Bowman*, 260 U.S. 94 (1922). Similarly, courts will not blind themselves to potential violations of international law where legislative intent is ambiguous. See *Murray v. The Schooner Charming Betsy*, 6 U.S. (2 Cranch) 64 (1804) ("[A]n act of congress ought never to be construed to violate the law of nations, if any other possible construction remains ...."). But the statute in question reflects an unmistakable congressional intent, consistent with treaty obligations of the United States, to authorize prosecution of those who take Americans hostage abroad no matter where the

offense occurs or where the offender is found. Our inquiry can go no further.

The Antihijacking Act provides for criminal punishment of persons who hijack aircraft operating wholly outside the "special aircraft jurisdiction" of the United States, provided that the hijacker is later "found in the United States." 49 U.S.C. App. § 1472(n). * * *

The Antihijacking Act of 1974 was enacted to fulfill this nation's responsibilities under the Convention for the Suppression of Unlawful Seizure of Aircraft (the "Hague Convention"), which requires signatory nations to extradite or punish hijackers "present in" their territory. Convention for the Suppression of Unlawful Seizure of Aircraft, Dec. 16, 1970, art. 4, para. 2, Dec. 16, 1970, 22 U.S.T. 1643, 1645, T.I.A.S. No. 7192. * * *

The district court correctly found that international law does not restrict this statutory jurisdiction to try Yunis on charges of air piracy. Aircraft hijacking may well be one of the few crimes so clearly condemned under the law of nations that states may assert universal jurisdiction to bring offenders to justice, even when the state has no territorial connection to the hijacking and its citizens are not involved. But in any event we are satisfied that the Antihijacking Act authorizes assertion of federal jurisdiction to try Yunis regardless of hijacking's status vel non as a universal crime. Thus, we affirm the district court on this issue.

Is the court's analysis correct? Does U.S. domestic law trump international law? Are U.S. courts obliged primarily by the U.S. Constitution? The U.S., like most states have always held that, while the domestic Constitution is the governing law, statutes will be interpreted to comply with international law, where possible. Does the D.C. Circuit hold that hijacking is a "universal" crime, giving rise to universal jurisdiction? Are there any other bases of jurisdiction that cover U.S. jurisdiction over this conduct?

2. Applying International Law in *Yousef***—Thoughts on Customary International Law.** The Second Circuit, in *Yousef*, stated:

Principles of customary international law reflect the practices and customs of States in the international arena that are applied in a consistent fashion and that are generally recognized by what used to be called "civilized states." That is, principles of customary international law consist of the "*settled* rule[s] of international law" as recognized through "the general assent of civilized nations.

Is this a correct definition of customary international law? The *Yousef* Court also stated:

In the event that there is no "controlling executive or legislative act or judicial decision [that the court must apply, a court should identify the norms of customary international law by looking to] the general usage and practice of nations [,] or by [looking to] judicial decisions recognizing and enforcing that law ... [, or by] consulting the works of jurists writing professedly on public law," *United States v. Smith,* 18 U.S. (5 Wheat.) 153, 5 L.Ed. 57 (1820) (Story, J.).

Is this a correct statement or definition of customary international law? U.S. Courts have long misunderstood the concept, but Justice Story comes close to a proper understanding, if he meant to include the term *opinio juris* in the concepts of law and norms. See our discussion of customary international law in the Introduction Chapter.

    3. Rejecting Universal Jurisdiction. The *Yousef* decision rejected the application of the universality theory of jurisdiction for Yousef's offenses. Moreover, the language of the Second Circuit seems to reject the universality theory for terrorism generally. Do you agree with this? What is the Court's argument for this position? Is there an argument for applying universal jurisdiction to terrorism? It is true that, notwithstanding an apparent use of the term "universal jurisdiction" in a multilateral treaty, at the beginning of such a treaty regime, true universal jurisdiction may not arise from the treaty. The International Court of Justice in the *"Arrest Warrant Case"* (*Case Concerning the Arrest Warrant of 11 Apr. 2000 (Democratic Republic of the Congo v. Belgium)*), 41 I.L.M. 536, 560 (2002), noted that, although the purpose of such treaties is to assure "universal punishment of the offenses in question ... [by denying] perpetrators ... refuge in all States," it is *incorrect* to denominate this jurisdiction as true universal jurisdiction. Judge Rosalyn Higgins, President of the International Court of Justice, makes this point, noting that such conventions do not actually create "actual or true 'universal jurisdiction,' or even 'treaty-based universal jurisdiction,' because the treaties create obligations only in states parties, not universally in all states." *See* Rosalyn Higgins, Problems and Process: International Law and How We Use It 64 (1994) (stating that jurisdiction created by treaty is never "universal jurisdiction *stricto sensu*" because only States parties are vested with jurisdiction by the treaty) (emphasis ours). On the other hand, treaties may recognize and codify already extant customary international law or they may begin an evolution that creates custom

    4. Universal Jurisdiction and Terrorism. Many multilateral treaties have condemned various international offenses that could be characterized as terrorism. One could argue that the responsibility to desist from promoting or committing terrorism and the obligation to combat it devolves on all nations universally. Terrorism consists of universally condemned conduct and, although no one multilateral treaty explicitly states as much, clearly the universality principle could apply to many of today's terrorist activities. Should it?

    Some of these treaties that may have created or evolved into a true universal crime or set of crimes that we would call terrorism. In addition, it would seem that intentional or wanton slaughter of innocents is a jus cogens crime. Crimes proscribed in treaties and domestic law might include hijacking and sabotaging civil aircraft, use of weapons of mass destruction, targeting or wantonly killing innocent civilians. History, the relevant treaties as well as others, and the domestic criminal law of all states, when considered as a whole, make it clear that terrorism—including hostage taking, kidnapping, intentional or wanton violence against innocent civilians—is often really a composite term that includes, or could be, any one of several separate universally condemned offenses. If the treaty becomes customary international law or is based on it already, or is based on a *jus cogens* principle, it establishes actual universality jurisdiction, requiring a nation that gains custody of an accused person to extradite or prosecute.

5. Terrorism and Bar Room Brawls. The legislative history of the Omnibus Antiterrorism Act and its progeny make it clear that the law does not "reach nonterrorist violence inflicted upon American victims. Simple barroom brawls or normal street crime, for example, are not intended to be covered by this provision...." Earlier draft bills applied a broad passive–personality principle theory of jurisdiction. This language was broad enough to include all common criminal violence against American nationals. This breadth was considered too expansive, so Congress passed 18 U.S.C. 2332 (d), which reads:

> (d) Limitation on Prosecution.—No prosecution for any offense described in this section shall be undertaken by the United States except on written certification of the Attorney General or the highest ranking subordinate of the Attorney General with responsibility for criminal prosecutions that, in the judgment of the certifying official, *such offense was intended to coerce, intimidate, or retaliate against a government or a civilian population.* (Emphasis added)

Several other laws, including the USA Patriot Act, provide for jurisdiction on the basis of several extraterritorial theories, including the protective principle. In *United States v. Martinelli*, 62 M.J. 52, 62 (C.A.A.F. 2005), discussed in Chapter Two, the court noted that:

> Congress has clearly expressed its intent in other criminal statutes as well: the Biological Weapons Anti–Terrorism Act of 1989 provides, "There is extraterritorial federal jurisdiction over an offense under this section committed by or against a national of the United States," 18 U.S.C. § 175(a) (2000); the Maritime Drug Law Enforcement Act provides, "This section is intended to reach acts of possession, manufacture, or distribution committed outside the territorial jurisdiction of the United States." 46 U.S.C. app. § 1903(h) (2000). Congress also amended 18 U.S.C. § 7 (2000), which defines the "special maritime and territorial jurisdiction" of the United States, as part of the [USA PATRIOT Act] ... The USA PATRIOT Act amendments inserted a new provision that, with respect to "offenses committed by or against a national of the United States," extends the special maritime and territorial jurisdiction of the United States under 18 U.S.C. § 7 to the "premises of ... diplomatic, consular, military or other ... missions ... in foreign States...." This is a clear expression of congressional intent that a crime committed in "the special maritime and

territorial jurisdiction" now includes conduct that may in some instances have occurred inside the boundaries of a foreign nation.

Thus, Congress has allowed jurisdiction over certain specific extraterritorial crimes. The legislation generally does not articulate the theoretical underpinnings of its jurisdiction, but these may be inferred. International law is passive on the issue of extraterritorial jurisdiction. That is, a state may provide for extraterritorial jurisdiction, unless an explicit rule of international law prohibits it. *The S.S. Lotus* (France v. Turkey), Permanent Court of International Justice (P.C.I.J.) (1927), P.C.I.J. Ser. A. No. 10. The U.S. Supreme Court has not yet addressed this issue.

6. Piracy and Universal Jurisdiction. Perhaps the most ancient offense of universal interest is piracy, a crime that may be considered analogous to terrorism or part of the set of terrorist offenses. Green Hackworth wrote: "It has long been recognized and well settled that persons and vessels engaged in piratical operations on the high seas are entitled to the protection of no nation and may be punished by any nation that may apprehend or capture them." 2 HACKWORTH DIGEST 681 (1940). The 1958 Geneva Convention on the High Seas Apr. 29, 1958 [1962] 13 U.S.T. 2312, T.I.A.S. No. 52,107 provides that:

On the high seas, or in any other place outside the jurisdiction of any State, every State may seize a pirate ship or aircraft, or a ship taken by piracy and under the control of pirates, and arrest the persons and seize the property on board. The courts of the State which carried out the seizure may decide upon the penalties to be imposed, and may also determine the action to be taken with regard to the ships, aircraft or property, subject to the rights of third parties acting in good faith.

7. Other Crimes. Like piracy, several other crimes are universally condemned and jurisdiction obtains in any nation that gains control of the accused. International conventions have provided jurisdiction for all parties to the conventions. Some of these offenses have become true universal crimes, through customary international law that has developed out of state practice (and *opinio juris*) following treaties. Some of these include participation in the slave trade, war crimes, and crimes against humanity, genocide, and apartheid. The *ad hoc* international criminal tribunals have helped to make the idea of universal jurisdiction more concrete and accessible for several offenses, and have helped to establish customary international law on the issue. Several multi-lateral treaties have been promulgated for the purpose of providing jurisdiction that is universal among the states parties. *See, e.g.,* Convention on Offenses and Certain Other Acts Committed on Board Aircraft, entered into force Dec. 4, 1969, 20 U.S.T. 2941, 704 U.N.T.S. 219; Convention for the Suppression of Unlawful Seizure of Aircraft (Hague Hijacking Convention), Dec. 16, 1970, 22 U.S.T. 1641; 860 U.N.T.S. 105 (entered into force in the U.S. Oct. 14, 1971); The Convention for the Suppression of Unlawful Acts Against the Safety of

Civil Aviation, Sept. 23, 1971, 24 U.S.T. 565, 974 U.N.T.S. 177 (entered into force in the U.S. Jan. 26, 1973).

Virtually all nations condemn, prosecute, and punish terrorist violence, when it is perpetrated against them or their nationals. Other international conventions proscribing genocide, apartheid, and hostage taking provide additional impetus toward the recognition of the universality theory of jurisdiction. The U.N. International Convention against the Taking of Hostages provides for the prosecution or extradition of any person who commits the offense of hostage-taking, without reference to the motive or identity of the victim. Some states have also taken measures to establish jurisdiction over the crime of hostage-taking and to provide appropriately severe penalties. The conventions relating to aircraft hijacking and sabotage provide examples of how universal jurisdiction is established among states parties, but that either reflects or develops into customary international law. The Hague Convention for the Suppression of Unlawful Seizure of Aircraft grants all contracting parties jurisdiction over unlawful seizures or control of aircraft and obligates the party obtaining custody of the alleged hijackers to prosecute or extradite them. All parties are to promulgate laws to "severely" punish the prohibited conduct. The Hague Convention also establishes priorities of jurisdiction. The state of the aircraft's registration and the state, in which it landed, if the criminal act occurred in the air, are made "primary" jurisdictions. Other states are so-called "substitutionary" jurisdictions that may assert jurisdiction if the primary jurisdiction cannot or will not assert it. The Montreal Convention extends the Hague Convention beyond hijacking and unlawful control of aircraft to include acts of sabotage. This spectrum of treaties has likely become customary international law, because virtually all nations consider themselves legally obliged to abide by their rules.

Domestic legislation has been promulgated to incorporate these conventions, notably in Europe and in the United States, but virtually throughout the world. The United Nations International Convention against the Taking of Hostages similarly provides, in strong language, for prosecution and extradition of offenders. The Convention provides that: "[t]he State Party in the territory of which the alleged offender is found shall, if it does not extradite him, be obliged, without exception whatsoever and whether or not the offence was committed in its territory, to submit the case to its competent authorities for the purpose of prosecution, through proceedings in accordance with the law of that State. Those authorities shall take their decision in the same manner as in the case of any ordinary offence of a grave nature under the law of that state." International Convention Against the Taking of Hostages, G.A. Res. 146, U.N. GAOR, 34th Sess., Supp. No. 46, at 246, U.N. Doc. A/34/146 (1979).

8.   State Terrorism. Governmental violence against innocents may justify revolution, but does not excuse or justify violence that targets innocents for their nationality, ethnicity, race, religion, gender, or allegiance to the ruling group. If conduct is illegal when committed against one's own, it is also illegal when committed *by* one's own. The fact that it may be committed against a group who are part of a nation or group who committed the original atrocity is not a justification or an excuse. A willful or wanton violence against innocents is terrorism per se. To target innocents or to use them as a shield is a war crime or crime against humanity during armed conflict, whether committed by a soldier or other government agent, or by a member of a political or guerilla group. It will be terrorism, if not committed in an armed conflict.

Most nation-states (as well as terrorist groups and guerilla warriors) try to define terrorism solely as a crime that *"others"* commit. One of the problems plaguing attempts to define terrorism has been that, although nations, governments, legislatures, and some scholars have been willing to call certain conduct terrorism as a generic, universal crime that ought to transcend time and space limitations, they have usually limited suppression or prosecution to a specified period of time and place. States or groups adopt universalist rhetoric based on international law and principles of universality, to condemn the conduct of others and legitimates their own counter-actions. It is extremely rare for a state or group to apply these principles in a universal way or one that might apply to their own people. See Gerry J. Simpson, *War Crimes: A Critical Introduction* ch. 1, *in* THE LAW OF WAR CRIMES: NATIONAL AND INTERNATIONAL APPROACHES 10 (Timothy L.H. McCormack & Gerry J. Simpson eds. 1997). Other scholars refuse to define terrorism, because they feel that it is impossible or too politically loaded. Similarly, legislation or treaties calling for universal jurisdiction often do so with a limitation based on racial, cultural, ethnic, or religious stereotyping (if not included in the acts, it is applied by action, such as in trials or arrests or deportations of the "exotic foreigner"—the "Islamic terrorist"—thus, incorporating bias and discrimination, and excluding "one's own kind.") The reason for this would appear to be that they only want to have "others" prosecuted, so that their own compatriots will not subject to the condemnation, because of the limitations. If the conduct were neutrally and universally condemned, anyone who committed it anytime would be subject to liability.

9. How Far Should Jurisdiction Extend? Consider the following scenarios and ask whether any of these acts should be subject to prosecution in the United States.

1. A terrorist group enters a U.S. military base in another country and plants an explosive device planted on a U.S. military transport plane. The device explodes shortly after takeoff, when the plane was no longer over the military base but in the air space of the host country, and all 250 soldiers on board were killed. If the perpetrators were captured and brought to the United States, for what crimes could they be charged, and

what would be the jurisdictional issues that a court might have to confront.

2.   Applying the same facts, the attackers planted a bomb on a civilian plane leaving Rome for the United States on which there were a large number of U.S. soldiers returning from duty in Iraq. Would this change the jurisdictional analysis? What additional facts would a prosecutor need to determine what charges to file?

3.   Applying the same facts, the attackers planted a bomb on a civilian plane leaving Rome for the United States on which there were a large number of U.S. soldiers returning from duty in Iraq. Would this change the jurisdictional analysis? What additional facts would a prosecutor need to determine what charges to file?

4.   A United States citizen, not an agent of the government, planted a bomb on a Pakistani Lear jet leaving from Lahore for Tehran, Iran. The perpetrator believed that terrorist operatives were aboard, although none were. The plane exploded over Afghanistan and all were killed. If the perpetrator were captured and brought to the United States, would the United States have proper jurisdiction? If so, upon what theoretical basis and for what crime? What additional facts might you need to determine what offenses to charge? Would your analysis be different if the perpetrator were a government agent? What if he were a contract "security" employee of the government?

5.   Apply the same facts as in problem 4, except that the plane *was* filled with terrorist operatives, traveling to a Black Sea resort to plan an attack that they intended to place one year from then in Moscow. If this perpetrator were captured and brought to the United States, would the United States have proper jurisdiction? If so, upon what theoretical basis and for what crime? What additional facts might you need to determine what offenses to file?

6.   Apply the same facts as in problem 4, except that a French national planted the bomb. If this perpetrator were captured and brought to the United States, would the United States have proper jurisdiction? If so, upon what theoretical basis and for what crime? What additional facts would you need to make this determination?

Chapter IV

GENOCIDE

A. INTRODUCTION TO GENOCIDE AND INTERNATIONAL CRIMINAL TRIBUNALS

The word "genocide" immediately evokes images of the Holocaust and other mass killings, such as occurred in Cambodia and Rwanda. Although large scale atrocities have occurred throughout history, the term "genocide" did not exist until after World War II. A Polish lawyer, Raphael Lemkin,[1] coined the word and began a determined campaign to convince the world to adopt a Convention on the Prevention and Punishment of Genocide.[2] Most of the world's countries have ratified the Convention and the definition of genocide in the Convention is considered to be customary international law. Genocide is a *jus cogens* crime calling for universal jurisdiction. The use of the term "genocide" in the media and on the political stage, however, is not always consistent with the legal definition.

In this chapter, you will study the legal definition of genocide as defined by customary international law and the treaty (convention) on genocide. As with other sources of law, such as constitutional or statutory provisions, there is a need for judicial interpretation of the terms and clauses of the definition. The judicial interpretations come from national court cases as with other domestic laws, but also come from a newer type of court, international criminal tribunals.

International criminal tribunals are new to the legal landscape, but are an increasingly important and permanent part of the

---

1. *See* Samantha Power, A PROBLEM FROM HELL (Harper Collins 2002) for an interesting account of Lemkin's struggle for a Genocide Convention.

2. Convention on the Prevention and Punishment of the Crime of Genocide,

Jan. 12, 1951, 78 U.N.T.S. 277, http://www.unhchr.ch/html/menu3/b/p_genoci.htm.

world's criminal justice system. The post-World War II trials of Nazi leaders at Nuremberg and of Japanese leaders in similar trials in the Far East were the first international criminal trials in modern times. See the brief history of international criminal tribunals in the introductory chapter. Although the Nuremberg and Far East trials were the seeds for developing international criminal law and tribunals, once those trials were completed, there were no other international criminal tribunals until 1993. In 1993, the Security Council of the United Nations created the International Criminal Tribunal for the former Yugoslavia (ICTY) as a means of establishing peace and security in the Balkans during the conflicts that raged during the breakup of Yugoslavia. In 1994, the Security Council acted again, creating the International Criminal Tribunal for Rwanda (ICTR) in the aftermath of large scale massacres of civilians during a major conflict within the country.

With the ICTY and ICTR paving the way, other international and semi-international criminal tribunals have followed. Tribunals now exist in Sierra Leone, East Timor, Kosovo, Bosnia, and Cambodia that are considered "hybrid" tribunals. Each one has a combination of international and national judges. The other major development was the establishment of the International Criminal Court (ICC) in 1998, which became operational in 2002.[3] The ICC is the first permanent international tribunal ever established. The other completely international tribunals, the ICTY and ICTR, are designed for a specific conflict and will close within a few years. Also, unlike the ICTY and ICTR that were created under the peace and security authority of the United Nations Security Council, the ICC was established by treaty, an agreement among the States Parties to create and maintain the court. As of November 2006, 102 nations had ratified the treaty for the ICC.[4] Notable among the countries that have not ratified is the United States. Even without the participation of the United States, the ICC is already undertaking investigations and adjudicating cases from conflicts in several countries.

Common to all of the international criminal tribunals is the jurisdiction to hear cases involving allegations of genocide, crimes against humanity, and war crimes. As a result, there is a growing body of jurisprudence on the elements of these crimes, theories of responsibility, and defenses. In this chapter, you will be reading cases from the ICTY and ICTR that will be relevant to analyzing the problem that is based on facts from the atrocities that occurred

---

3. Established by Rome Statute of the International Criminal Court, July 17, 1998, 2187 U.N.T.S. 3, http://www.icc-cpi.int. Statute entered into force on July 1, 2002.

4. http://www.icc-cpi.int/asp/states parties.html. Another ratification is likely in the near future. Japan announced in September 2006 that it is ready to ratify the treaty.

during the reign of the Khmer Rouge in Cambodia. As you read
through the materials in this chapter, consider the similarities and
differences between criminal law concepts in the United States and
criminal law concepts on an international level.

B. INTRODUCTION TO THE KHMER ROUGE TRIBUNAL AND GENOCIDE PROBLEM

In 1975, the Khmer Rouge took over the government of Cambodia. The Khmer Rouge leadership were communists who believed
in creating economic equality. To further that end, the Khmer
Rouge ordered the evacuation of virtually the entire population of
the capital city, Phnom Penh. The urban population, which the
Khmer Rouge viewed as a privileged economic class, was ordered to
villages in the countryside. The theory was that the privileged class
would be "re-educated" to work alongside peasants on an equal
footing. In order to purge Cambodian society of negative elements,
the Khmer Rouge leadership initially ordered the execution of
leaders from the prior government and military. Ultimately, there
were communications from the leadership to discover and execute
traitors, who included alleged spies for the CIA and other enemy
agents. The reach of the executions was then expanded to anyone
who was presumed to be opposed to the government, including
those who simply lived near the border with Vietnam.[1]

The ultimate authority for the Khmer Rouge government was
the Central Committee of the party. Under the aegis of the Central
Committee, the members of the Standing Committee were the key
government officials. Pol Pot was the General Secretary of the
Standing Committee and the Prime Minister of the government.
Underneath the Standing Committee were the security units, military units, and administrative zones. The Zone Secretaries were
responsible for supervising the geographical levels of sector, district, and local, each a smaller unit of the former.

Somewhere between 1 and 3 million people died during the
reign of the Khmer Rouge, approximately 20% of the total population of the country. Many were executed and many others died of
starvation. In 1979, the Vietnamese ousted the Khmer Rouge and
installed a new government. After about a decade, the Vietnamese
withdrew from Cambodia and, after various negotiations assisted
by the United Nations, a fully independent Cambodian government
came into power.

1. *See* CRAIG ETCHESON, AFTER THE
KILLING FIELDS: LESSONS FROM THE CAMBODI-
AN GENOCIDE at 87–106 (Praeger 2005).

A special chamber of the Cambodian judicial system was authorized by agreement between the government of Cambodia and the United Nations in 2003. This tribunal, the Extraordinary Chambers in the Courts of Cambodia for the Prosecution of Crimes Committed during the Period of Democratic Kampuchea (ECDK), is charged with trying "senior leaders ... and those who were the most responsible" for the mass killings and deaths during the period of the Khmer Rouge. The tribunal is also called the Khmer Rouge Tribunal (KRT). A combination of Cambodian and international judges will hear the cases. In May 2006, the United Nations and Cambodia selected the judges and co-prosecutors. Investigations are underway, and proceedings are expected to commence in 2007. The jurisdiction of the tribunal is limited to crimes committed between April 17, 1975 and January 6, 1979. Substantively, the tribunal's jurisdiction extends to a limited number of crimes, including the major post-conflict crimes of genocide, crimes against humanity, and grave breaches of the Geneva Conventions.[2] Pol Pot died in 1998, but other senior leaders of the Khmer Rouge are still alive and could be brought to trial. The Problem below is based on possible charges and defenses in the prosecution of the leaders of the Khmer Rouge.

Genocide Problem[3]

Assume that four defendants are being tried in the KRT for genocide. The following facts are presented in the trial:

2. The other crimes within the jurisdiction of the tribunal include the internationally-defined crimes of destruction of cultural property and crimes against internationally protected persons and the domestic crimes of homicide, torture, and religious persecution as defined in the Cambodian Penal Code. Law on the Establishment of Extraordinary Chambers of the Courts of Cambodia for the Prosecution of Crimes Committed During the Period of Democratic Kampuchea, art. 3–8 (2004), *available at* http://www. cambodia.gov. kh/krt/english/ lawönëstab lishment.htm.

3. The facts in the hypothetical are based on historical events, but modified for the hypothetical problem. Sources consulted included: Mann (Mac) Bunyanunda, *The Khmer Rouge on Trial: Whither the Defense?,* 74 S. CAL. L. REV. 1581 (2001); Stephen Heder, *Reassesing the Role of Senior Leaders and Local Officials in Democratic Kampuchea Crimes: Cambodian Accountability in Comparative Perspective,* in AWAITING

JUSTICE: ESSAYS ON ACCOUNTABILITY IN CAMBODIA(Jason Abrams, Jaya Ramji & Beth Van Schaack eds. 2005); Scott Luftglass, *Crossroads in Cambodia: The United Nation's Responsibility to Withdraw Involvement from the Establishment of a Cambodian Tribunal to Prosecute the Khmer Rouge,* 90 VA. L. REV. 893 (2004); Beth Van Schaack, *The Crime of Political Genocide: Repairing the Genocide Convention's Blind Spot,* 106 YALE L.J. 2259 (1997); Craig Etcheson, AFTER THE KILLING FIELDS: LESSONS FROM THE CAMBODIAN GENOCIDE (Praeger 2005); Stephen Heder and Brian D. Tittemore, SEVEN CANDIDATES FOR PROSECUTION:‗ ACCOUNTABILITY FOR THE CRIMES OF THE KHMER ROUGE (War Crimes Research Office, American University and Documentation Center of Cambodia 2004); Ben Kiernan, THE POL POT REGIME: RACE, POWER AND GENOCIDE UNDER THE KHMER ROUGE, 1975–79 (Yale University Press 1996); and information from the Documentation Center of Cambodia.

Sar was a member of the Standing Committee and the Deputy Prime Minister for Foreign Affairs.

Kek was the Chief of Government Security and the warden of the S–21 Interrogation Center, located in the Phnom Penh Special Zone.

Peah was a guard who worked at S–21.

Mok was the Secretary of the Southwest Zone.

Evidence is presented that at least 16,000 people were detained at S–21 and then executed. Only 7 people are known to have survived from the detainees at S–21. Approximately 4,000 written "confessions" were discovered in the records of S–21. Evidence from testimony, photographs, and written records indicates that the detainees were tortured with beatings, electrocution, near-drowning, burning of skin, and other methods in order to obtain "confessions." The "confessions" stated ways in which the detainee was an enemy of the state, including that the detainee worked with the CIA, that the detainee stole from the government, or other such acts. Many photographs were introduced into the record that showed severe injuries to the detainees or dead bodies. The vast majority of detainees at S–21 were Khmer (most Cambodians are ethnic Khmer), but approximately 500 ethnic Vietnamese were also imprisoned and killed at S–21.

In 1975, there were approximately 160,000 ethnic Vietnamese living in Cambodia out of a total national population of about 7,000,000 people. At the outset of the Khmer Rouge reign, about 150,000 of the ethnic Vietnamese were forced to leave the country. Of the 10,000 remaining in Cambodia, it is believed that none survived the Khmer Rouge rule.

In addition to political opponents, the Khmer Rouge tried to disband all religions in Cambodia. The dominant religion was Buddhism. Buddhist monks were sent into the villages and it is estimated that 25,000–50,000 monks died out of a total of approximately 60,000 monks in Cambodia in 1975. Most of the monks died from starvation. Cambodian Cham, who are Muslim, were also forbidden to practice their religion. Of the approximately 250,000 Cham in Cambodia at the time, it is estimated that about 90,000 Cham died from starvation or execution.

Within the Southwest Zone, exact statistics are not available for the death tolls. It is known, however, that thousands died, predominantly Khmer, but also ethnic Vietnamese, Buddhist monks, and Cham.

Peah admits that he tortured and killed many of the detainees at S–21. He claims, however, that he was ordered to do this and only did so out of fear for his own life. At trial, other former guards testified that Kek verbally threatened to kill any guard who refused to carry out interrogations and executions on many occasions. The former guards also testified that Peah was present when a guard was executed when he refused to participate. Peah testified that he was never at a meeting on a higher level; his understanding was that the detainees had been arrested for being enemies of the state and deserved death as traitors.

Kek admits that he was in charge of S–21. He claims that those executed were properly found to have committed the crime of treason and were accordingly executed pursuant to law. He denies that torture occurred in the interrogations. Kek attended some of the meetings of the Standing Committee and Central Committee. He testified that his immediate superior was Chea, the Deputy Secretary of the Central Committee. He testified that Sar was present at some of those meetings during which the policies of re-education and execution of enemies of the state were discussed and reports were distributed from the zones indicating the number of persons executed. Kek further testified, however, that Sar was not part of planning the policy or giving directives that executions occur. Kek also testified that, at one meeting, Sar argued that there should not be so many executions. Sar, however, was largely ignored.

Sar claims that he was not aware of the mass executions occurring in the country. He testified that Pol Pot was the architect of the policies of the Khmer Rouge, which were then carried out by Kek and others.

Mok testified that he relayed orders from the Standing Committee to the leaders of the sectors, districts and local levels. Those orders included the execution of former government and military officials and the execution of those who could not be re-educated and posed a threat to the government. He claimed that he did not directly order the execution of anyone. Moreover, he claimed that the ethnic Vietnamese, Buddhist monks, and Cham were never the subject of an order that he transmitted. He did admit that he was aware of a historic discrimination against ethnic Vietnamese in Cambodia and of the overall prohibition of religious practices.

Evaluate the likelihood of convicting Sar, Kek, Peah, and Mok for the crimes of genocide and conspiracy to commit genocide. Can the mens rea for the crimes be proved for each defendant? What is the targeted group? Which of the defendants is the most likely to be convicted?

What defenses might be raised for each defendant and what would be the likelihood of success?

Which defendants are most likely to be convicted as aiding and abetting genocide? Which defendants might be liable as co-perpetrators of a joint criminal enterprise? What is the potential liability of any of the defendants under the theory of command responsibility?

C. SOURCES OF LAW

With any legal problem, it is important to determine what law governs the proceedings. In your study of domestic criminal cases that are prosecuted on a U.S. state level in the United States, you have studied state statutes, case law and at times, federal constitutional law. Although it is far less common, treaties entered into by the United States and "customary international law" would also be binding on the courts in a state prosecution if pertinent to the case. The most common sources of law, however, in a U.S. state prosecution will be state statutory and case law. In the arena of international crimes, such as genocide, the dominant sources of law are treaties and customary international law. The elements of genocide are found in the Convention on the Prevention and Punishment of the Crime of Genocide of 1948, but genocide is also considered to be a crime as a matter of customary international law, which is binding on all countries in the world.[8]

The trial of genocide cases could occur in a domestic criminal court under a domestic statute or pursuant to customary international law. However, under the U.S. Constitution, customary international law is not sufficient by itself for prosecution. A statute would be required, incorporating the customary rule before the proscribed conduct could be prosecuted. The U.S. statute prohibiting genocide is set forth in Section D, *infra*. Although the U.S. statute provides only for a limited jurisdiction over genocide cases in U.S. courts, customary international law includes a concept of "universal jurisdiction" for crimes such as genocide that are universally condemned. Under universal jurisdiction, any country conceivably could try a defendant for genocide. For instance, Canada is currently trying a Rwandan for alleged acts of genocide that occurred in Rwanda under a Canadian statute that provides for universal jurisdiction of genocide crimes.[9]

The tribunal in Cambodia is a hybrid court, with both Cambodian and international judges hearing the cases. The trials will be governed by a combination of international law and Cambodian penal law and procedure. The Cambodian law that is the most

8. It is important to note the issue of dualism versus monism, discussed in BLAKESLEY, ET AL. THE INTERNATIONAL LEGAL SYSTEM, Ch. 17, and in the Terrorism Chapter of this book. Many domestic systems require incorporation of the international rule before it is functional or, at least, that there not be a domestic rule that contradicts the customary rule. *See, e.g.,* The Paquete Habana, The Lola, 175 U.S. 677, 20 S.Ct. 290, 44 L.Ed. 320 (1900) (holding that customary international law is part of the law of the United States to the limited extent that "where there is *no treaty,* and *no controlling executive or legislative act or judicial decision,* resort must be had to the customs and usages of civilized nations.") (emphasis added). On the other hand, any nation-state taking a position contrary to customary international law is illegal under international law and will ultimately receive a sanction of some sort.

9. *See, e.g.,* "RCMP Charges Foreign National with War Crimes," Ottawa October 2005, more information available at RCMP's War Crimes website: http://www.rcmp.ca/news/2005/n_0525_e.htm.

detailed is referred to as the **ECDK Law** (this refers to the Extraordinary Chambers described earlier). The ECDK Law incorporates the basic definition of genocide from the Convention. Because the ICTY and ICTR have interpreted the elements of the crime of genocide in the cases before them, the jurisprudence of these two tribunals will also be relevant to the decisions in the Cambodian tribunal.

The next two sections provide the pertinent provisions of the ECDK Law and the case law from the ICTY and ICTR that you should use to evaluate the criminal culpability of the defendants in the Problem.

1. ECDK Law Provisions

a. ECDK Law Article 4: Genocide

The Extraordinary Chambers shall have the power to bring to trial all Suspects who committed the crimes of genocide as defined in the Convention on the Prevention and Punishment of the Crime of Genocide of 1948, and which were committed during the period from 17 April 1975 to 6 January 1979.

The acts of genocide, which have no statute of limitations, mean any acts committed with the intent to destroy, in whole or in part, a national, ethnical, racial or religious group, as such.

The specific acts are:

—Killing members of the group;

—Causing serious bodily or mental harm to members of the group;

—Deliberately inflicting on the group conditions of life calculated to bring about its physical destruction in whole or in part;

—Imposing measures intended to prevent births within the group;

—Forcibly transferring children from one group to another group.

The following acts shall be punishable under this Article:

—attempts to commit acts of genocide;

—conspiracy to commit acts of genocide;

—participation in acts of genocide.

b. ECDK Law Article 29: Responsibility

Any Suspect who planned, instigated, ordered, aided and abetted, or committed the crimes referred to in article ... 4 ... of this law shall be individually responsible for the crime.

The position or rank of any Suspect shall not relieve such person of criminal responsibility or mitigate punishment.

The fact that any of the acts referred to in Articles ... 4 ... of this law were committed by a subordinate does not relieve the superior of personal criminal responsibility if the superior had effective command and control or authority and control over the subordinate, and the superior knew or had reason to know that the subordinate was about to commit such acts or had done so and the superior failed to take the necessary and reasonable measures to prevent such acts or to punish the perpetrators.

The fact that a Suspect acted pursuant to an order of the Government of Democratic Kampuchea or of a superior shall not relieve the Suspect of individual criminal responsibility.

2. Case Materials on Genocide

a. *The Elements of Genocide and Conspiracy to Commit Genocide*

The two cases in this section raise issues about the meaning of the elements of genocide and conspiracy to commit genocide. Genocide requires an "intent to destroy, in whole or in part, a national, ethnical, racial or religious group, as such" and a specific act (e.g., killing members of the group). In the first case, *Krstic*, the ICTY must interpret the meaning of an intent to destroy "in part" an identifiable group under the statutory definition—in this case, Bosnian Muslims. In the second case, *Nahimana*, the ICTR analyzes the elements of the separate crime of conspiracy to commit genocide.

International Criminal Tribunal for the Former Yugoslavia in the Appeals Chamber

PROSECUTOR v. RADISLAV KRSTIC

Judgement: 19 April 2004

Before: Presiding Judge Theodor Meron, Judge Fausto Pocar, Judge Mohamed Shahabuddeen, Judge Mehmet Guney, Judge Wolfgang Schomburg

I. Introduction

1.   The Appeals Chamber of the International Tribunal for the Prosecution of Persons Responsible for Serious Violations of Inter-

national Humanitarian Law Committed in the Territory of the Former Yugoslavia Since 1991 is seised of two appeals from the written Judgement rendered by the Trial Chamber on 2 August 2001 in the case of *Prosecutor v. Radislav Krstic*, Case No. IT–98–33–T ("Trial Judgement"). Having considered the written and oral submissions of the Prosecution and the Defence, the Appeals Chamber hereby renders its Judgement.

2.   Srebrenica is located in eastern Bosnia and Herzegovina. It gave its name to a United Nations so-called safe area, which was intended as an enclave of safety set up to protect its civilian population from the surrounding war. Since July 1995, however, Srebrenica has also lent its name to an event the horrors of which form the background to this case. The depravity, brutality and cruelty with which the Bosnian Serb Army ("VRS") treated the innocent inhabitants of the safe area are now well known and documented. Bosnian women, children and elderly were removed from the enclave, and between 7,000—8,000 Bosnian Muslim men were systematically murdered.

3.   Srebrenica is located in the area for which the Drina Corps of the VRS was responsible. Radislav Krstic was a General–Major in the VRS and Commander of the Drina Corps at the time the crimes at issue were committed. For his involvement in these events, the Trial Chamber found Radislav Krstic guilty of genocide; persecution through murders, cruel and inhumane treatment, terrorising the civilian population, forcible transfer and destruction of personal property; and murder as a violation of the laws or customs of war. Radislav Krstic was sentenced to forty-six years of imprisonment.
* * *

II.   THE TRIAL CHAMBER'S FINDING THAT GENOCIDE OCCURRED IN SREBRENICA

5.   The Defence appeals Radislav Krstic's conviction for genocide committed against Bosnian Muslims in Srebrenica. The Defence argues that the Trial Chamber both misconstrued the legal definition of genocide and erred in applying the definition to the circumstances of this case. With respect to the legal challenge, the Defence's argument is two-fold. First, Krstic contends that the Trial Chamber's definition of the part of the national group he was found to have intended to destroy was unacceptably narrow. Second, the Defence argues that the Trial Chamber erroneously enlarged the term "destroy" in the prohibition of genocide to include the geographical displacement of a community.

A. The Definition of the Part of the Group

6. Article 4 of the Tribunal's Statute, like the Genocide Convention, covers certain acts done with "intent to destroy, in whole or in part, a national, ethnical, racial or religious group, as such." The Indictment in this case alleged, with respect to the count of genocide, that Radislav Krstic "intend[ed] to destroy a part of the Bosnian Muslim people as a national, ethnical, or religious group." The targeted group identified in the Indictment, and accepted by the Trial Chamber, was that of the Bosnian Muslims. The Trial Chamber determined that the Bosnian Muslims were a specific, distinct national group, and therefore covered by Article 4. This conclusion is not challenged in this appeal.

7. As is evident from the Indictment, Krstic was not alleged to have intended to destroy the entire national group of Bosnian Muslims, but only a part of that group. The first question presented in this appeal is whether, in finding that Radislav Krstic had genocidal intent, the Trial Chamber defined the relevant part of the Bosnian Muslim group in a way which comports with the requirements of Article 4 and of the Genocide Convention.

8. It is well established that where a conviction for genocide relies on the intent to destroy a protected group "in part," the part must be a substantial part of that group. The aim of the Genocide Convention is to prevent the intentional destruction of entire human groups, and the part targeted must be significant enough to have an impact on the group as a whole. Although the Appeals Chamber has not yet addressed this issue, two Trial Chambers of this Tribunal have examined it. In *Jelisic*, the first case to confront the question, the Trial Chamber noted that, "[g]iven the goal of the [Genocide] Convention to deal with mass crimes, it is widely acknowledged that the intention to destroy must target at least a *substantial* part of the group."[10] The same conclusion was reached by the *Sikirica* Trial Chamber: "This part of the definition calls for evidence of an intention to destroy a substantial number relative to the total population of the group."[11] As these Trial Chambers

10. Jelisic Trial Judgement, para. 82 (citing Report of the International Law Commission on the Work of its Forty–Eighth Session, 6 May—26 July 1996, G.A.O.R., 51st session, Supp. No. 10 (A/51/10) (1996), p. 89; Nehemiah Robinson, The Genocide Convention: A Commentary (1960) (1st ed. 1949), p. 63; Genocide Convention, Report of the Committee on Foreign Relations, U.S. Senate, (18 July 1981), p. 22). The Jelisic Trial Judgement was reversed in part by the Appeals Chamber on other grounds. See Jelisic Appeal Judgement, para. 72. The Trial Chamber's definition of what constitutes an appropriate part of the group protected by the Genocide Convention was not challenged.

11. Sikirica Judgement on Defence Motions to Acquit, para. 65.

explained, the substantiality requirement both captures genocide's defining character as a crime of massive proportions and reflects the Convention's concern with the impact the destruction of the targeted part will have on the overall survival of the group.

9.   The question has also been considered by Trial Chambers of the ICTR, whose Statute contains an identical definition of the crime of genocide.[13] These Chambers arrived at the same conclusion. In *Kayishema*, the Trial Chamber concluded, after having canvassed the authorities interpreting the Genocide Convention, that the term " 'in part' requires the intention to destroy a considerable number of individuals who are part of the group." This definition was accepted and refined by the Trial Chambers in *Bagilishema* and *Semanza*, which stated that the intent to destroy must be, at least, an intent to destroy a substantial part of the group.[15]

10.   This interpretation is supported by scholarly opinion. The early commentators on the Genocide Convention emphasized that the term "in part" contains a substantiality requirement. Raphael Lemkin, a prominent international criminal lawyer who coined the term "genocide" and was instrumental in the drafting of the Genocide Convention, addressed the issue during the 1950 debate in the United States Senate on the ratification of the Convention. Lemkin explained that "the destruction in part must be of a substantial nature so as to affect the entirety." He further suggested that the Senate clarify, in a statement of understanding to accompany the ratification, that "the Convention applies only to actions undertaken on a mass scale." Another noted early commentator, Nehemiah Robinson, echoed this view, explaining that a perpetrator of genocide must possess the intent to destroy a substantial number of individuals constituting the targeted group. In discussing this requirement, Robinson stressed, as did Lemkin, that "the act must be directed toward the destruction of a group," this formulation being the aim of the Convention.

11.   Recent commentators have adhered to this view. The International Law Commission, charged by the UN General Assem-

---

13.   See Art. 2 of the ICTR Statute (defining the specific intent requirement of genocide as the "intent to destroy, in whole or in part, a national, ethnical, racial or religious group, as such").

15.   See Bagilishema Trial Judgement, para. 64 ("the intention to destroy must target at least a substantial part of the group") (citing Kayishema and Ruzindana Trial Judgement, para. 97); Semanza Trial Judgement and Sentence, para. 316 ("The intention to destroy must be, at least, to destroy a substan-

tial part of the group") (citing Bagilishema Trial Judgement, para. 64). While Kayishema used the term "considerable number" rather than "substantial part," Semanza and Bagilishema make it clear that Kayishema did not intend to adopt a different standard with respect to the definition of the term "a part." The standard adopted by the Trial Chambers of the ICTR is therefore consistent with the jurisprudence of this Tribunal.

bly with the drafting of a comprehensive code of crimes prohibited by international law, stated that "the crime of genocide by its very nature requires the intention to destroy at least a substantial part of a particular group."[20] The same interpretation was adopted earlier by the 1985 report of Benjamin Whitaker, the Special Rapporteur to the United Nations Sub–Commission on Prevention of Discrimination and Protection of Minorities.[21]

12.   The intent requirement of genocide under Article 4 of the Statute is therefore satisfied where evidence shows that the alleged perpetrator intended to destroy at least a substantial part of the protected group. The determination of when the targeted part is substantial enough to meet this requirement may involve a number of considerations. The numeric size of the targeted part of the group is the necessary and important starting point, though not in all cases the ending point of the inquiry. The number of individuals targeted should be evaluated not only in absolute terms, but also in relation to the overall size of the entire group. In addition to the numeric size of the targeted portion, its prominence within the group can be a useful consideration. If a specific part of the group is emblematic of the overall group, or is essential to its survival, that may support a finding that the part qualifies as substantial within the meaning of Article 4.[22]

13.   The historical examples of genocide also suggest that the area of the perpetrators' activity and control, as well as the possible extent of their reach, should be considered. Nazi Germany may have intended only to eliminate Jews within Europe alone; that ambition probably did not extend, even at the height of its power, to an undertaking of that enterprise on a global scale. Similarly, the perpetrators of genocide in Rwanda did not seriously contemplate

---

20. Report of the International Law Commission on the Work of Its Forty–Eighth Session, 6 May—26 July 1996, p. 89. The Draft Code of Crimes Against the Peace and Security of Mankind, adopted by the International Law Commission, contains a prohibition of the offence of genocide substantively similar to the prohibition present in the Genocide Convention. The Draft code is not binding as a matter of international law, but is an authoritative instrument, parts of which may constitute evidence of customary international law, clarify customary rules, or, at the very least, "be indicative of the legal views of eminently qualified publicists representing the major legal systems of the world." Furundzija Trial Judgement, para. 227.

21. Benjamin Whitaker, Revised and Updated Report on the Question of the Prevention and Punishment of the Crime of Genocide, U.N. Doc. E/CN.4/Sub.2/1985/6, para. 29 (" 'In part' would seem to imply a reasonably significant number, relative to the total of the group as a whole, or else a significant section of a group, such as its leadership."); see also Jelisic Trial Judgement, para. 65 (quoting the report); Trial Judgement, para. 587 (same).

22. The Trial Chambers in Jelisic and Sikirica referred to this factor as an independent consideration which is sufficient, in and of itself, to satisfy requirement of substantiality. See Jelisic Trial Judgement, para. 82; Sikirica Trial Judgement, para. 65. Properly understood, this factor is only one of several which may indicate whether the substantiality requirement is satisfied.

the elimination of the Tutsi population beyond the country's borders. The intent to destroy formed by a perpetrator of genocide will always be limited by the opportunity presented to him. While this factor alone will not indicate whether the targeted group is substantial, it can—in combination with other factors—inform the analysis.

14.   These considerations, of course, are neither exhaustive nor dispositive. They are only useful guidelines. The applicability of these factors, as well as their relative weight, will vary depending on the circumstances of a particular case.

15.   In this case, having identified the protected group as the national group of Bosnian Muslims, the Trial Chamber concluded that the part the VRS Main Staff and Radislav Krstic targeted was the Bosnian Muslims of Srebrenica, or the Bosnian Muslims of Eastern Bosnia.[24] This conclusion comports with the guidelines outlined above. The size of the Bosnian Muslim population in Srebrenica prior to its capture by the VRS forces in 1995 amounted to approximately forty thousand people.[25] This represented not only the Muslim inhabitants of the Srebrenica municipality but also many Muslim refugees from the surrounding region.[26] Although this population constituted only a small percentage of the overall Muslim population of Bosnia and Herzegovina at the time, the importance of the Muslim community of Srebrenica is not captured

24.   Trial Judgement, para. 560 ("The Chamber concludes that the protected group, within the meaning of Article 4 of the Statute, must be defined, in the present case, as the Bosnian Muslims. The Bosnian Muslims of Srebrenica or the Bosnian Muslims of Eastern Bosnia constitute a part of the protected group under Article 4."). See also Trial Judgement, para. 591. Although the Trial Chamber did not delineate clearly the interrelationship between these two alternative definitions, an explanation can be gleaned from its Judgement. As the Trial Chamber found, "most of the Bosnian Muslims residing in Srebrenica at the time of the [Serbian] attack were not originally from Srebrenica but from all around the central Podrinje region." Trial Judgement, para. 559; see also ibid., para. 592 (speaking about "the Bosnian Muslim community of Srebrenica and its surrounds"). The Trial Chamber used the term "Bosnian Muslims of Srebrenica" as a short-hand for the Muslims of both Srebrenica and the surrounding areas, most of whom had, by the time of the Serbian attack against

the city, sought refuge with the enclave. This is also the sense in which the term will be used in this Judgement.

25.   While the Trial Chamber did not make a definitive determination as to the size of the Bosnian Muslim community in Srebrenica, the issue was not in dispute. The Prosecution estimated the number to be between 38,000 and 42,000. See Trial Judgement, para. 592. The Defence's estimate was 40,000. See ibid., para. 593.

26.   The pre-war Muslim population of the municipality of Srebrenica was 27,000. Trial Judgement, para. 11. By January 1993, four months before the UN Security Council declared Srebrenica to be a safe area, its population swelled to about 50,000—60,000, due to the influx of refugees from nearby regions. Ibid., para. 14. Between 8,000 and 9,000 of those who found shelter in Srebrenica were subsequently evacuated in March—April 1993 by the UN High Commissioner for Refugees. Ibid., para. 16.

solely by its size.[27] As the Trial Chamber explained, Srebrenica (and the surrounding Central Podrinje region) were of immense strategic importance to the Bosnian Serb leadership. Without Srebrenica, the ethnically Serb state of Republica Srpska they sought to create would remain divided into two disconnected parts, and its access to Serbia proper would be disrupted. The capture and ethnic purification of Srebrenica would therefore severely undermine the military efforts of the Bosnian Muslim state to ensure its viability, a consequence the Muslim leadership fully realized and strove to prevent. Control over the Srebrenica region was consequently essential to the goal of some Bosnian Serb leaders of forming a viable political entity in Bosnia, as well as to the continued survival of the Bosnian Muslim people. Because most of the Muslim inhabitants of the region had, by 1995, sought refuge within the Srebrenica enclave, the elimination of that enclave would have accomplished the goal of purifying the entire region of its Muslim population.

16. In addition, Srebrenica was important due to its prominence in the eyes of both the Bosnian Muslims and the international community. The town of Srebrenica was the most visible of the "safe areas" established by the UN Security Council in Bosnia. By 1995 it had received significant attention in the international media. In its resolution declaring Srebrenica a safe area, the Security Council announced that it "should be free from armed attack or any other hostile act."[29] This guarantee of protection was re-affirmed by the commander of the UN Protection Force in Bosnia (UNPROFOR) and reinforced with the deployment of UN troops. The elimination of the Muslim population of Srebrenica, despite the assurances given by the international community, would serve as a potent example to all Bosnian Muslims of their vulnerability and defenselessness in the face of Serb military forces. The fate of the Bosnian Muslims of Srebrenica would be emblematic of that of all Bosnian Muslims.

17. Finally, the ambit of the genocidal enterprise in this case was limited to the area of Srebrenica. While the authority of the VRS Main Staff extended throughout Bosnia, the authority of the Bosnian Serb forces charged with the take-over of Srebrenica did not extend beyond the Central Podrinje region. From the perspec-

---

27. The Muslim population of Bosnia and Herzegovina in 1995, when the attack against Srebrenica took place, was approximately 1,400,000. See http://www.unhabitat.org/habrdd/conditions/southeurope/bosnia.htm, accessed 26/03/2004 (estimating that the Muslims constituted 40 percent of the 1995 population of 3,569,000). The Bosnian Muslims of Srebrenica therefore formed about 2.9 percent of the overall population.

29. Security Council Resolution 819, UN Doc. S/RES/819 (1993), quoted in Trial Judgement, para. 18 & n. 17. The two other protected enclaves created by the Security Council were Zepa and Gorazde. See Security Council Resolution 824, UN Doc. S/RES/824 (1993); Trial Judgement, para. 18 & n. 18.

tive of the Bosnian Serb forces alleged to have had genocidal intent in this case, the Muslims of Srebrenica were the only part of the Bosnian Muslim group within their area of control.

18.   In fact, the Defence does not argue that the Trial Chamber's characterization of the Bosnian Muslims of Srebrenica as a substantial part of the targeted group contravenes Article 4 of the Tribunal's Statute. Rather, the Defence contends that the Trial Chamber made a further finding, concluding that the part Krstic intended to destroy was the Bosnian Muslim men of military age of Srebrenica. In the Defence's view, the Trial Chamber then engaged in an impermissible sequential reasoning, measuring the latter part of the group against the larger part (the Bosnian Muslims of Srebrenica) to find the substantiality requirement satisfied. The Defence submits that if the correct approach is properly applied, and the military age men are measured against the entire group of Bosnian Muslims, the substantiality requirement would not be met.

19.   The Defence misunderstands the Trial Chamber's analysis. The Trial Chamber stated that the part of the group Radislav Krstic intended to destroy was the Bosnian Muslim population of Srebrenica. The men of military age, who formed a further part of that group, were not viewed by the Trial Chamber as a separate, smaller part within the meaning of Article 4. Rather, the Trial Chamber treated the killing of the men of military age as evidence from which to infer that Radislav Krstic and some members of the VRS Main Staff had the requisite intent to destroy all the Bosnian Muslims of Srebrenica, the only part of the protected group relevant to the Article 4 analysis.

20.   In support of its argument, the Defence identifies the Trial Chamber's determination that, in the context of this case, "the intent to kill the men [of military age] amounted to an intent to destroy a substantial part of the Bosnian Muslim group." The Trial Chamber's observation was proper. As a specific intent offense, the crime of genocide requires proof of intent to commit the underlying act and proof of intent to destroy the targeted group, in whole or in part. The proof of the mental state with respect to the commission of the underlying act can serve as evidence from which the fact-finder may draw the further inference that the accused possessed the specific intent to destroy.

21.   The Trial Chamber determined that Radislav Krstic had the intent to kill the Srebrenica Bosnian Muslim men of military age. This finding is one of intent to commit the requisite genocidal act—in this case, the killing of the members of the protected group, prohibited by Article 4(2)(a) of the Statute. From this intent to kill, the Trial Chamber also drew the further inference that Krstic shared the genocidal intent of some members of the VRS Main Staff

to destroy a substantial part of the targeted group, the Bosnian Muslims of Srebrenica.

22. It must be acknowledged that in portions of its Judgement, the Trial Chamber used imprecise language which lends support to the Defence's argument.[36] The Trial Chamber should have expressed its reasoning more carefully. As explained above, however, the Trial Chamber's overall discussion makes clear that it identified the Bosnian Muslims of Srebrenica as the substantial part in this case.

23. The Trial Chamber's determination of the substantial part of the protected group was correct. The Defence's appeal on this issue is dismissed.

B. The Determination of the Intent to Destroy

24. The Defence also argues that the Trial Chamber erred in describing the conduct with which Radislav Krstic is charged as genocide. The Trial Chamber, the Defence submits, impermissibly broadened the definition of genocide by concluding that an effort to displace a community from its traditional residence is sufficient to show that the alleged perpetrator intended to destroy a protected group. By adopting this approach, the Defence argues, the Trial Chamber departed from the established meaning of the term genocide in the Genocide Convention—as applying only to instances of physical or biological destruction of a group—to include geographic displacement.

25. The Genocide Convention, and customary international law in general, prohibit only the physical or biological destruction of a human group.[39] The Trial Chamber expressly acknowledged

---

36. See, e.g., para. 581 ("Since in this case primarily the Bosnian Muslim men of military age were killed, a second issue is whether this group of victims represents a sufficient part of the Bosnian Muslim group so that the intent to destroy them qualifies as an 'intent to destroy the group in whole or in part' under Article 4 of the Statute."); para. 634 ("[T]he Trial Chamber has concluded that, in terms of the requirement of Article 4(2) of the Statute that an intent to destroy only part of the group must nevertheless concern a substantial part thereof, either numerically or qualitatively, the military aged Bosnian Muslim men of Srebrenica do in fact constitute a substantial part of the Bosnian Muslim group, because the killing of these men inevitably and fundamentally would result in the annihilation of the entire Bosnian Muslim community at Srebrenica.").

39. The International Law Commission, when drafting a code of crimes which it submitted to the ICC Preparatory Committee, has examined closely the travaux preparatoires of the Convention in order to elucidate the meaning of the term "destroy" in the Convention's description of the requisite intent. The Commission concluded: "As clearly shown by the preparatory work for the Convention, the destruction in question is the material destruction of a group either by physical or by biological means, not the destruction of the national, linguistic, cultural or other identity of a particular group." Report of the International Law Commission on the Work of its Forty–Eighth Session, 6 May—26 July 1996, G.A.O.R., 51st session, Supp. No. 10 (A/51/10) (1996), pp. 90–91.

this limitation, and eschewed any broader definition. The Chamber stated: "[C]ustomary international law limits the definition of genocide to those acts seeking the physical or biological destruction of all or part of the group. [A]n enterprise attacking only the cultural or sociological characteristics of a human group in order to annihilate these elements which give to that group its own identity distinct from the rest of the community would not fall under the definition of genocide."

26. Given that the Trial Chamber correctly identified the governing legal principle, the Defence must discharge the burden of persuading the Appeals Chamber that, despite having correctly stated the law, the Trial Chamber erred in applying it. The main evidence underlying the Trial Chamber's conclusion that the VRS forces intended to eliminate all the Bosnian Muslims of Srebrenica was the massacre by the VRS of all men of military age from that community. The Trial Chamber rejected the Defence's argument that the killing of these men was motivated solely by the desire to eliminate them as a potential military threat. The Trial Chamber based this conclusion on a number of factual findings, which must be accepted as long as a reasonable Trial Chamber could have arrived at the same conclusions. The Trial Chamber found that, in executing the captured Bosnian Muslim men, the VRS did not differentiate between men of military status and civilians. Though civilians undoubtedly are capable of bearing arms, they do not constitute the same kind of military threat as professional soldiers. The Trial Chamber was therefore justified in drawing the inference that, by killing the civilian prisoners, the VRS did not intend only to eliminate them as a military danger. The Trial Chamber also found that some of the victims were severely handicapped and, for that reason, unlikely to have been combatants. This evidence further supports the Trial Chamber's conclusion that the extermination of these men was not driven solely by a military rationale.

27. Moreover, as the Trial Chamber emphasized, the term "men of military age" was itself a misnomer, for the group killed by the VRS included boys and elderly men normally considered to be outside that range. Although the younger and older men could still be capable of bearing arms, the Trial Chamber was entitled to conclude that they did not present a serious military threat, and to draw a further inference that the VRS decision to kill them did not stem solely from the intent to eliminate them as a threat. The killing of the military aged men was, assuredly, a physical destruction, and given the scope of the killings the Trial Chamber could legitimately draw the inference that their extermination was motivated by a genocidal intent.

28.   The Trial Chamber was also entitled to consider the long-term impact that the elimination of seven to eight thousand men from Srebrenica would have on the survival of that community. In examining these consequences, the Trial Chamber properly focused on the likelihood of the community's physical survival. As the Trial Chamber found, the massacred men amounted to about one fifth of the overall Srebrenica community.[46] The Trial Chamber found that, given the patriarchal character of the Bosnian Muslim society in Srebrenica, the destruction of such a sizeable number of men would "inevitably result in the physical disappearance of the Bosnian Muslim population at Srebrenica." Evidence introduced at trial supported this finding, by showing that, with the majority of the men killed officially listed as missing, their spouses are unable to remarry and, consequently, to have new children. The physical destruction of the men therefore had severe procreative implications for the Srebrenica Muslim community, potentially consigning the community to extinction.

29.   This is the type of physical destruction the Genocide Convention is designed to prevent. The Trial Chamber found that the Bosnian Serb forces were aware of these consequences when they decided to systematically eliminate the captured Muslim men. The finding that some members of the VRS Main Staff devised the killing of the male prisoners with full knowledge of the detrimental consequences it would have for the physical survival of the Bosnian Muslim community in Srebrenica further supports the Trial Chamber's conclusion that the instigators of that operation had the requisite genocidal intent.

30.   The Defence argues that the VRS decision to transfer, rather than to kill, the women and children of Srebrenica in their custody undermines the finding of genocidal intent. This conduct, the Defence submits, is inconsistent with the indiscriminate approach that has characterized all previously recognized instances of modern genocide.

31.   The decision by Bosnian Serb forces to transfer the women, children and elderly within their control to other areas of Muslim-controlled Bosnia could be consistent with the Defence argument. This evidence, however, is also susceptible of an alternative interpretation. As the Trial Chamber explained, forcible transfer could be an additional means by which to ensure the physical destruction of the Bosnian Muslim community in Srebrenica. The transfer completed the removal of all Bosnian Muslims from Srebrenica, thereby eliminating even the residual possibility that the

---

46. See Ibid., paras. 592—594 (finding, on the basis of the parties' estimates, the number of the killed men to be approximately 7,500 and the overall size of the Srebrenica community, augmented by refugees from the surrounding areas, to be approximately 40,000).

Muslim community in the area could reconstitute itself. The decision not to kill the women or children may be explained by the Bosnian Serbs' sensitivity to public opinion. In contrast to the killing of the captured military men, such an action could not easily be kept secret, or disguised as a military operation, and so carried an increased risk of attracting international censure.

32. In determining that genocide occurred at Srebrenica, the cardinal question is whether the intent to commit genocide existed. While this intent must be supported by the factual matrix, the offence of genocide does not require proof that the perpetrator chose the most efficient method to accomplish his objective of destroying the targeted part. Even where the method selected will not implement the perpetrator's intent to the fullest, leaving that destruction incomplete, this ineffectiveness alone does not preclude a finding of genocidal intent. The international attention focused on Srebrenica, combined with the presence of the UN troops in the area, prevented those members of the VRS Main Staff who devised the genocidal plan from putting it into action in the most direct and efficient way. Constrained by the circumstances, they adopted the method which would allow them to implement the genocidal design while minimizing the risk of retribution.

33. The Trial Chamber—as the best assessor of the evidence presented at trial—was entitled to conclude that the evidence of the transfer supported its finding that some members of the VRS Main Staff intended to destroy the Bosnian Muslims in Srebrenica. The fact that the forcible transfer does not constitute in and of itself a genocidal act does not preclude a Trial Chamber from relying on it as evidence of the intentions of members of the VRS Main Staff. The genocidal intent may be inferred, among other facts, from evidence of "other culpable acts systematically directed against the same group."

34. The Defence also argues that the record contains no statements by members of the VRS Main Staff indicating that the killing of the Bosnian Muslim men was motivated by genocidal intent to destroy the Bosnian Muslims of Srebrenica. The absence of such statements is not determinative. Where direct evidence of genocidal intent is absent, the intent may still be inferred from the factual circumstances of the crime. The inference that a particular atrocity was motivated by genocidal intent may be drawn, moreover, even where the individuals to whom the intent is attributable are not precisely identified. If the crime committed satisfies the other requirements of genocide, and if the evidence supports the inference that the crime was motivated by the intent to destroy, in whole or in part, a protected group, a finding that genocide has occurred may be entered.

35.   In this case, the factual circumstances, as found by the Trial Chamber, permit the inference that the killing of the Bosnian Muslim men was done with genocidal intent. As already explained, the scale of the killing, combined with the VRS Main Staff's awareness of the detrimental consequences it would have for the Bosnian Muslim community of Srebrenica and with the other actions the Main Staff took to ensure that community's physical demise, is a sufficient factual basis for the finding of specific intent. The Trial Chamber found, and the Appeals Chamber endorses this finding, that the killing was engineered and supervised by some members of the Main Staff of the VRS. The fact that the Trial Chamber did not attribute genocidal intent to a particular official within the Main Staff may have been motivated by a desire not to assign individual culpability to persons not on trial here. This, however, does not undermine the conclusion that Bosnian Serb forces carried out genocide against the Bosnian Muslims.

36.   Among the grievous crimes this Tribunal has the duty to punish, the crime of genocide is singled out for special condemnation and opprobrium. The crime is horrific in its scope; its perpetrators identify entire human groups for extinction. Those who devise and implement genocide seek to deprive humanity of the manifold richness its nationalities, races, ethnicities and religions provide. This is a crime against all of humankind, its harm being felt not only by the group targeted for destruction, but by all of humanity.

37.   The gravity of genocide is reflected in the stringent requirements which must be satisfied before this conviction is imposed. These requirements—the demanding proof of specific intent and the showing that the group was targeted for destruction in its entirety or in substantial part—guard against a danger that convictions for this crime will be imposed lightly. Where these requirements are satisfied, however, the law must not shy away from referring to the crime committed by its proper name. By seeking to eliminate a part of the Bosnian Muslims, the Bosnian Serb forces committed genocide. They targeted for extinction the forty thousand Bosnian Muslims living in Srebrenica, a group which was emblematic of the Bosnian Muslims in general. They stripped all the male Muslim prisoners, military and civilian, elderly and young, of their personal belongings and identification, and deliberately and methodically killed them solely on the basis of their identity. The Bosnian Serb forces were aware, when they embarked on this genocidal venture, that the harm they caused would continue to plague the Bosnian Muslims. The Appeals Chamber states unequivocally that the law condemns, in appropriate terms, the deep and lasting injury inflicted, and calls the massacre at Srebrenica by its

proper name: genocide. Those responsible will bear this stigma, and it will serve as a warning to those who may in future contemplate the commission of such a heinous act.

38.   In concluding that some members of the VRS Main Staff intended to destroy the Bosnian Muslims of Srebrenica, the Trial Chamber did not depart from the legal requirements for genocide. The Defence appeal on this issue is dismissed.

From: https://www.cia.gov/cia/publications/mapspub/maps/Cental_Balkin_Region.htm, presented in http://www.reisenett.no/map_collection/europe/Central_Balkan_pol98.jpg

Introductory Note on the Conflict in Rwanda

Rwanda's population consists primarily of people identified as Hutu and Tutsi (with a small population of a third group, the Twa). During the time when Rwanda was a Belgian colony, identity cards were issued for Hutu and Tutsi. There is great debate about whether there really is an ethnic difference between Hutu and Tutsi, or whether the identities were more of a socioeconomic difference. Nevertheless, the identity cards solidified certain political differences between the groups that existed even after Rwanda was granted independence in 1962.

In 1994, an airplane carrying the President of Rwanda was shot down. His death unleashed 100 days of fighting, during which close to 1 million people died. Most of the killing was directed toward the Tutsi minority in Rwanda. Ultimately, an army of largely Tutsi refugees, with leaders including the current President of Rwanda, took control and stabilized the country.

Much of the killing in Rwanda occurred at roadblocks and in churches. At the roadblocks, people were asked for their identity cards. Those with Tutsi identity cards were treated harshly and many were killed. Similarly, Tutsis and moderate Hutus who fled to churches for refuge were killed, either on a large scale in the church or by pulling out individuals for execution.

The United Nations established the International Criminal Tribunal for Rwanda (ICTR) to prosecute those who were the most responsible for genocide, crimes against humanity, and war crimes. The next case is from the ICTR. The case involves high level political leaders who were accused of conspiracy to commit genocide against the Tutsi population.

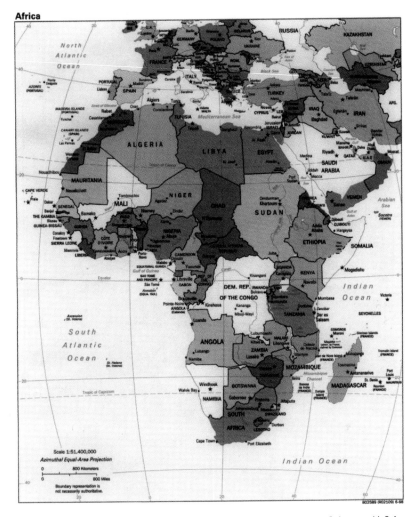

From: https://www.cia.gov/cia/publications/mapspub/maps/Africa.
htm, presented in http://www.reisenett.no/map_collection/africa/
Africa_pol98.jpg

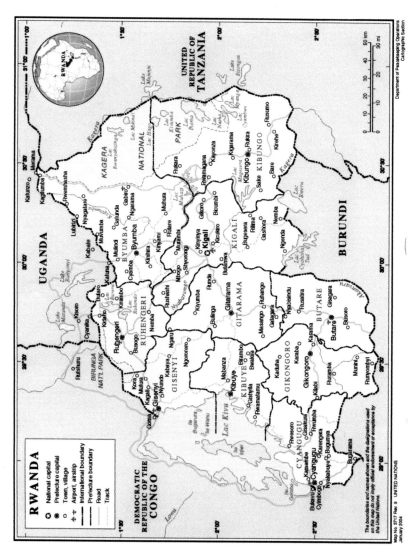

International Criminal Tribunal for Rwanda
Trial Chamber I

THE PROSECUTOR v. FERDINAND NAHIMANA
JEAN-BOSCO BARAYAGWIZA
HASSAN NGEZE

Judgement of: 3 December 2003

Before: PRESIDING JUDGES NAVANETHEM PILLAY, ERIK MOOSE, ASOKA DE ZOYSA GUNAWARDANA

[Ed. Notes of Explanation:

RTLM was a radio station in Rwanda. Defendants Barayagwiza and Nahimana were the top management of the radio station.

Kangura was a newspaper published in Rwanda from 1990 to 1995, with a wide circulation in French and Kinyarwandan. Defendant Hassan Ngeze was the editor-in-chief of the newspaper.

CDR was the Coalition for the Defence of the Republic, a political party created in 1992. Defendant Barayagwiza was actively involved with CDR. Defendant Ngeze was involved to a lesser extent.]

* * *

RTLM

949. The Chamber found, . . . that RTLM broadcasts engaged in ethnic stereotyping in a manner that promoted contempt and hatred for the Tutsi population and called on listeners to seek out and take up arms against the enemy. The enemy was defined to be the Tutsi ethnic group. These broadcasts called explicitly for the extermination of the Tutsi ethnic group. In 1994, both before and after 6 April, RTLM broadcast the names of Tutsi individuals and their families, as well as Hutu political opponents who supported the Tutsi ethnic group. In some cases these persons were subsequently killed. A specific causal connection between the RTLM broadcasts and the killing of these individuals—either by publicly naming them or by manipulating their movements and directing that they, as a group, be killed—has been established. . . .

Kangura

950. The Chamber found, . . . that *The Appeal to the Conscience of the Hutu and The Ten Commandments*, published in *Kangura* No. 6 in December 1990, conveyed contempt and hatred for the Tutsi ethnic group, and for Tutsi women in particular as enemy agents, and called on readers to take all necessary measures to stop the enemy, defined to be the Tutsi population. Other editorials and articles published in *Kangura* echoed the contempt and hatred for Tutsi found in *The Ten Commandments* and were clearly intended to fan the flames of ethnic hatred, resentment and fear against the Tutsi population and Hutu political opponents who supported the Tutsi ethnic group. The cover of *Kangura* No. 26 promoted violence by conveying the message that the machete should be used to eliminate the Tutsi, once and for all. This was a call for the destruction of the Tutsi ethnic group as such. Through fear-mongering and hate propaganda, *Kangura* paved the way for genocide in Rwanda, whipping the Hutu population into a killing frenzy.

CDR

951.   The Hutu Power movement, spearheaded by CDR, created a political framework for the killing of Tutsi and Hutu political opponents. The CDR and its youth wing, the *Impuzamugambi*, convened meetings and demonstrations, established roadblocks, distributed weapons, and systematically organized and carried out the killing of Tutsi civilians. The genocidal cry of *"tubatsembatsembe"* or "let's exterminate them", referring to the Tutsi population, was chanted consistently at CDR meetings and demonstrations. As well as orchestrating particular acts of killing, the CDR promoted a Hutu mindset in which ethnic hatred was normalized as a political ideology. The division of Hutu and Tutsi entrenched fear and suspicion of the Tutsi and fabricated the perception that the Tutsi population had to be destroyed in order to safeguard the political gains that had been made by the Hutu majority.

Causation

952.   The nature of media is such that causation of killing and other acts of genocide will necessarily be effected by an immediately proximate cause in addition to the communication itself. In the Chamber's view, this does not diminish the causation to be attributed to the media, or the criminal accountability of those responsible for the communication.

953.   The Defence contends that the downing of the President's plane and the death of President Habyarimana precipitated the killing of innocent Tutsi civilians. The Chamber accepts that this moment in time served as a trigger for the events that followed. That is evident. But if the downing of the plane was the trigger, then RTLM, *Kangura* and CDR were the bullets in the gun. The trigger had such a deadly impact because the gun was loaded. The Chamber therefore considers the killing of Tutsi civilians can be said to have resulted, at least in part, from the message of ethnic targeting for death that was clearly and effectively disseminated through RTLM, *Kangura* and CDR, before and after 6 April 1994.

Acts of Jean-Bosco Barayagwiza

954.   . . . Barayagwiza came to Gisenyi, one week after 6 April, with a truckload of weapons that were distributed to the local population and used to kill individuals of Tutsi ethnicity. Barayagwiza played a leadership role in the distribution of these weapons, which formed part of a predefined and structured plan to kill Tutsi civilians. From Barayagwiza's critical role in this plan, orchestrating the delivery of the weapons to be used for destruction, the Chamber finds that Barayagwiza was involved in planning this killing. . . . Barayagwiza supervised roadblocks manned by the Impuzamugambi, established to stop and kill Tutsi.

Acts of Hassan Ngeze

955.   ... Hassan Ngeze on the morning of 7 April 1994 ordered the *Interahamwe* in Gisenyi to kill Tutsi civilians. Many were killed in the attacks that happened immediately thereafter and later on the same day, among whom were Witness EB's mother, brother and pregnant sister, whose body was sexually violated with an umbrella rod. On the basis of these acts, the Chamber finds that Ngeze ordered the killing of Tutsi civilians.

956.   ... Hassan Ngeze helped secure and distribute, stored, and transported weapons to be used against the Tutsi population. He set up, manned and supervised roadblocks in Gisenyi in 1994 that identified targeted Tutsi civilians who were subsequently taken to and killed at the *Commune Rouge*. On the basis of these acts, the Chamber finds that Ngeze aided and abetted the killing of Tutsi civilians.

Genocidal Intent

957.   In ascertaining the intent of the Accused, the Chamber has considered their individual statements and acts, as well as the message they conveyed through the media they controlled.

* * *

963.   Kangura and RTLM explicitly and repeatedly, in fact relentlessly, targeted the Tutsi population for destruction. Demonizing the Tutsi as having inherently evil qualities, equating the ethnic group with "the enemy" and portraying its women as seductive enemy agents, the media called for the extermination of the Tutsi ethnic group as a response to the political threat that they associated with Tutsi ethnicity.

964.   The genocidal intent in the activities of the CDR was expressed through the phrase "tubatsembasembe" or "let's exterminate them", a slogan chanted repeatedly at CDR rallies and demonstrations. At a policy level, CDR communiques called on the Hutu population to "neutralize by all means possible" the enemy, defined to be the Tutsi ethnic group.

* * *

966.   ... As the mastermind of RTLM, Nahimana set in motion the communications weaponry that fought the "war of media, words, newspapers and radio stations" he described in his Radio Rwanda broadcast of 25 April as a complement to bullets. Nahimana also expressed his intent through RTLM, where the words broadcast were intended to kill on the basis of ethnicity, and that is what they did.

967. Jean–Bosco Barayagwiza said in public meetings, "let's exterminate them" with "them" being understood by those who heard it as a reference to the Tutsi population. After separating the Tutsi from the Hutu and humiliating the Tutsi by forcing them to perform the Ikinyemera, their traditional dance, at several public meetings, Barayagwiza threatened to kill them and said it would not be difficult. . . .

968. Hassan Ngeze wrote many articles and editorials, and made many statements that openly evidence his genocidal intent. . . . His Radio Rwanda broadcast of 12 June 1994 called on listeners not to mistakenly kill Hutu rather than Tutsi. Crass references to the physical and personal traits of Tutsi ethnicity permeate Kangura and his own writings in Kangura. Ngeze harped on the broad nose of the Hutu as contrasted with the aquiline nose of the Tutsi, and he incessantly described the Tutsi as evil. His role in saving Tutsi individuals whom he knew does not, in the Chamber's view, negate his intent to destroy the ethnic group as such. . . . Witness AEU heard Ngeze on a megaphone, saying that he was going to kill and exterminate all the Inyenzi, by which he meant the Tutsi, and as set forth above, Ngeze himself ordered an attack on Tutsi civilians in Gisenyi, evidencing his intent to destroy the Tutsi population.

969. Based on the evidence set forth above, the Chamber finds beyond a reasonable doubt that Ferdinand Nahimana, Jean–Bosco Barayagwiza and Hassan Ngeze acted with intent to destroy, in whole or in part, the Tutsi ethnic group. The Chamber considers that the association of the Tutsi ethnic group with a political agenda, effectively merging ethnic and political identity, does not negate the genocidal animus that motivated the Accused. To the contrary, the identification of Tutsi individuals as enemies of the state associated with political opposition, simply by virtue of their Tutsi ethnicity, underscores the fact that their membership in the ethnic group, as such, was the sole basis on which they were targeted.

* * *

Kangura

1036. Many of the writings published in Kangura combined ethnic hatred and fear-mongering with a call to violence to be directed against the Tutsi population, who were characterized as the enemy or enemy accomplices. The Appeal to the Conscience of the Hutu and the cover of Kangura No. 26 are two notable examples in which the message clearly conveyed to the readers of Kangura was that the Hutu population should "wake up" and take the measures necessary to deter the Tutsi enemy from decimating the Hutu. The Chamber notes that the name *Kangura* itself means "to wake up others". What it intended to wake the Hutu up to is evidenced by its content, a litany of ethnic denigration presenting the Tutsi population as inherently evil and calling for the extermination of the Tutsi as a preventive measure. The Chamber notes the increased attention in 1994 issues of *Kangura* to the fear of an RPF attack and the threat that killing of innocent Tutsi civilians that would follow as a consequence.

1037.   The Chamber notes that not all of the writings published in *Kangura* and highlighted by the Prosecution constitute direct incitement. A Cockroach Cannot Give Birth to a Butterfly, for example, is an article brimming with ethnic hatred but did not call on readers to take action against the Tutsi population.

1038.   As founder, owner and editor of *Kangura*, Hassan Ngeze directly controlled the publication and all of its contents, for which he has largely acknowledged responsibility. The Chamber has found that Ngeze acted with genocidal intent, as set forth in paragraph 969. Ngeze used the publication to instill hatred, promote fear, and incite genocide. It is evident that Kangura played a significant role, and was seen to have played a significant role, in creating the conditions that led to acts of genocide. Accordingly, the Chamber finds Hassan Ngeze guilty of direct and public incitement to genocide, under Article 2(3)(c) and in accordance with Article 6(1) of the Statute.

Acts of Hassan Ngeze

1039.   As set forth in paragraph 837, Hassan Ngeze often drove around with a megaphone in his vehicle, mobilizing the Hutu population to come to CDR meetings and spreading the message that the *Inyenzi* would be exterminated, *Inyenzi* meaning, and being understood to mean, the Tutsi ethnic minority. For these acts, which called for the extermination of the Tutsi population, the Chamber finds Hassan Ngeze guilty of direct and public incitement to genocide, under Article 2(3)(c) and in accordance with Article 6(1) of the Statute.

4.   Conspiracy to Commit Genocide

1040.   Count 1 of the Indictments charge the Accused with conspiracy to commit genocide pursuant to Article 2(3)(b) of the Statute, in that they conspired with each other, and others, to kill and cause serious bodily or mental harm to members of the Tutsi population with the intent to destroy, in whole or in part, a racial or ethnic group as such.

1041.   In *Musema*, the Tribunal reviewed the history of the inclusion of the crime of conspiracy in the Convention for the

Prevention and Punishment of the Crime of Genocide, noting that in view of the serious nature of the crime of genocide, it was felt that the mere agreement to commit genocide should be punishable even if no preparatory act had taken place. After considering the civil law and common law definitions of conspiracy, the *Musema* judgement defined conspiracy to commit genocide as an agreement between two or more persons to commit the crime of genocide.

1042. The requisite intent for the crime of conspiracy to commit genocide is the same intent required for the crime of genocide. That the three Accused had this intent has been found beyond a reasonable doubt and is set forth in paragraph 969.

1043. The Appeals Chamber in *Musema* has affirmed that distinct crimes may justify multiple convictions, provided that each statutory provision that forms the basis for a conviction has a materially distinct element not contained in the other. The Chamber notes that planning is an act of commission of genocide, pursuant to Article 6(1) of the Statute. The offence of conspiracy requires the existence of an agreement, which is the defining element of the crime of conspiracy. Accordingly, the Chamber considers that the Accused can be held criminally responsible for both the act of conspiracy and the substantive offence of genocide that is the object of the conspiracy.

1044. The Chamber notes that as set forth in paragraphs 100–104 conspiracy is an inchoate offence, and as such has a continuing nature that culminates in the commission of the acts contemplated by the conspiracy. For this reason, acts of conspiracy prior to 1994 that resulted in the commission of genocide in 1994 fall within the temporal jurisdiction of the Tribunal.

1045. The essence of the charge of conspiracy is the agreement among those charged. It is a well established principle of the Anglo–American jurisprudence on conspiracy that the existence of a formal or express agreement is not needed to prove the charge of conspiracy. An agreement can be inferred from concerted or coordinated action on the part of the group of individuals. A tacit understanding of the criminal purpose is sufficient.

1046. In *Niyitegeka*, the Tribunal inferred the existence of a conspiracy to commit genocide based on circumstantial evidence, including various actions of the Accused, such as his participation and attendance at meetings to discuss the killing of Tutsi, his planning of attacks against Tutsi, his promise and distribution of weapons to attackers to be used in attacks against Tutsi, and his leadership role in conducting and speaking at the meetings.

1047. The Chamber considers that conspiracy to commit genocide can be inferred from coordinated actions by individuals who have a common purpose and are acting within a unified framework.

A coalition, even an informal coalition, can constitute such a framework so long as those acting within the coalition are aware of its existence, their participation in it, and its role in furtherance of their common purpose.

1048.   The Chamber further considers that conspiracy to commit genocide can be comprised of individuals acting in an institutional capacity as well as or even independently of their personal links with each other. Institutional coordination can form the basis of a conspiracy among those individuals who control the institutions that are engaged in coordinated action. The Chamber considers the act of coordination to be the central element that distinguishes conspiracy from "conscious parallelism", the concept put forward by the Defence to explain the evidence in this case.

1049.   Nahimana and Barayagwiza collaborated closely as the two most active members of the Steering Committee (*Comite d' Initiative*), or provisional board, of RTLM. They were together in meetings at which they represented RTLM, and they were the two officials signing checks for the organization. They both attended clandestine meetings at the Ministry of Transport. In June 1994, they were together in Geneva and met with Prosecution Witness Dahinden, a Swiss journalist, to talk about RTLM. Barayagwiza also collaborated closely with Ngeze in the CDR. They were together at CDR meetings and demonstrations, as documented not only by the evidence of witnesses but also by various photographs of Barayagwiza and Ngeze together on podiums at CDR functions.

1050.   The Chamber finds that Barayagwiza was the lynchpin among the three Accused, collaborating closely with both Nahimana and Ngeze. Nahimana and Ngeze met with Barayagwiza at his office in the Ministry of Foreign Affairs, and Ngeze also met Barayagwiza at his home. They discussed RTLM, CDR and *Kangura* as all playing a role in the struggle of the Hutu against the Tutsi. All three participated together in an MRND rally in Nyamirambo Stadium in 1993 where they were introduced within the framework of the emerging Hutu solidarity movement called "Hutu Power". All three were depicted by Ngeze on the cover of *Kangura* in connection with the creation of RTLM in a cartoon which showed the three Accused as representing the new radio initiative within the framework of advancing a common Hutu agenda.

1051.   Institutionally also, there were many links that connected the Accused to each other. *Kangura* was a shareholder, albeit limited one, of RTLM, and the newspaper and radio closely collaborated. *Kangura* welcomed the creation of RTLM as an initiative in which *Kangura* had a role. RTLM promoted issues of *Kangura* to its listeners. *Kangura* and RTLM undertook a joint initiative in March 1994, a competition to make readers and listen-

ers familiar with the contents of past issues of *Kangura* and to
survey readers and listeners on their views regarding RTLM broad-
casters. One of the prizes offered was for CDR members only.

1052. *Kangura* also worked together with CDR, welcoming its
creation with a special issue devoted to it. The newspaper urged its
readers to join CDR, and it publicly identified Ngeze with CDR,
through editorials, photographs, and the publication of letters and
communiques. An article signed by *Kangura* in May 1992 told
readers "The island is none other than the CDR. So now grab your
oars, Hutus." It called for a mental revolution among the Hutu, to
deal with the intractable Tutsi "who has a desiccated heart where
the Nazi worm nibbles in tranquility".

1053. There were several triangular links as well among the
three institutions effectively controlled by the three Accused. *Kangura* interacted extensively with both RTLM and CDR. Although
RTLM was primarily made up of MRND shareholders, the few CDR
shareholders involved in RTLM were key officials in both RTLM
and CDR. In addition to Barayagwiza, who had a controlling role in
both RTLM and CDR, Stanislas Simbizi, a member of the CDR
Executive Committee, became a member of the RTLM Steering
Committee following the General Assembly of RTLM on 11 July
1993. Simbizi was also a member of the editorial board of Kangura.
An article signed by Ngeze and published in *Kangura* in January
1994 links all three entities: "*Kangura* has been supported by CDR
and then RTLM radio station was established . . . The entire Hutu
youth now have been taught how the Hutu youth can confront the
Inyenzis. . . ." As a political institution CDR provided an ideological
framework for genocide, and the two media institutions formed
part of the coalition that disseminated the message of CDR that the
destruction of the Tutsi was essential to the survival of the Hutu.

1054. This evidence establishes, beyond a reasonable doubt,
that Nahimana, Barayagwiza and Ngeze consciously interacted
with each other, using the institutions they controlled to promote a
joint agenda, which was the targeting of the Tutsi population for
destruction. There was public presentation of this shared purpose
and coordination of efforts to realize their common goal.

1055. The Chamber finds that Nahimana, Ngeze and Barayagwiza, through personal collaboration as well as interaction among
institutions within their control, namely RTLM, *Kangura* and CDR,
are guilty of conspiracy to commit genocide under Article 2(3)(b)
and pursuant to Article 6(1) of the Statute.

b. Theories of Responsibility

Individuals can be held culpable for criminal offenses that they directly commit and also for those offenses in which there is indirect liability. For example, you have studied accomplice liability in American law. The materials in this section cover theories of indirect culpability for the crime of genocide and other crimes within the jurisdiction of the tribunals. These theories include *joint criminal enterprise, aiding and abetting* a crime, and *command responsibility.*

(i) Joint Criminal Enterprise and Aiding and Abetting.

The ICTY and ICTR have recognized *joint criminal enterprise* (JCE) as a theory of responsibility even though it is not expressly stated in their statutes. JCE is considered a form of "commission" of a crime. What is a JCE?

A joint criminal enterprise is a plurality of persons who act in furtherance of a common purpose that constitutes a crime within the jurisdiction of the tribunal. Each person is called a *co-perpetrator* of the crime. For example, assume that five guards at a prison camp participate in the torture of detainees. Three of the guards inflict the torture; one guard stands watch to signal if someone is coming during the torture; and the other guard falsely documents the detainees' injuries as self-inflicted. Each guard has contributed to the crime of torture, even though in different ways. If, in addition, each of the guards is intending to further the torture of the detainees, then each will be considered guilty of torture pursuant to a theory of co-perpetration of a joint criminal enterprise. The critical elements are a plurality of persons; a common purpose to commit a prohibited crime; an intent that the crime occur; and a contribution to the commission of the crime.[10]

How does JCE differ from *aiding and abetting*? The ICTY Appeals Chamber has explained that aiding and abetting a crime is a lesser form of responsibility than co-perpetrating a JCE. Aiding and abetting requires knowledge of the criminal purpose of the perpetrator and a substantial contribution to the commission of the crime.

As explained in *Prosecutor v. Kvocka*, Case No. IT–98–30/1–A (Feb. 28, 2005), http://www.un.org/icty-/kvocka/appeal/judgement/index.htm at para.89, *citing Prosecutor v. Vasiljevic*, Case No. IT–98–32–A (Feb. 25 2004), http://www.un.org/icty/vasiljevic/-appeal/judgement/index.htm at para. 102:

"The Appeals Chamber notes that in the *Vasiljevic* Appeal Judgement, the Appeals Chamber discussed the correct distinction

---

10. *Prosecutor v. Kvocka*, Case No. IT–98–30/1–A, (Feb. 28, 2005), http://www.un.org/icty-/kvocka/appeal/judgement/index.htm at para. 96.

between co-perpetration by means of a joint criminal enterprise and aiding and abetting:

(i) The aider and abettor carries out acts specifically directed to assist, encourage or lend moral support to the perpetration of a certain specific crime (murder, extermination, rape, torture, wanton destruction of civilian property, etc.), and this support has a substantial effect upon the perpetration of the crime. By contrast, it is sufficient for a participant in a joint criminal enterprise to perform acts that in some way are directed to the furtherance of the common design.

(ii) In the case of aiding and abetting, the requisite mental element is knowledge that the acts performed by the aider and abettor assist the commission of the specific crime of the principal. By contrast, in the case of participation in a joint criminal enterprise, i.e. as a co-perpetrator, the requisite *mens rea* is intent to pursue a common purpose."

For instance, in *Kvocka*, the Appeals Chamber affirmed the Trial Chamber's finding that Kvocka was a co-perpetrator of a JCE to commit the crime against humanity of persecution. Kvocka was a Bosnian Serb police officer who was assigned to the Omarska detention camp. He functioned as the deputy commander of the guards at the camp. Kvocka argued that he did not have the discriminatory intent required for the crime of persecution (the intent to discriminate on racial, religious, or political grounds). Facts that supported a finding that Kvocka intended to discriminate included his awareness of the harsh treatment of the non-Serb detainees; his participation in the operation of the camp that allowed the abuse to occur; and his authority over the guards and ability to prevent the harm.[11]

Another important aspect of JCE is the scope of liability of co-perpetrators. Co-perpetrators are liable not only for the crime that is the object of the common purpose, but also for crimes that are a "natural and foreseeable consequence of the common purpose."[12] This means that a person who commits torture as a co-perpetrator of a JCE might also be guilty of murder under the same theory if the murder of a detainee is considered to be a natural and foreseeable consequence of the joint criminal enterprise of torture. Note that, under this extended liability, the defendant need not intend that the murder occur. His culpability is based on his intent and participation in the joint criminal enterprise of torture. In contrast, an aider and abettor is liable only for the crimes of which the

11. *Id.* at para. 244. **12.** *Id.* at para. 83.

person has knowledge and assists. There is no extended liability for an aider and abettor.[13]

As you read the *Krstic* case, consider the following questions:

1.   Why is Krstic's level of responsibility for genocide that of an aider and abettor and not as a co-perpetrator of a joint criminal enterprise?

2.   What is the difference between joint criminal enterprise and conspiracy to commit genocide?

3.   Note that Krstic is found to be a co-perpetrator of a joint criminal enterprise to forcibly remove Bosnian Muslim civilians. What is the scope of his liability for acts committed in furtherance of that JCE?

International Criminal Tribunal for the Former Yugoslavia in the Appeals Chamber

PROSECUTOR v. RADISLAV KRSTIC

Judgement: 19 April 2004

Before: PRESIDING JUDGE THEODOR MERON, JUDGE FAUSTO POCAR, JUDGE MOHAMED SHAHABUDDEEN, JUDGE MEHMET GUNEY, JUDGE WOLFGANG SCHOMBURG

* * *

D.   The Appeals Chamber's Analysis of Radislav Krstic's Criminal Responsibility

79.   It remains for the Appeals Chamber to determine whether the Trial Chamber erred in finding that Radislav Krstic shared the genocidal intent of a joint criminal enterprise to commit genocide against the Bosnian Muslims of Srebrenica. The Appeals Chamber will now proceed with its analysis of Krstic's criminal responsibility in light of its findings above.

1.   The Trial Chamber's finding that Radislav Krstic shared the intent of a joint criminal enterprise to commit genocide

80.   The Defence argues that in finding that Radislav Krstic shared the intent to commit genocide, the Trial Chamber failed to accord to him the presumption of innocence. The Defence identifies a number of instances in which the Trial Chamber used the language "must have known," "could not have failed to know," and "could only surmise" as illustrative of this failure. The Defence argues that the Trial Chamber adopted this language to mask the

13. *Id.* at 90.

lack of a proper evidentiary basis for its finding that Krstic possessed the intent to commit genocide.

81. The Trial Chamber properly articulated the standard of proof to be applied to the Defence as being one of proof beyond reasonable doubt. The Trial Chamber's reliance upon language such as "must have known" is indicative of the nature of the case against Krstic being one based upon circumstantial evidence. While the Trial Chamber should have used less ambiguous language when making findings concerning Krstic's knowledge and intent, the regrettable choice of phraseology alone is not sufficient to overturn the Trial Chamber's findings.

82. The Defence argues, however, that even if the Trial Chamber properly articulated the standard of proof, its conclusion that Krstic shared the genocidal intent of the joint criminal enterprise is erroneous. The Appeals Chamber therefore considers the evidence on which the Trial Chamber relied to establish that Krstic shared the intent of the joint criminal enterprise to commit genocide.

83. As already stated, the case against Radislav Krstic was one based on circumstantial evidence, and the finding of the Trial Chamber was largely based upon a combination of circumstantial facts. In convicting Krstic as a participant in a joint criminal enterprise to commit genocide, the Trial Chamber relied upon evidence establishing his knowledge of the intention on the part of General Mladic and other members of the VRS Main Staff to execute the Bosnian Muslims of Srebrenica, his knowledge of the use of personnel and resources of the Drina Corps to carry out that intention given his command position, and upon evidence that Radislav Krstic supervised the participation of his subordinates in carrying out those executions.

2. Contacts between Radislav Krstic and other participants in the joint criminal enterprise

84. The Trial Chamber found the contacts between Krstic and General Mladic to be crucial to establishing Radislav Krstic's genocidal intent. The parties agreed that General Mladic was the main figure behind the killings. The Trial Chamber found that Generals Krstic and Mladic were in constant contact throughout the relevant period. The Trial Chamber concluded that "if General Mladic knew about the killings, it would be natural for Krstic to know as well".

(a) Radislav Krstic's presence at the meetings in the Hotel Fontana

85. Reaching this conclusion, the Trial Chamber first relied upon the presence of Krstic at the second and third of three meetings convened by General Mladic at the Hotel Fontana on 11

and 12 July 1995. The fate of the Bosnian Muslims following the fall of Srebrenica was discussed at these meetings. Based on his presence at two of these meetings, the Trial Chamber concluded that Radislav Krstic "was put on notice that the survival of the Bosnian Muslim population was in question following the take-over of Srebrenica."

86.   All three meetings convened by General Mladic were attended by UNPROFOR leaders and Bosnian civilians leaders selected by UNPROFOR. At the first of these meetings, at which Krstic was not present, Colonel Karremans of Dutch-bat sought assurances from General Mladic that the Bosnian Muslim population of Srebrenica, together with Dutch-bat personnel, would be allowed to withdraw from the area. General Mladic stated that the Bosnian Muslim civilian population was not the target of his actions, and he asked UNPROFOR if they could provide buses for the transportation of the civilian population. It was at the second meeting, at which Krstic was present, that the plan to transport the civilian population crystallised.

87.   The most that Radislav Krstic's presence at these meetings established is his knowledge about General Mladic's decisions to transfer the population from Potocari to Muslim-held territory on buses, and to screen the male members of this population prior to transportation for war criminals. As the Trial Chamber acknowledged, the decision to screen was neither criminal nor unreasonable. The Bratunac Brigade had drawn up a list of over 350 suspected war criminals thought to be in the Srebrenica area. Although General Mladic also announced that the survival of the population depended upon the complete surrender of the ABiH, it is unlikely that General Mladic would be disclosing his genocidal intent in the presence of UNPROFOR leaders and foreign media, or that those present at the meeting, including Krstic, would have interpreted his comments in that light. There was no evidence to suggest that at this time Radislav Krstic knew about the intent on the part of General Mladic to execute the Bosnian Muslim civilians who were to be transferred.

88.   There was, however, evidence to suggest that Krstic was aware of the intention of the members of the Main Staff to take total control of Srebrenica and make the situation unbearable for the Bosnian Muslims in Srebrenica, both military and civilian. In March 1995, the President of Republika Srpska, Radovan Karadzic, in reaction to the pressure of the international community to end the war and create a peace agreement, issued a directive to the VRS, "Directive 7" setting out the long-term strategy of the VRS. Directive 7 specified that the VRS was to "complete the physical separation of Srebrenica from Zepa as soon as possible, preventing even communication between individuals in the two enclaves. By

planned and well-thought out combat operations, create an unbearable situation of total insecurity with no hope of further survival or life for the inhabitants of Srebrenica.''

89.   Part of the plan included the blocking of aid convoys. The Directive declared that

> the relevant State and military organs responsible for the work of UNPROFOR and humanitarian organisations shall, through planned and unobtrusively restrictive issuing of permits, reduce and limit the logistics support of UNPROFOR to the enclaves and the supply of material resources to the Muslim population, making them dependent on our good will while at the same time avoiding the condemnation of the international community and international public opinion.

On 31 March 1995, the VRS Main Staff issued Directive 7.1. This Directive, signed by General Mladic, sought to implement Directive 7 and directed the Drina Corps to conduct "active combat operations . . . around the enclaves."

90.   Directives 7 and 7.1 are insufficiently clear to establish that there was a genocidal intent on the part of the members of the Main Staff who issued them. Indeed, the Trial Chamber did not even find that those who issued Directive 7 and 7.1 had genocidal intent, concluding instead that the genocidal plan crystallised at a later stage. At most, Krstic's knowledge of these Directives alerted him to the military plan to take over Srebrenica and Zepa, and to create conditions that would lead to the total defeat of the Bosnian Muslim military forces in the area, without whose protection the civilian population would be compelled to leave the area. It also alerted Radislav Krstic to the intention of the Main Staff to obstruct humanitarian aid to the civilians of Srebrenica so that their conditions would become unbearable and further motivate them to leave the area.

91.   It is reasonable to infer that the meetings at Hotel Fontana were a further step in the implementation of the goals of the Directive. At each of those meetings, General Mladic called for the total surrender of the Bosnian Military forces in the area. In the two meetings at which Krstic was present, General Mladic's primary concern was securing the surrender of the Bosnian military forces in the area. In the second meeting, General Mladic said that the population had to choose whether to stay or whether to go, and he demanded that all ABiH troops in the area surrender their weapons, and emphasised that the survival of the civilian population in the enclave was linked to the surrender of the ABiH troops. At the third meeting, he again made it clear that the survival of the civilian population in the area was conditional upon the capitulation of the ABiH forces. He said "you can either survive or

disappear ... For your survival, I request: that all your armed men who attacked and committed crimes and many did against our people, hand over their weapons to the Army of the Republika Srpska ... on handing over weapons you may ... choose to stay in the territory ... or, if it suits you, go where you want. The wish of every individual will be observed, no matter how many of you there are." To secure the surrender of the ABiH forces General Mladic was willing to threaten severe repercussions for the civilian population that chose to remain in the area but was also willing to facilitate their removal. As already stated, however, the public nature of the meeting at which these threats were made, and particularly, the presence of members of the international community, make it difficult to conclude that General Mladic was in fact publicly stating his genocidal intent.

* * *

(e) The Trial Chamber's other findings militating against a finding of genocidal intent

131.   The Trial Chamber also made numerous findings that militate against a conclusion that Radislav Krstic had genocidal intent. It found that although Krstic was not a reluctant participant in the forcible transfer of the Bosnian Muslim population, he did appear concerned to ensure that the operation was conducted in an orderly fashion. He simply wanted the civilian population out of the area and he had no interest in mistreating them along the way. The Trial Chamber acknowledged, moreover, that the evidence could not establish that "Radislav Krstic himself ever envisaged that the chosen method of removing the Bosnian Muslims from the enclave would be to systematically execute part of the civilian population" and that he "appeared as a reserved and serious career officer who is unlikely to have ever instigated a plan such as the one devised for the mass execution of Bosnian Muslim men, following the take-over of Srebrenica in July 1995." The Trial Chamber found that "left to his own devices, it seems doubtful that Krstic would have been associated with such a plan at all."

132.   The Trial Chamber also found that Radislav Krstic made efforts to ensure the safety of the Bosnian Muslim civilians transported out of Potocari. In an intercept of 12 July 1995, he was heard ordering that no harm must come to the civilians and, in the interview he gave in Potocari on 12 July 1995, guaranteed their safe transportation out. The Trial Chamber found that Krstic showed similar concerns for the Bosnian Muslim civilians during the Zepa campaign. In an intercept of 25 July 1995 he was heard to order that a convoy of civilians bound for Kladanj be treated in a civilised manner, "so that nothing of the kind of problem we had before happens." The Trial Chamber concluded that while this

intercept suggested that Radislav Krstic was anxious for the transfer to proceed properly, it also indicated that he was aware of problems with earlier transfers. The conclusion that he was "aware of problems with earlier transfers," and now took steps to avoid mistreatment, goes against the Trial Chamber's conclusion that Krstic had been a willing participant in a joint criminal enterprise of genocide.

133. Finally, the Trial Chamber referred to the evidence of a Defence witness that on 13 July 1995 he had a conversation about the Bosnian Muslim column with Krstic, who had expressed the view that the VRS should allow the column to pass so that the situation could be "ended as it should." The Trial Chamber relied on the evidence as indicating awareness on the part of Radislav Krstic that attempts were being made to capture the men from the column. The evidence, however, indicates that Krstic harboured no genocidal intent. His own particular intent was directed to a forcible displacement. Some other members of the VRS Main Staff harboured the same intent to carry out forcible displacement, but viewed this displacement as a step in the accomplishment of their genocidal objective. It would be erroneous, however, to link Krstic's specific intent to carry out forcible displacement with the same intent possessed by other members of the Main Staff, to whom the forcible displacement was a means of advancing the genocidal plan.

(f) The Appeals Chamber's preliminary conclusion regarding the Trial Chamber's finding of Radislav Krstic's genocidal intent

134. As has been demonstrated, all that the evidence can establish is that Krstic was aware of the intent to commit genocide on the part of some members of the VRS Main Staff, and with that knowledge, he did nothing to prevent the use of Drina Corps personnel and resources to facilitate those killings. This knowledge on his part alone cannot support an inference of genocidal intent. Genocide is one of the worst crimes known to humankind, and its gravity is reflected in the stringent requirement of specific intent. Convictions for genocide can be entered only where that intent has been unequivocally established. There was a demonstrable failure by the Trial Chamber to supply adequate proof that Radislav Krstic possessed the genocidal intent. Krstic, therefore, is not guilty of genocide as a principal perpetrator.

E. The Criminal Responsibility of Radislav Krstic: Aiding and Abetting Genocide

135. The issue that arises now is the level of Radislav Krstic's criminal responsibility in the circumstances as properly established. All of the crimes that followed the fall of Srebrenica occurred in the Drina Corps zone of responsibility. There was no evidence that the

Drina Corps devised or instigated any of the atrocities, and the evidence strongly suggested that the criminal activity was being directed by some members of the VRS Main Staff under the direction of General Mladic. At the time the executions commenced Krstic was engaged in preparing for combat activities at Zepa and, from 14 July 1995 onwards, directing the attack itself.

136. At trial the Defence had argued that, given the involvement of General Mladic, Radislav Krstic could do nothing to prevail upon General Mladic and stop the executions. The Trial Chamber however found evidence of General Mladic's orders being challenged by the Drina Corps Command, and in particular, evidence of Krstic countering an order issued by the Main Staff. The Trial Chamber also found evidence of Radislav Krstic's continued loyalty to General Mladic despite his knowledge of General Mladic's role in the genocide at Srebrenica.

137. As has been found above, it was reasonable for the Trial Chamber to conclude that, at least from 15 July 1995, Radislav Krstic had knowledge of the genocidal intent of some of the Members of the VRS Main Staff. Radislav Krstic was aware that the Main Staff had insufficient resources of its own to carry out the executions and that, without the use of Drina Corps resources, the Main Staff would not have been able to implement its genocidal plan. Krstic knew that by allowing Drina Corps resources to be used he was making a substantial contribution to the execution of the Bosnian Muslim prisoners. Although the evidence suggests that Radislav Krstic was not a supporter of that plan, as Commander of the Drina Corps he permitted the Main Staff to call upon Drina Corps resources and to employ those resources. The criminal liability of Krstic is therefore more properly expressed as that of an aider and abettor to genocide, and not as that of a perpetrator. This charge is fairly encompassed by the indictment, which alleged that Radislav Krstic aided and abetted in the planning, preparation or execution of genocide against the Bosnian Muslims in Srebrenica.

138. Krstic's responsibility is accurately characterized as aiding and abetting genocide under Article 7(1) of the Statute, not as complicity in genocide under Article 4(3)(e). The charge of complicity was also alleged in the indictment, as Count 2. The Trial Chamber did not enter a conviction on this count, concluding that Radislav Krstic's responsibility was that of a principal perpetrator. As the Trial Chamber observed, there is an overlap between Article 4(3) as the general provision enumerating punishable forms of participation in genocide and Article 7(1) as the general provision for criminal liability which applies to all the offences punishable under the Statute, including the offence of genocide. There is support for a position that Article 4(3) may be the more specific provision (lex specialis) in relation to Article 7(1). There is, howev-

er, also authority indicating that modes of participation enumerated in Article 7(1) should be read, as the Tribunal's Statute directs, into Article 4(3), and so the proper characterization of such individual's criminal liability would be that of aiding and abetting genocide.

139. The Appeals Chamber concludes that the latter approach is the correct one in this case. Article 7(1) of the Statute, which allows liability to attach to an aider and abettor, expressly applies that mode of liability to any "crime referred to in articles 2 to 5 of the present Statute," including the offence of genocide prohibited by Article 4. Because the Statute must be interpreted with the utmost respect to the language used by the legislator, the Appeals Chamber may not conclude that the consequent overlap between Article 7(1) and Article 4(3)(e) is a result of an inadvertence on the part of the legislator where another explanation, consonant with the language used by the Statute, is possible. In this case, the two provisions can be reconciled, because the terms "complicity" and "accomplice" may encompass conduct broader than that of aiding and abetting.[233] Given the Statute's express statement in Article 7(1) that liability for genocide under Article 4 may attach through the mode of aiding and abetting, Radislav Krstic's responsibility is properly characterized as that of aiding and abetting genocide.[234]

140. This, however, raises the question of whether, for liability of aiding and abetting to attach, the individual charged need only possess knowledge of the principal perpetrator's specific genocidal intent, or whether he must share that intent. The Appeals Chamber has previously explained, on several occasions, that an individual who aids and abets a specific intent offense may be held responsible if he assists the commission of the crime knowing the intent behind the crime.[235] This principle applies to the Statute's prohibi-

---

233. See Krnojelac Appeal Judgement, para. 70 ("The Appeals Chamber notes first of all that, in the case-law of the Tribunal ... this term [accomplice] has different meanings depending on the context and may refer to a co-perpetrator or an aider and abettor.") (citing Tadic Appeal Judgement, paras. 220, 229).

234. In this Appeal, the Appeals Chamber is concerned solely with the application to Article 4(3) of only one mode of liability deriving from Article 7(1), that of aiding and abetting. The Appeals Chamber expresses no opinion regarding other modes of liability listed in Article 7(1).

235. See Krnojelac Appeal Judgement, para. 52 ("the aider and abettor

in persecution, an offence with a specific intent, must be aware ... of the discriminatory intent of the perpetrators of that crime," but "need not share th[at] intent"); Vasiljevic Appeal Judgement, para. 142 ("In order to convict [the accused] for aiding and abetting the crime of persecution, the Appeals Chamber must establish that [he] had knowledge that the principal perpetrators of the joint criminal enterprise intended to commit the underlying crimes, and by their acts they intended to discriminate...."); see also Tadic Appeal Judgement, para. 229 ("In the case of aiding and abetting, the requisite mental element is knowledge that the acts performed by the aider and abettor assist the commission of a specific crime by the principal.").

tion of genocide, which is also an offence requiring a showing of specific intent. The conviction for aiding and abetting genocide upon proof that the defendant knew about the principal perpetrator's genocidal intent is permitted by the Statute and case-law of the Tribunal.

141.   Many domestic jurisdictions, both common and civil law, take the same approach with respect to the *mens rea* for aiding and abetting, and often expressly apply it to the prohibition of genocide. Under French law, for example, an aider and abettor need only be aware that he is aiding the principal perpetrator by his contribution,[236] and this general requirement is applied to the specific prohibition of the crime of genocide.[237] German law similarly requires that, in offences mandating a showing of a specific intent (*dolus specialis*), an aider and abettor need not possess the same degree of *mens rea* as the principal perpetrator, but only to be aware of the perpetrator's intent.[238] This general principle is applied to the prohibition of genocide in Section 6 of the German Code of Crimes Against International Law.[239] The criminal law of Switzerland takes the same position, holding that knowledge of another's specific intent is sufficient to convict a defendant for having aided a crime.[240] Among the common law jurisdictions, the criminal law of England follows the same approach, specifying that an aider and abettor need only have knowledge of the principal perpetrator's intent. This general principle again applies to the prohibition of genocide under the domestic English law.[242] The English approach

236.   Code Penal, Art. 121–7 ("Est complice d'un crime ou d'un delit la personne qui sciemment, par aide ou assistance, en a facilite la preparation ou la consommation."); see also Cour de Cassation, Chambre criminelle, 1st October 1984, summary 96.

237.   Code Penal, Art. 211–1.

238.   See section 27(1) of the German Penal Code (Strafgesetzbuch). According to section 2 of the German Code of Crimes Against International Law (CCIL), section 27(1) of the German Penal Code is applicable to crimes of genocide. See Albin Eser & Helmut Kreicker, Nationale Strafverfolgung Volkerrechtlicher Verbrechen (Freiburg 2003), Vol. I, pp. 107, 108.

239.   With the implementation of the Statute of the International Criminal Court (ICC) in Germany, Section 6 of the CCIL recently replaced former section 220a of the German Penal Code. See Gerhard Werle & Florian Jessberger "International Criminal Justice Is Com-

ing Home: The New German Code of Crimes Against International Law," Criminal Law Forum 13, (2002), pp. 201—202. The new provision is substantively similar. See ibid., pp. 191—223. This article also provides a full reprint of the CCIL in English. The text is also available, both in English and in several other languages, at http:// www.iuscrim. mpg.de/forsch/online_pub.html.

240.   See Arts. 25, 65 of the Swiss Criminal Code (Schweizerisches Strafgesetzbuch) ("La peine pourra etre attenuee (art 65) a l'egard de celui qui aura intentiollement prete assistance pour commetre un crime ou un delit."); see also Jidgement of the Swiss Federal Supreme court (Schweizerisches Bundesgericht) of 17 February 1995, Decisions of the Swiss Federal Supreme Court (Bundesgerichtsentscheide, 121 IV, pp. 109, 120).

242.   See Arts. 25, 65 of the Swiss Criminal Code (Schweizerisches Strafgesetzbuch) ("La peine pourra etre attenuee (art 65) a l'egard de celui qui

to the *mens rea* requirement in cases of aiding and abetting has been followed in Canada and Australia,[243] and in some jurisdictions in the United States.[244]

142.   By contrast, there is authority to suggest that complicity in genocide, where it prohibits conduct broader than aiding and abetting, requires proof that the accomplice had the specific intent to destroy a protected group. Article 4 of the Statute is most naturally read to suggest that Article 4(2)'s requirement that a perpetrator of genocide possess the requisite "intent to destroy" a protected group applies to all of the prohibited acts enumerated in Article 4(3), including complicity in genocide.[245] There is also evidence that the drafters of the Genocide Convention intended the charge of complicity in genocide to require a showing of genocidal intent. The U.K. delegate in the Sixth Committee of the General Assembly "proposed adding the word 'deliberate' before 'complicity,'" explaining that "it was important to specify that complicity must be deliberate, because there existed some systems where complicity required intent, and others where it did not. Several delegates [representing Luxembourg, Egypt, Soviet Union, Yugoslavia] said that this was unnecessary, because there had never been any doubt that complicity in genocide must be intentional. The United Kingdom eventually withdrew its amendment, 'since it was understood that, to be punishable, complicity in genocide must be deliberate.'" The texts of the Tribunal's Statute and of the Genocide Convention, combined with the evidence in the Convention's *travaux preparatoires*, provide additional support to the conclusion that the drafters of the Statute opted for applying the notion of aiding and abetting to the prohibition of genocide under Article 4.[247]

aura intentiollement prete assistance pour commetre un crime ou un delit."); see also Jidgement of the Swiss Federal Supreme court (Schweizerisches Bundesgericht) of 17 February 1995, Decisions of the Swiss Federal Supreme Court (Bundesgerichtsentscheide, 121 IV, pp. 109, 120).

243. See Schedule 8, Art. 6 of the International Criminal Court Act of 2001 (specifying that a determination of liability in aiding and abetting genocide follows the general regulations of Section 8 of the Accessories and Abettors Act of 1861). The approach was the same under the pre-ICC English law. See Genocide Act of 1969 (replaced by the International Criminal Court Act on 31 August 2001); Official Report, Fifth Series, Parliamentary debates, Commons 1968–69, Vol. 777, 3—14 February 1969, pp. 480–509 (explaining that sec-

ondary liability with respect to genocide will be governed by the general principles of the English criminal law).

244. See Candace Courteau, Note, The Mental Element Required for Accomplice Liability, 59 La. L. Rev. 325, 334 (1998) (while the majority of federal and state jurisdictions in the United States require a showing that an aider and abettor shared the principal perpetrator's intent, some states still find knowledge to be sufficient).

245. The same analysis applies to the relationship between Article II of the Genocide Convention, which contains the requirement of specific intent, and the Convention's Article III, which lists the proscribed acts, including that of complicity.

247. As it is not at issue in this case, the Appeals Chamber takes no position

143. The fact that the Trial Chamber did not identify individual members of the Main Staff of the VRS as the principal participants in the genocidal enterprise does not negate the finding that Radislav Krstic was aware of their genocidal intent. A defendant may be convicted for having aided and abetted a crime which requires specific intent even where the principal perpetrators have not been tried or identified.[248] In *Vasiljevic*, the Appeals Chamber found the accused guilty as an aider and abettor to persecution without having had the alleged principal perpetrator on trial and without having identified two other alleged co-perpetrators. Accordingly, the Trial Chamber's conviction of Krstic as a participant in a joint criminal enterprise to commit genocide is set aside and a conviction for aiding and abetting genocide is entered instead.[250]

144. The Appeals Chamber's examination of Radislav Krstic's participation in the crime of genocide has implications for his criminal responsibility for the murders of the Bosnian Muslim civilians under Article 3, violations of the laws or customs of war, and for extermination and persecution under Article 5, all of which arise from the executions of the Bosnian Muslims of Srebrenica between 13 and 19 July 1995. As the preceding factual examination has established, there was no evidence that Krstic ordered any of these murders, or that he directly participated in them. All the

on the mens rea requirement for the conviction for the offence of complicity in genocide under Article 4(3) of the Statute where this offense strikes broader than the prohibition of aiding and abetting.

248. See, e,g., Krnojelac Trial Judgement, paras. 489–490 (finding a defendant liable for having aided and abetted the crime of persecution, which requires the specific intent to discriminate, where the principal perpetrators of the crime were not identified). Although the Appeals Chamber, on unrelated grounds, increased the defendant's level of responsibility to that of a co-perpetrator, it rejected the defendant's appeal against his conviction as an aider and abettor. See Krnojelac Appeal Judgement, paras. 35–53. See also Stakic Trial Judgement, para. 534 (stating that "an individual can be prosecuted for complicity even where the perpetrator has not been tried or even identified") (citing Musema Trial Judgement, para. 174); Akayesu Trial Judgement, para. 531 (same).

250. In entering a conviction against General Krstic as a participant in a joint criminal enterprise to commit genocide under Article 7(1) the Trial Chamber

stated that he could also bear responsibility as a Commander pursuant to Article 7(3). The Trial Chamber concluded, however, that a conviction under Article 7(1) sufficiently expressed General Krstic's criminality. Trial Judgement, para. 652. The Appeals Chamber's determination that General Krstic is responsible as an aider and abettor is also based on Article 7(1). Even if General Krstic is also found to be responsible as a Commander, the Appeals Chamber concludes, as did the Trial Chamber, that the mode of liability under Article 7(1) best encapsulates General Krstic's criminality. This is because the most he could have done as a Commander was to report the use of his personnel and assets, in facilitating the killings, to the VRS Main Staff and to his superior, General Mladic, the very people who ordered the executions and were active participants in them. Further, although General Krstic could have tried to punish his subordinates for their participation in facilitating the executions, it is unlikely that he would have had the support of his superiors in doing so. See Krnojelac Trial Judgement, para. 127; not disturbed on appeal, see Krnojelac Appeal Judgement.

evidence can establish is that he knew that those murders were occurring and that he permitted the Main Staff to use personnel and resources under his command to facilitate them. In these circumstances the criminal responsibility of Radislav Krstic is that of an aider and abettor to the murders, extermination and persecution, and not of a principal co-perpetrator.

F. Radislav Krstic's Criminal Responsibility for the Opportunistic Crimes Committed at Potocari

145. The Defence also contests the findings of the Trial Chamber in relation to Krstic's criminal responsibility for the crimes committed on 12 and 13 July 1995 at Potocari. The Trial Chamber found that Radislav Krstic was a participant in a joint criminal enterprise to forcibly remove the Bosnian Muslim civilians from Potocari, and so incurred criminal responsibility for the murders, beatings and abuses committed there as natural and foreseeable consequences of that joint criminal enterprise. The Defence argues that these crimes were not natural and foreseeable consequences of the ethnic cleansing campaign, and that the Trial Chamber's finding that Krstic was aware of them is contrary to the presumption of innocence.

146. According to the Defence, the evidence established that he was at Potocari on 12 July 1995 for at most two hours. There was no evidence to support the conclusion of the Trial Chamber that he had "first-hand knowledge that the refugees were being mistreated by VRS or other armed forces," or that he witnessed the inhumane conditions of the White House and the killing of civilians there. The Defence argues that, to the contrary, the evidence establishes that there were orders from the military authorities to treat the civilians humanely. The Defence refers to an order of 9 July 1995 issued by Mr. Karadzic as Supreme Commander of the Serb forces, which expressly provided that the civilian population was to be treated in accordance with the Geneva Conventions, the evidence of Drazen Erdemovic that soldiers entering the town of Srebrenica were explicitly told not to fire at civilians, the intercept of 12 July 1995 in which Radislav Krstic stated that nothing must happen to the civilians transported from Potocari, and the statements he made in an interview given on 12 July 1995 during the bussing operation, that the Drina Corps had guaranteed the safety of the civilian population.

147. The ethnic cleansing of the Bosnian Muslim civilians from Srebrenica was part of the Krivaja 95 operation in which Krstic was found to have played a leading role. Radislav Krstic knew that the shelling of Srebrenica would force tens of thousands of Bosnian Muslim civilians into Potocari because of the UN presence there. He was also well aware that there were inadequate

facilities at Potocari to accommodate the Bosnian civilians. As such, the Trial Chamber found he was responsible for setting the stage at Potocari for the crimes that followed. Further, from his presence at two meetings convened by General Mladic at the Hotel Fontana he knew that the Bosnian Muslim civilians were in fact facing a humanitarian crisis at Potocari. There was, therefore, sufficient evidence for the Trial Chamber to be satisfied that Radislav Krstic was aware that the Bosnian Muslim civilians at Potocari would be subject to other criminal acts.

148. As the Defence has argued, the Trial Chamber could only establish that Radislav Krstic was present in Potocari for one or two hours in the afternoon of 12 July. At this time he was involved in overseeing the bussing operation along with other VRS Officers, including General Mladic. However, VRS soldiers were generally mistreating the Bosnian Muslim civilians, and the situation facing the Bosnian Muslim civilians at Potocari was so obviously appalling that the Trial Chamber concluded that these conditions must have been apparent to him. Further, while he was found to have been physically present for only a short period of time, the evidence established that he played a principal role in procuring and monitoring the movement of the buses throughout that day. It also established that Drina Corp units under his command were heavily involved in organising and monitoring the transfer of the Bosnian civilians from Potocari. While the Trial Chamber found that this aspect of the operation appeared to be one of the more disciplined ones, and that it could not be satisfied that the Drina Corps was directly involved in any of the opportunistic crimes committed, the Trial Chamber nevertheless found that the Drina Corp units present at Potocari were also in a position to observe the pervasive mistreatment of the Bosnian Muslim civilians by other Serb forces. While the evidence established that on two occasions Krstic issued orders that the Bosnian Muslim civilians being transported on the buses were not to be harmed, there was no evidence of any attempts being made on the part of Radislav Krstic to ensure that these orders were respected. There was also no evidence of Drina Corps units under his command taking any steps to ensure that the orders of their Commander were respected, or to report any contravention of these orders to him.

149. In these circumstances, the Defence's argument that the crimes committed against the civilian population of Potocari were not natural and foreseeable consequences of the joint criminal enterprise to forcibly transfer the Bosnian civilians is not convincing. The Trial Chamber reasonably found that the creation of a humanitarian crisis in Potocari fell within the scope of the intended joint criminal enterprise to forcibly transfer the civilian population. The Trial Chamber expressly found that, "given the circumstances

at the time the plan was formed, Radislav Krstic must have been aware that an outbreak of these crimes would be inevitable given the lack of shelter, the density of the crowds, the vulnerable condition of the refugees, the presence of many regular and irregular military and paramilitary units in the area and sheer lack of sufficient numbers of UN soldiers to provide protection." The Appeals Chamber agrees with this finding. Further, given Krstic's role in causing the humanitarian crisis in Potocari, the issuance of orders directing that civilians not be harmed is not sufficient to establish that the crimes which occurred were not a natural and foreseeable consequence of the plan to forcibly transfer the civilians.

150. The Defence further argues that he cannot be held responsible for crimes that he was unaware were actually occurring. In making this argument, the Defence misunderstands the third category of joint criminal enterprise liability. For an accused to incur criminal responsibility for acts that are natural and foreseeable consequences of a joint criminal enterprise, it is not necessary to establish that he was aware in fact that those other acts would have occurred. It is sufficient to show that he was aware that those acts outside the agreed enterprise were a natural and foreseeable consequence of the agreed joint criminal enterprise, and that the accused participated in that enterprise aware of the probability that other crimes may result. As such, it was unnecessary for the Trial Chamber to conclude that Radislav Krstic was actually aware that those other criminal acts were being committed; it was sufficient that their occurrence was foreseeable to him and that those other crimes did in fact occur.

151. The Defence further asserts that Radislav Krstic should not be found guilty with respect to the crimes committed at Potocari on 12 and 13 July 1995 because General Zivanovic was Commander of the Drina Corps until 13 July 1995. This argument is inapposite. The responsibility of Radislav Krstic for the crimes committed at Potocari arose from his individual participation in a joint criminal enterprise to forcibly transfer civilians. The opportunistic crimes were natural and foreseeable consequences of that joint criminal enterprise. His conviction for these crimes does not depend upon the rank Krstic held in the Drina Corps staff at the time of their commission. Radislav Krstic's appeal against his convictions for the opportunistic crimes that occurred at Potocari as a natural and foreseeable consequence of his participation in the joint criminal enterprise to forcibly transfer is dismissed.

(ii) Command Responsibility. In many cases that come
before international criminal tribunals, the accused are high-level
military or civilian leaders. As the leaders, they generally do not
commit the acts that constitute the crimes themselves. Instead,
their responsibility is based on their leadership role. In addition to
the theories of aiding and abetting and joint criminal enterprise,
another theory of responsibility is *command responsibility.* The
ICTY Statute defines command responsibility as:

> The fact that any of the acts referred to in articles 2 to 5 [the
> covered crimes] of the present Statute was committed by a
> subordinate does not relieve his superior of criminal responsi-
> bility if he knew or had reason to know that the subordinate
> was about to commit such acts or had done so and the superior
> failed to take the necessary and reasonable measures to pre-
> vent such acts or to punish the perpetrators thereof.

ICTY Statute, Article 7(3).

The necessary elements to establish command responsibility
are:

    1. A superior-subordinate relationship;

    2. Knowledge or reason to know that the subordinates
were about to commit or had committed a crime of genocide,
crimes against humanity, or war crimes;

    3. A failure to take necessary and reasonable measures to
either prevent the acts or to punish the perpetrators after the
acts.

Each element raises its own interpretational issues. For instance,
when is a military leader a "superior"? Similarly, when would a
political leader, such as a defense minister be a "superior" for the
actions of troops? The ICTY and ICTR jurisprudence has found
that a person is a superior when he or she has "effective control"
over the subordinates (either civilian or military). Effective control
exists when there is a "material ability" to prevent and punish
transgressions by the subordinates.[14]

Another issue involves the *mens rea* part of command responsibility. What does it mean to "have reason to know" of the subordinates' actions? Is this comparable to a negligence standard in
American criminal law? A recklessness standard or higher? Again,
the ICTY and ICTR have had occasion to address this issue. In

14. *See* Prosecutor v. Bagilishema,
Case No. ICTR–95–1A–A (Jul. 3, 2002),
http://69.94.11.53/ENGLISH/cases/Bagili
shema/judgment/acjudge/131202.htm, at
para. 50–52.

Prosecutor v. Bagilishema,[15] the Appeals Chamber of the ICTR rejected the argument that criminal negligence sufficed for "had reason to know." Instead, the ICTR found that the superior would have reason to know if there is "some general information...available to him which would put him on notice of possible unlawful acts by his subordinates [and he] did not take the necessary and reasonable measures to prevent the acts or to punish the perpetrators therof."[16] How does this standard differ from negligence? Is it comparable to recklessness as defined in the Model Penal Code or, given the nature of the offenses, to the common law concept of "depraved heart" as malice aforethought? Is it another way of stating the "knowledge" standard? Or is the standard *sui generis*?

Would the accused be responsible for genocide under command responsibility in the following situation? Defendant is the commander of armed forces for the Croatian Defense Council in Central Bosnia. In addition to the troops under his direct control, there are also military police working in conjunction with the regular armed forces. Members of the military police commit serious crimes against humanity against civilians in communities in Central Bosnia.

How does the following evidence affect your analysis?

—Testimony that Defendant had control over the military police.

—Defendant's admission that the military police were assigned to him on an ad hoc basis.

—Defendant had a duty to report abuse by any member of the military police to the commander of that group.

—Testimony that Defendant secured the release of one of his generals who had been detained by the military police.

—Contradictory testimony that the military police refused to release the general on Defendant's order.

—An order from Defendant instructing a commander of a unit of the military police to conduct an investigation into abuses.

—Testimony that, in general, the military police are under the authority of the central government, such as the minister of the interior, and not under the command of the armed forces.

—Testimony that military police units refused to allow humanitarian convoys to pass on Defendant's order; instead, they demanded the authority of one of the political leaders of the Croatian leadership in that part of Bosnia.

15. *Id.*   **16.** *Id.* At para. 33.

—Sounds of gunfire and smoke from the surrounding areas were due both to legitimate military conflict and to criminal killing of civilians and burning of homes by the military police.

—Defendant received information about a massacre in the town of Ahmici 10–15 days after it occurred. The population of the town was predominantly Muslim. During the attack, 103 people were killed, including 33 women and children. Houses were burned down and groups of soldiers went from house to house to torch, evict, and kill.[17]

—Defendant asked the commander of the military police to do an investigation of crimes committed in that massacre. That report was never given to Defendant; it was sent to the Military Police Administration.

See Prosecutor v. Blaskic, Case No.IT–95–14–A (July 29, 2004), http://www.un.org/icty/blaskic/appeal/judgement/index.htm.

Also consider this situation with a civilian leader: Defendant is the *bourgmestre* (mayor) of a commune in Rwanda. During the conflict between the largely Tutsi RPF force and the largely Hutu government forces, members of the *gendarmerie* (national police force) are assigned to protect each commune. If members of the *gendarmerie* kill Tutsi civilians at a roadblock in the commune, is the Defendant responsible under command responsibility? What facts would you want to know? *See Prosecutor v. Bagilishema,* Case No. ICTR–95–1A–A (Jul. 3, 2002), http://69.94.11.53/ENGLISH/cases/Bagilishema/judgment/acjudge/131202.htm.

c. Duress

In this section, you will read the *Erdemovic* case from the ICTY. Erdemovic was part of an execution squad for the Bosnian Serb army. His squad was involved in the execution of 7–8,000 men and boys at Srebrenica. At first, Erdemovic refused to participate in killing the unarmed men and boys. Erdemovic's commander told him: "if you are sorry for them, stand up, line up with them and we will kill you too." Erdemovic then participated in the killings.[18]

The issue posed is whether duress can be an affirmative defense to murder. As you read this decision, compare the ICTY's use of precedent from the post-World War II era with the typical use of precedent in an American court. What is the value of the precedent in the ICTY case? Also notice the role of national laws of

17. *Prosecutor v. Blastic,* Case No. IT–95–14–A (July 29, 2004), http://www.un.org/icty/blaskic/appeal/judgement/index.htm at para. 2.

18. *Prosecutor v. Erdemovic,* Case No. IT–96–22, (Oct. 7, 1997), http:// www.un.org/icty/erdemovic/appeal/judgement/erd-aj971007e.htm at para. 3–4.

various countries in the ICTY's decision-making process. How are the national laws relevant to the ICTY decision? After reading *Erdemovic*, what do you consider the strongest argument to allow duress as a defense to homicide? What do you consider the strongest argument not to allow duress as a defense to homicide?

How does Erdemovic's situation compare with the historic criminal law case of *Regina v. Dudley & Stephens?* In *Dudley & Stephens,* 14 Q.B.D. 373 (1884), four sailors were stranded in a lifeboat with no rescue apparent to them. Two of the sailors (Dudley and Stephens) killed the young cabin boy who was close to death and then all three of the living sailors ate the boy in order to survive. Dudley and Stephens were convicted of murder and sentenced to death. They argued for a defense of necessity—that killing one person to save three people was a lesser evil than the deaths of all four persons. The court rejected their defense, but ultimately, their sentences were commuted to six months imprisonment. Should the threat to Erdemovic's life be taken into account in sentencing?

International Criminal Tribunal for the Former Yugoslavia IN THE APPEALS CHAMBER

PROSECUTOR v. DRAZEN ERDEMOVIC

Judgement of: 7 October 1997

Before: JUDGE ANTONIO CASSESE, PRESIDING, JUDGE GABRIELLE KIRK MCDONALD, JUDGE HAOPEI LI, JUDGE NINIAN STEPHEN, JUDGE LAL CHAND VOHRAH

JOINT SEPARATE OPINION OF JUDGE MCDONALD and JUDGE VOHRAII

* * *

A.   THE APPLICABLE LAW

40.   The sources of international law are generally considered to be exhaustively listed in Article 38 of the Statute of the International Court of Justice ('ICJ Statute') which reads:

1.   The Court, whose function is to decide in accordance with international law such disputes as are submitted to it, shall apply:

a.   international conventions, whether general or particular, establishing rules expressly recognised by the contesting states;

b.   international custom, as evidence of a general practice accepted as law;

    c. the general principles of law recognised by civilised nations;

    d. subject to the provisions of Article 59, judicial decisions and the teachings of the most highly qualified publicists of the various nations, as subsidiary means for the determination of rules of law.

2. This provision shall not prejudice the power of the Court to decide a case *ex aequo et bono*, if the parties agree thereon.[40]

B. CUSTOMARY INTERNATIONAL LAW (ARTICLE 38(1)(b) OF ICJ STATUTE)

41. The Prosecution submits that 'under international law duress cannot afford a complete defence to a charge of crimes against humanity and war crimes when the underlying offence is the killing of an innocent human being'. The Prosecution contends that the relevant case-law of the post-Second World War military tribunals does not recognise duress as a defence to a charge involving the killing of innocent persons. Given also that there is no conventional international law which resolves the question of duress as a defence to murder, it is the submission of the Prosecution that customary international law, as contained in the decisions of the post-World War Two military tribunals, clearly precludes duress as such a defence. Although the Prosecution does not confine its arguments to the specific question as to whether duress is a complete defence for a soldier who has been charged under international law with killing innocent persons, we would, however, so limit our inquiry in this appeal.

42. The Trial Chamber states in the *Sentencing Judgement* that "[a] review by the United Nations War Crimes Commission of the post-World War Two international military case-law, as reproduced in the 1996 report of the International Law Commission (Supplement No.10 (A/51/10) p. 93) shows that the post-World War Two military tribunals of nine nations considered the issue of duress as constituting a complete defence". This interpretation of the conclusions of the United Nations War Crimes Commission does not bear close scrutiny. In Volume XV of the Law Reports of Trials of War Criminals by the United Nations War Crimes Commission, 1949, what is stated is merely the following:

> The general view seems therefore to be that duress may prove a defence if (a) the act charged was done to avoid an immediate danger both serious and irreparable; (b) there was no other

---

40. Statute of the International Court of Justice, I.C.J. Acts and Documents, No. 5 ('ICJ Statute'). Article 59 provides: 'The decision of the Court has no binding force except between the parties and in respect of that particular case'.

adequate means of escape; (c) the remedy was not disproportionate to the evil.

The United Nations War Crimes Commission did not specifically address the question whether duress afforded a defence to crimes involving the killing of innocent persons in its expression of this "general view". Furthermore, the authorities which the United Nations War Crimes Commission surveyed in fact support the position that duress may not be pleaded as a defence to a war crime involving the killing of innocent persons generally, regardless of whether the accused was or was not a soldier. Express statements that duress is no defence to a crime involving the killing of innocent persons may be found in the opinions of the Judge–Advocate–Generals in the *Stalag Luft III* case and the *Feurstein* case, both before British military tribunals. These cases constitute lex posteriori and overrule the earlier 1946 British military tribunal decision in the *Jepson* case which asserted a contrary position without reference to any authority. We further note the express rejection of duress as a defence to the killing of innocent persons by the Judge–Advocate–General in the *Holzer* case decided in 1946 before Canadian military tribunal.

43.   We find that the only express affirmation of the availability of duress as a defence to the killing of innocent persons in post-World War Two military tribunal cases appears in the *Einsatzgruppen* case before a United States military tribunal. There the tribunal stated:

> Let it be said at once that there is no law which requires that an innocent man must forfeit his life or suffer serious harm in order to avoid committing a crime which he condemns. The threat, however, must be imminent, real and inevitable. No court will punish a man who, with a loaded pistol at his head, is compelled to pull a lethal lever.

In our view, however, the value of this authority is cast into some considerable doubt by the fact that the United States military tribunal in the *Einsatzgruppen* case did not cite any authority for its opinion that duress may constitute a complete defence to killing an innocent individual. The military tribunal certainly could not have relied on any authority from the common law of the United States in which it has been established since the 1890s that duress is no defence to murder in the first degree. Moreover, even if the tribunal's views regarding duress as a defence to murder had been supportable in its time, these views cannot presently constitute good authority in light of the development of the law. Rule 916 (h) of the Manual for Courts–Martial United States 1984 (1994 ed.) now clearly provides that duress is a defence "to any offence except killing an innocent person". The laws of all but a handful of state jurisdictions in the United States definitively reject duress as a complete defence for a principal in the first degree to murder. The comments of the most qualified publicists, recognised as a subsidiary source of international law in Article 38(1)(d) of the ICJ Statute, are also informative. Two years after the *Einsatzgruppen* decision in the *opus classicum* on international law, Professor Hersch Lauterpacht wrote that "[n]o principle of justice and, in most civilised communities, no principle of law permits the individual person to avoid suffering or even to save his life at the expense of the life—or, as revealed in many war crimes trials, of a vast multitude of lives—of or sufferings, on a vast scale, of others" and, in particular, that there is "serious objection to this [contrary] reasoning of the Tribunal" in the *Einsatzgruppen* case.

44.   We, accordingly, find that the *Einsatzgruppen* decision is in discord with the preponderant view of international authorities. There is no other precedent in the case-law of international post-World War Two military tribunals which could be cited as authority for the proposition that duress is a complete defence to the killing of innocent persons in international law.

45.   For completeness, reference must be made to the following observation of the International Military Tribunal at Nuremberg:

> That a soldier was ordered to kill or torture in violation of the international laws of war has never been recognised as a valid defence to such acts of brutality, though, as the Charter here provides, the order may be urged in mitigation of the punishment. The true test, which is found in varying degrees in the criminal law of most nations, is not the existence of the order, but whether moral choice was in fact possible.

This unelaborated statement, in our view, makes no significant contribution to the jurisprudence on this issue. It does little to support the contention that the decisions of post-World War Two international military tribunals established a clear rule recognising duress as a defence to the killing of innocent persons which would then by now have become customary international law. This is recognised by the International Law Commission in its treatment of the issue of duress in the commentary to the Draft Code of Crimes Against the Peace and the Security of Mankind, wherein it cites the Nuremberg dicta and then states:

> There are different views as to whether even the most extreme duress can ever constitute a valid defence or extenuating circumstance with respect to a particularly heinous crime, such as killing an innocent human being.

1. No customary international law rule can be derived on the question of duress as a defence to the killing of innocent persons

46. The Prosecution strongly contends that the opinions of the post-World War Two military tribunals on the question of duress as a defence to murder have become part of customary international law. It matters not, the Prosecution urges, that this custom was based originally on common law authorities. It is worth setting out its contention on this point in full.

> I wish simply to emphasise also that the Common Law pedigree of international law in this respect should in no way put into question the position of international law on the admissibility of duress as a defence. Such an argument, the argument that the court must somehow reject the overwhelming weight of authority of this case law, simply because it has a Common Law orientation, would overlook the essentially eclectic character of international criminal law, borrowing, as it does, from various legal systems, often haphazardly ... To quickly give but one example, the law of conspiracy when it was discussed in 1944, during the preparatory work of the Nuremberg Charter, was considered by the French delegation, and I quote from Bradley Smith, a leading commentator, "as a barbarous concept unworthy of modern law". The Soviet delegation was outright shocked at the concept of conspiracy. Nevertheless it was retained in the charter and it was developed through the case law both of the international military Tribunal and the courts under control council law number 10. It cannot now be argued that conspiracy, because of its Common Law pedigree, should not be admitted as a concept under international criminal law. I would submit, your Honour, that the same clearly applies to the defence of duress. The fact that the position of international law concurs by virtue of historical or other circumstances with the Common Law position, the fact that duress clearly cannot be a defence to murder under international law, cannot be in any way challenged because of the pedigree or origins of that concept.

47. A number of war crimes cases have been brought to our attention as supporting the position that duress is a complete defence to the killing of innocent persons in international law: the *Llandovery Castle* case before the German Supreme Court at Leipzig; *Mueller et al.* before the Belgium Military Court of Brussels and the Belgium Court of Cassation; the *Eichmann* case before the Supreme Court of Israel; the Papon case before the French Court of Cassation; *Retzlaff et al.* before the Soviet Military Tribunal in Kharkov; *Sablic et al.* before the Military Court of Belgrade; the cases *Bernadi* and *Randazzo*, Sra et al. and *Masetti* before the

Italian Courts of Assize and the Court of Cassation; the German cases *S.* and *K.* before the Landesgericht of Ravensburg; the *Warsaw ghetto* case before the Court of Assize attached to the District Court of Dortmund; and *Wetzling et al.* before the Court of Assize of Arnsberg.

(a) Questionable relevance and authority of a number of these cases

48.   The cases set out in paragraph 62 touch upon the issue of duress in varying degrees. In our view, however, these cases are insufficient to support the finding of a customary rule providing for the availability of the defence of duress to the killing of innocent persons. We would note that a number of the cases are of questionable relevance and authority. Firstly, in the *Papon* case, the accused was not charged with murder as a principal in the first degree but merely as an accomplice in the extermination of Jews during the World War Two by his actions as a police officer who rounded up and deported French Jews to Germany. Secondly, in the *Retzlaff* and *Sablic* cases, the defence of duress did not succeed and there was no clear statement by the courts as to the reason for this failure. Thirdly, the decision in the *S.* and *K.* case was in fact quashed by the superior court in the French Zone for contravening Control Council Law No.10 and thus is of doubtful authority. Finally, the accused in the *Warsaw ghetto* case were held merely to be accomplices in murder and thus the application of duress in that case is only authoritative in respect of complicity to murder and not murder in the first degree.

(b) No consistent and uniform state practice underpinned by opinio juris

49.   Although some of the above mentioned cases may clearly represent the positions of national jurisdictions regarding the availability of duress as a complete defence to the killing of innocent persons, neither they nor the principles on this issue found in decisions of the post-World War Two military tribunals are, in our view, entitled to be given the status of customary international law. For a rule to pass into customary international law, the International Court of Justice has authoritatively restated in the *North Sea Continental Shelf cases* that there must exist extensive and uniform state practice underpinned by *opinio juris sive necessitatis*. To the extent that the domestic decisions and national laws of States relating to the issue of duress as a defence to murder may be regarded as state practice, it is quite plain that this practice is not at all consistent. The defence in its Notice of Appeal surveys the criminal codes and legislation of 14 civil law jurisdictions in which necessity or duress is prescribed as a general exculpatory principle applying to all crimes. The surveyed jurisdictions comprise those of

Austria, Belgium, Brazil, Greece, Italy, Finland, the Netherlands, France, Germany, Peru, Spain, Switzerland, Sweden and the former Yugoslavia. Indeed, the war crimes decisions cited in the Separate Opinion of Judge Cassese are based upon the acceptance of duress as a general defence to all crimes in the criminal codes of France, Italy, Germany, the Netherlands and Belgium. In stark contrast to this acceptance of duress as a defence to the killing of innocents is the clear position of the various countries throughout the world applying the common law. These common law systems categorically reject duress as a defence to murder. The sole exception is the United States where a few states have accepted Section 2.09 of the United States Penal Code which currently provides that duress is a general defence to all crimes. Indeed, the rejection of duress as a defence to the killing of innocent human beings in the *Stalag Luft III* and the *Feurstein* cases, both before British military tribunals, and in the Holzer case before a Canadian military tribunal, reflects in essence the common law approach.

50.   Not only is State practice on the question as to whether duress is a defence to murder far from consistent, this practice of States is not, in our view, underpinned by *opinio juris*. Again to the extent that state practice on the question of duress as a defence to murder may be evidenced by the opinions on this question in decisions of national military tribunals and national laws, we find quite unacceptable any proposition that States adopt this practice because they "feel that they are conforming to what amounts to a legal obligation" at an international level.

51.   To answer the Prosecution's submission regarding conspiracy during oral argument, we are of the view that conspiracy owes its status as customary international law to the fact that it was incorporated in the Nuremberg Charter which subsequently obtained recognition as custom and not to the fact that the objections of the civil law system were rejected in the process. Moreover, conspiracy was clearly established as a principle in the Nuremberg Charter. In the present case, duress, either as a general notion or specifically as it applies to murder, is not contained in any international treaty or instrument subsequently recognised to have passed into custom.

* * *

C.   GENERAL PRINCIPLES OF LAW RECOGNISED BY CIVILISED
NATIONS (ARTICLE 38(1)(C) OF ICJ STATUTE)

56.   It is appropriate now to inquire whether the "general principles of law recognised by civilised nations", established as a source of international law in Article 38(1)(c) of the ICJ Statute, may shed some light upon this intricate issue of duress. Paragraph

58 of the Report of the Secretary–General of the United Nations presented on 3 May 1993 expressly directs the International Tribunal to this source of law:

> The International Tribunal itself will have to decide on various personal defences which may relieve a person of individual criminal responsibility, such as minimum age or mental incapacity, drawing upon general principles of law recognised by all nations.

Further, Article 14 of the International Law Commission's Draft Code of Crimes Against the Peace and Security of Mankind provides:

> The competent court shall determine the admissibility of defences in accordance with the general principles of law, in the light of the character of each crime.

57.   A number of considerations bear upon our analysis of the application of "general principles of law recognised by civilised nations" as a source of international law. First, although general principles of law are to be derived from existing legal systems, in particular, national systems of law, it is generally accepted that the distillation of a "general principle of law recognised by civilised nations" does not require the comprehensive survey of all legal systems of the world as this would involve a practical impossibility and has never been the practice of the International Court of Justice or other international tribunals which have had recourse to Article 38(1)(c) of the ICJ Statute. Second, it is the view of eminent jurists, including Baron Descamps, the President of the Advisory Committee of Jurists on Article 38(1)(c), that one purpose of this article is to avoid a situation of *non-liquet*, that is, where an international tribunal is stranded by an absence of applicable legal rules. Third, a "general principle" must not be confused with concrete manifestations of that principle in specific rules. As stated by the Italian–Venezuelan Mixed Claims Commission in the *Gentini* case:

> A rule ... is essentially practical and, moreover, binding; there are rules of art as there are rules of government, while a principle expresses a general truth, which guides our action, serves as a theoretical basis for the various acts of our life, and the application of which to reality produces a given consequence.

In light of these considerations, our approach will necessarily not involve a direct comparison of the specific rules of each of the world's legal systems, but will instead involve a survey of those jurisdictions whose jurisprudence is, as a practical matter, accessible to us in an effort to discern a general trend, policy or principle underlying the concrete rules of that jurisdiction which comports with the object and purpose of the establishment of the International Tribunal.

As Lord McNair pointed out in his Separate Opinion in the *South-West Africa Case*,

> it is never a question of importing into international law private law institutions "lock, stock and barrel", ready made and fully equipped with a set of rules. It is rather a question of finding in the private law institutions indications of legal policy and principles appropriate to the solution of the international problem at hand. It is not the concrete manifestation of a principle in different national systems—which are anyhow likely to vary—but the general concept of law underlying them that the international judge is entitled to apply under paragraph (c). (Emphasis added.)

It is thus generally the practice of international tribunals to employ the general principle in its formulation of a legal rule applicable to the facts of the particular case before it. This practice is most evident in the treatment of the general principle of 'good faith and equity' in cases before the International Court of Justice and the Permanent Court of International Justice. For example in the *North Sea Continental Shelf Cases* before the International Court of Justice, the Court had regard to "equitable principles" in its formulation of the rule delimiting the boundaries of continental shelves. In the *Diversion of Water from the Meuse Case (Netherlands v. Belgium)* before the Permanent Court of International Justice, Judge Hudson in his Individual Opinion, after accepting that equity is a "general principle of law recognised by civilised nations", stated:

> It would seem to be an important principle of equity that where two parties have assumed an identical or a reciprocal obligation, one party which is engaged in a continuing non-performance of that obligation should not be permitted to take advantage of a similar non-performance of that obligation by the other party.

In the *Chorzow Factory Case (Merits)*, the Permanent Court observed that "it is a principle of international law, and even a general conception of law, that any breach of an engagement involves an obligation to make reparation".

In the *Corfu Channel Case (Merits)*, the International Court stated that

> the other State, the victim of a breach of international law, is often unable to furnish direct proof of facts giving rise to responsibility. Such a State should be allowed a more liberal recourse to inferences of fact and circumstantial evidence. This

indirect evidence is admitted in all systems of law, and its use is recognized by international decisions.

58.   In order to arrive at a general principle relating to duress, we have undertaken a limited survey of the treatment of duress in the world's legal systems. This survey is necessarily modest in its undertaking and is not a thorough comparative analysis. Its purpose is to derive, to the extent possible, a "general principle of law" as a source of international law.

* * *

3.   What is the general principle?

66.   Having regard to the above survey relating to the treatment of duress in the various legal systems, it is, in our view, a general principle of law recognised by civilised nations that an accused person is less blameworthy and less deserving of the full punishment when he performs a certain prohibited act under duress. We would use the term "duress" in this context to mean "imminent threats to the life of an accused if he refuses to commit a crime" and do not refer to the legal terms of art which have the equivalent meaning of the English word "duress" in the languages of most civil law systems. This alleviation of blameworthiness is manifest in the different rules with differing content in the principal legal systems of the world as the above survey reveals. On the one hand, a large number of jurisdictions recognise duress as a complete defence absolving the accused from all criminal responsibility. On the other hand, in other jurisdictions, duress does not afford a complete defence to offences generally but serves merely as a factor which would mitigate the punishment to be imposed on a convicted person. Mitigation is also relevant in two other respects. Firstly, punishment may be mitigated in respect of offences which have been specifically excepted from the operation of the defence of duress by the legislatures of some jurisdictions. Secondly, courts have the power to mitigate sentences where the strict elements of a defence of duress are not made out on the facts.

It is only when national legislatures have prescribed a mandatory life sentence or death penalty for particular offences that no consideration is given in national legal systems to the general principle that a person who commits a crime under duress is less blameworthy and less deserving of the full punishment in respect of that particular offence.

4.   What is the applicable rule?

67.   The rules of the various legal systems of the world are, however, largely inconsistent regarding the specific question whether duress affords a complete defence to a combatant charged with a war crime or a crime against humanity involving the killing of

innocent persons. As the general provisions of the numerous penal codes set out above show, the civil law systems in general would theoretically allow duress as a complete defence to all crimes including murder and unlawful killing. On the other hand, there are laws of other legal systems which categorically reject duress as a defence to murder. Firstly, specific laws relating to war crimes in Norway and Poland do not allow duress to operate as a complete defence but permit it to be taken into account only in mitigation of punishment. Secondly, the Ethiopian Penal Code of 1957 provides in Article 67 that only "absolute physical coercion" may constitute a complete defence to crimes in general. Where the coercion is "moral", which we would interpret as referring to duress by threats, the accused is only entitled to a reduction of penalty. This reduction of penalty may extend, where appropriate, even to a complete discharge of the offender from punishment. Thirdly, the common law systems throughout the world, with the exception of a small minority of jurisdictions of the United States which have adopted without reservation Section 2.09 of the United States Model Penal Code, reject duress as a defence to the killing of innocent persons.

* * *

71.   Given that duress has been held at common law not to negate *mens rea*, the availability of the defence turns on the question whether, in spite of the elements of the offence being strictly made out, the conduct of the defendant should be justified or excused. The second aspect of the common law stance against permitting duress as a defence to murder is the assertion in law of a moral absolute. This moral point has been pressed consistently in a long line of authorities in English law and is accepted by courts in other common law jurisdictions as the basis for the rejection of duress as a defence to murder.[152]

152. In the United States, the traditional common law approach generally follows the English authorities and categorically rejects duress as a defence to a charge of first degree murder: Rumble v. Smith, 905 F.2d 176, 180 (8th Cir. 1990); R.I. Recreation Center Inc. v. Aetna Casualty & Sur. Co., 177 F.2d 603, 605 (1st Cir. 1949), where the court said: "[i]t appears to be established . . . that although coercion or necessity will never excuse taking the life of an innocent person, it will excuse lesser crimes"; Thomas v. State, 246 Ga. 484, 486, 272 S.E.2d.68, 70 (1980) where it was stated that '[the] common law approach [is that] one should die himself before killing an innocent victim'. The prevailing view in the United States that duress is no defence to first degree murder is best evidenced, however, by the rejection by an overwhelming majority of state jurisdictions of Section 2.09 of the Model Penal Code which allows duress as a general defence to all crimes including murder. As to the law in the Australian states without a criminal code, see R v. Brown [1968] SASR 467 (FC); R v. Harding [1976] VR 129 (FC); R v. McConnell [1977] 1 NSWLR 714 (CCA).

(c) No consistent rule from the principal legal systems of the world

72. It is clear from the differing positions of the principal legal systems of the world that there is no consistent concrete rule which answers the question whether or not duress is a defence to the killing of innocent persons. It is not possible to reconcile the opposing positions and, indeed, we do not believe that the issue should be reduced to a contest between common law and civil law.

We would therefore approach this problem bearing in mind the specific context in which the International Tribunal was established, the types of crimes over which it has jurisdiction, and the fact that the International Tribunal's mandate is expressed in the Statute as being in relation to "serious violations of international humanitarian law".

D. THE RULE APPLICABLE TO THIS CASE

1. A normative mandate for international criminal law

* * *

76. It might be urged that although the civil law jurisdictions allow duress as a defence to murder, there is no evidence that crimes such as murder and terrorism are any more prevalent in these societies than in common law jurisdictions. We are not persuaded by this argument. We are concerned primarily with armed conflict in which civilian lives, the lives of the most vulnerable, are at great risk. Historical records, past and recent, concerned with armed conflict give countless examples of threats being brought to bear upon combatants by their superiors when confronted with any show of reluctance or refusal on the part of the combatants to carry out orders to perform acts which are in clear breach of international humanitarian law. It cannot be denied that in an armed conflict, the frequency of situations in which persons are forced under duress to commit crimes and the magnitude of the crimes they are forced to commit are far greater than in any peacetime domestic environment.

77. Practical policy considerations compel the legislatures of most common law jurisdictions to withhold the defence of duress not only from murder but from a vast array of offences without engaging in a complex and tortuous investigation into the relationship between law and morality. As indicated in the survey of the treatment of duress in various legal systems, the common law in England denies recognition of duress as a defence not only for murder but also for certain serious forms of treason. In Malaysia, duress is not available as a defence in respect not only of murder but also of a multitude of offences against the State which are punishable by death. In the states of Australia which have criminal

codes, the statutory provisions contain a list of excepted offences, with the Criminal Code of Tasmania having the longest, making the defence unavailable to persons charged with murder, attempted murder, treason, piracy, offences deemed to be piracy, causing grievous bodily harm, rape, forcible abduction, robbery with violence, robbery and arson.

Legislatures which have denied duress as a defence to specific crimes are therefore content to leave the interest of justice to be satisfied by mitigation of sentence.

78. We do not think our reference to considerations of policy are improper. It would be naive to believe that international law operates and develops wholly divorced from considerations of social and economic policy. There is the view that international law should distance itself from social policy and this view has been articulated by the International Court of Justice in the South West Africa Cases, where it is stated that "[l]aw exists, it is said, to serve a social need; but precisely for that reason it can do so only through and within the limits of its own discipline". We are of the opinion that this separation of law from social policy is inapposite in relation to the application of international humanitarian law to crimes occuring during times of war. It is clear to us that whatever is the distinction between the international legal order and municipal legal orders in general, the distinction is imperfect in respect of the criminal law which, both at the international and the municipal level, is directed towards consistent aims. At the municipal level, criminal law and criminal policy are closely intertwined. There is no reason why this should be any different in international criminal law. We subscribe to the views of Professor Rosalyn Higgins (as she then was) when she argued:

> Reference to the "correct legal view" or "rules" can never avoid the element of choice (though it can seek to disguise it), nor can it provide guidance to the preferable decision. In making this choice one must inevitably have consideration for the humanitarian, moral, and social purposes of the law ... Where there is ambiguity or uncertainty, the policy-directed choice can properly be made.

It appears that the essence of this thesis is not that policy concerns dominate the law but rather, where appropriate, are given due consideration in the determination of a case. This is precisely the approach we have taken to the question of duress as a defence to the killing of innocent persons in international law. Even if policy concerns are entirely ignored, the law will nevertheless fail in its ambition of neutrality "for even such a refusal [to acknowledge political and social factors] is not without political and social consequences. There is no avoiding the essential relationship between law and politics".

2.   An exception where the victims will die regardless of the participation of the accused?

79.   It was suggested during the hearing of 26 May 1997 that neither the English national cases nor the post-World War Two military tribunal decisions specifically addressed the situation in which the accused faced the choice between his own death for not obeying an order to kill or participating in a killing which was inevitably going to occur regardless of whether he participated in it or not. It has been argued that in such a situation where the fate of the victim was already sealed, duress should constitute a complete defence. This is because the accused is then not choosing that one innocent human being should die rather than another. In a situation where the victim or victims would have died in any event, such as in the present case where the victims were to be executed by firing squad, there would be no reason for the accused to have sacrificed his life. The accused could not have saved the victim's life by giving his own and thus, according to this argument, it is unjust and illogical for the law to expect an accused to sacrifice his life in the knowledge that the victim/s will die anyway. The argument, it is said, is vindicated in the Italian case of *Masetti* which was decided by the Court of Assize in "Aquila". The accused in that case raised duress in response to the charge of having organised the execute of two partisans upon being ordered to do so by the battalion commander. The Court of Assize acquitted the accused on the ground of duress and said:

> . . . the possible sacrifice [of their lives] by Masetti and his men [those who comprised the execution squad] would have been in any case to no avail and without any effect in that it would have had no impact whatsoever on the plight of the persons to be shot, who would have been executed anyway even without him [the accused].

We have given due consideration to this approach which, for convenience, we will label "the Masetti approach". For the reasons given below we would reject the *Masetti* approach.

3.   Rejection of utilitarianism and proportionality where human life must be weighed

80.   The *Masetti* approach proceeds from the starting point of strict utilitarian logic based on the fact that if the victim will die anyway, the accused is not at all morally blameworthy for taking part in the execution; there is absolutely no reason why the accused should die as it would be unjust for the law to expect the accused to die for nothing. It should be immediately apparent that the assertion that the accused is not morally blameworthy where the victim would have died in any case depends entirely again upon a view of

morality based on utilitarian logic. This does not, in our opinion, address the true rationale for our rejection of duress as a defence to the killing of innocent human beings. The approach we take does not involve a balancing of harms for and against killing but rests upon an application in the context of international humanitarian law of the rule that duress does not justify or excuse the killing of an innocent person. Our view is based upon a recognition that international humanitarian law should guide the conduct of combatants and their commanders. There must be legal limits as to the conduct of combatants and their commanders in armed conflict. In accordance with the spirit of international humanitarian law, we deny the availability of duress as a complete defence to combatants who have killed innocent persons. In so doing, we give notice in no uncertain terms that those who kill innocent persons will not be able to take advantage of duress as a defence and thus get away with impunity for their criminal acts in the taking of innocent lives.

(a) Proportionality?

81.   The notion of proportionality is raised with great frequency in the limited jurisprudence on duress. Indeed, a central issue regarding the question of duress in the *Masetti* decision was whether the proportionality requirement in Article 54 of the Italian Penal Code was satisfied where innocent lives where taken. By the Masetti approach, the killing of the victims by the accused is apparently proportional to the fate faced by the accused if the victims were going to die anyway.

Proportionality is merely another way of referring to the utilitarian approach of weighing the balance of harms and adds nothing to the debate when it comes to human lives having to be weighed and when the law must determine, because a certain legal consequence will follow, that one life or a set of lives is more valuable than another. The Prosecution draws attention to the great difficulty in judging proportionality when it is human lives which must be weighed in the balance:

> [O]ne immediately sees even from a philosophical point of view the immensely difficult balancing which a court would have to engage in such a circumstance. It would be really a case of a numbers game, if you like, of: "Is it better to kill one person and save ten? Is it better to save one small child, let us say, as opposed to elderly people? Is it better to save a lawyer as opposed to an accountant?" One could engage in all sorts of highly problematical philosophical discussions.

These difficulties are clear where the court must decide whether or not duress is a defence by a straight answer, "yes" or "no". Yet, the difficulties are avoided somewhat when the court is instead asked not to decide whether or not the accused should have a complete defence but to take account of the circumstances in the flexible but effective facility provided by mitigation of punishment.

    4. Mitigation of punishment as a clear, simple and uniform approach

* * *

    85. Finally, we think, with respect, that it is inaccurate to say that by rejecting duress as a defence to the killing of innocent persons, the law "expects" a person who knows that the victims will die anyway to throw his life away in vain. If there were a mandatory life sentence which we would be bound to impose upon a person convicted of killing with only an executive pardon available to do justice to the accused, it may well be said that the law "expects" heroism from its subjects. Indeed, such a mandatory life-term was prescribed for murder in England at the time the relevant English cases were decided and featured prominently in the considerations of the judges. We are not bound to impose any such mandatory term. One cannot superficially gauge what the law "expects" by the existence of only two alternatives: conviction or acquittal. In reality, the law employs mitigation of punishment as a far more sophisticated and flexible tool for the purpose of doing justice in an individual case. The law, in our view, does not "expect" a person whose life is threatened to be hero and to sacrifice his life by refusing to commit the criminal act demanded of him. The law does not "expect" that person to be a hero because in recognition of human frailty and the threat under which he acted, it will mitigate his punishment. In appropriate cases, the offender may receive no punishment at all. We would refer again to the opinion of Lord Simon in *Lynch v. DPP for Northern Ireland* where he stated:

> Any sane and humane system of criminal justice must be able to allow for all such situations as the following, and not merely for some of them. A person, honestly and reasonably believing that a loaded pistol is at his back which will in all probability be used if he disobeys, is ordered to do and act prima facie criminal. Similarly, a person whose child has been kidnapped, and whom as a consequence of threats he honestly and reasonably believes to be in danger of death or mutilation if he does not perform an act prima facie criminal. Or his neighbour's child in such a situation. Or any child. Or any human being? Or his home, a national heritage, threatened to be blown up? Or a stolen masterpiece of art destroyed. Or his son financially ruined? Or his savings for himself and his wife put in peril. In other words, a sane and humane system of criminal justice needs some general flexibility, and not merely some quirks of deference to certain odd and arbitrarily defined human weak-

nesses. In fact our own system of criminal justice has such flexibility, provided that it is realised that it does not consist only in the positive prohibitions and injunctions of the criminal law, but extends also to its penal sanctions. May it not be that the infinite variety of circumstances in which the lawful wish of the actor is overborne could be accommodated with far greater flexibility, with much less anomaly, and with avoidance of the social evils which would attend acceptance of the appellant's argument (that duress is a general criminal defence), by taking those circumstances into account in the sentence of the court? Is not the whole rationale of duress as a criminal defence that it recognises that an act prohibited by the criminal law may be morally innocent? Is not an absolute discharge just such an acknowledgement of moral innocence? (Emphasis added.)

86. In other words, the fact that justice may be done in ways other than admitting duress as a complete defence was always apparent to judges in England who rejected duress as a defence to murder. They have consistently argued that in cases of murder, duress could in appropriate cases be taken into account in mitigation of sentence, executive pardon or recommendations to the Parole Board: see Lord Hailsham of Marylebone LC in *R v. Howe.*

87. Indeed, we would note that Stephen in his classic work argued that duress should never constitute a defence to any crime but merely as a ground in mitigation. The merit of this view was acknowledged by Lord Morris of Borth-y-Gest in D.P.P. for Northern Ireland v. Lynch where he stated:

A tenable view might be that duress should never be regarded as furnishing an excuse from guilt but only where established as providing reasons why after conviction a court could mitigate its consequences or absolve from punishment. Some writers including Stephen . . . have so thought.

E. Our conclusions

88. After the above survey of authorities in the different systems of law and exploration of the various policy considerations which we must bear in mind, we take the view that duress cannot afford a complete defence to a soldier charged with crimes against humanity or war crimes in international law involving the taking of innocent lives. We do so having regard to our mandated obligation under the Statute to ensure that international humanitarian law, which is concerned with the protection of humankind, is not in any way undermined.

89. In the result, we do not consider the plea of the Appellant was equivocal as duress does not afford a complete defence in

international law to a charge of a crime against humanity or a war crime which involves the killing of innocent human beings.

90. Our discussion of the issues relating to the guilty plea entered by the Appellant is sufficient to dispose of the present appeal. It is not necessary for us to engage ourselves in the remaining issues raised by the parties. We would observe, however, that in rejecting the evidence of the Appellant that he had committed the crime under a threat of death from his commanding officer and consequently in refusing to take the circumstance of duress into account in mitigation of the Appellant's sentence, the Trial Chamber appeared to require corroboration of the Appellant's testimony as a matter of law. There is, with respect, nothing in the Statute or the Rules which requires corroboration of the exculpatory evidence of an accused person in order for that evidence to be taken into account in mitigation of sentence.

91. We would allow the appeal on the ground that the plea was not informed. The case is hereby remitted to another Trial Chamber where the Appellant must be given the opportunity to replead in full knowledge of the consequences of pleading guilty per se and of the inherent difference between the alternative charges.

D. FEDERAL GENOCIDE STATUTE

As part of the ratification of the Genocide Convention by the United States, Congress passed a law defining a crime of genocide, 18 U.S.C.A. § 1091. The elements of the crime are:

(a) **Basic offense.**—Whoever, whether in time of peace or in time of war, in a circumstance described in subsection (d) and with the specific intent to destroy, in whole or in substantial part, a national, ethnic, racial, or religious group as such—

(1) kills members of that group;

(2) causes serious bodily injury to members of that group;

(3) causes the permanent impairment of the mental faculties of members of the group through drugs, torture, or similar techniques;

(4) subjects the group to conditions of life that are intended to cause the physical destruction of the group in whole or in part;

(5) imposes measures intended to prevent births within the group; or

(6) transfers by force children of the group to another group;

or attempts to do so, shall be punished as provided in subsection (b).

(b) Punishment for basic offense.—The punishment for an offense under subsection (a) is—

(1) in the case of an offense under subsection (a)(1) where death results, by death or imprisonment for life and a fine of not more than $1,000,000, or both; and

(2) a fine of not more than $1,000,000 or imprisonment for not more than twenty years, or both, in any other case.

(c) Incitement offense.—Whoever in a circumstance described in subsection (d) directly and publicly incites another to violate subsection (a) shall be fined not more than $500,000 or imprisoned not more than five years, or both.

(d) Required circumstance for offenses.—The circumstance referred to in subsections (a) and (c) is that—

(1) the offense is committed within the United States; or

(2) the alleged offender is a national of the United States (as defined in section 101 of the Immigration and Nationality Act (8 U.S.C. 1101)).

(e) Nonapplicability of certain limitations.—Notwithstanding section 3282 of this title, in the case of an offense under subsection (a)(1), an indictment may be found, or information instituted, at any time without limitation.

––––––

Notes and Questions

1. Limitations on Federal Prosecutions of Genocide. Under what circumstances, if any, could the defendants in the Problem in Section B be prosecuted for genocide in the United States? Why do you think Congress imposed the limitations in subpart (d) of the statute on the ability to prosecute genocide case?

2. Crimes Against Humanity. Crimes Against Humanity were recognized at Nuremberg and are important in international criminal law. There is no treaty, however, that sets forth an accepted definition as there is for genocide. In general, the elements of crimes against humanity include:

1. For the purpose of this Statute, "crime against humanity" means any of the following acts when committed as part of a widespread or systematic attack directed against any civilian population, with knowledge of the attack:

(a) Murder;

(b) Extermination;

(c) Enslavement;

(d) Deportation or forcible transfer of population;

(e) Imprisonment or other severe deprivation of physical liberty in violation of fundamental rules of international law;

(f) Torture;

(g) Rape, sexual slavery, enforced prostitution, forced pregnancy, enforced sterilization, or any other form of sexual violence of comparable gravity;

(h) Persecution against any identifiable group or collectivity on political, racial, national, ethnic, cultural, religious, gender as defined in paragraph 3, or other grounds that are universally recognized as impermissible under international law, in connection with any act referred to in this paragraph or any crime within the jurisdiction of the Court;

(i) Enforced disappearance of persons;

(j) The crime of apartheid;

(k) Other inhumane acts of a similar character intentionally causing great suffering, or serious injury to body or to mental or physical health.

2. For the purpose of paragraph 1:

(a) "Attack directed against any civilian population" means a course of conduct involving the multiple commission of acts referred to in paragraph 1 against any civilian population, pursuant to or in furtherance of a State or organizational policy to commit such attack;

(b) "Extermination" includes the intentional infliction of conditions of life, inter alia the deprivation of access to food and medicine, calculated to bring about the destruction of part of a population;

(c) "Enslavement" means the exercise of any or all of the powers attaching to the right of ownership over a person and includes the exercise of such power in the course of trafficking in persons, in particular women and children;

(d) "Deportation or forcible transfer of population" means forced displacement of the persons concerned by expulsion or other coercive acts from the area in which they are lawfully present, without grounds permitted under international law;

(e) "Torture" means the intentional infliction of severe pain or suffering, whether physical or mental, upon a person in the custody or under the control of the accused; except that torture shall not include pain or suffering arising only from, inherent in or incidental to, lawful sanctions;

(f) "Forced pregnancy" means the unlawful confinement of a woman forcibly made pregnant, with the intent of affecting the ethnic composition of any population or carrying out other grave violations of international law. This definition shall not in any way be interpreted as affecting national laws relating to pregnancy;

(g) "Persecution" means the intentional and severe deprivation of fundamental rights contrary to international law by reason of the identity of the group or collectivity;

(h) "The crime of apartheid" means inhumane acts of a character similar to those referred to in paragraph 1, committed in the context of an institutionalized regime of systematic oppression and domination by one racial group over any other racial group or groups and committed with the intention of maintaining that regime;

(i) "Enforced disappearance of persons" means the arrest, detention or abduction of persons by, or with the authorization, support or acquiescence of, a State or a political organization, followed by a refusal to acknowledge that deprivation of freedom or to give information on the fate or whereabouts of those persons, with the intention of removing them from the protection of the law for a prolonged period of time.

3. For the purpose of this Statute, it is understood that the term "gender" refers to the two sexes, male and female, within the context of society. The term "gender" does not indicate any meaning different from the above.

Rome Statute of the International Criminal Court, Article 7: Crimes Against Humanity.

What is the likelihood that the defendants in the KRT Problem would be criminally culpable for crimes against humanity?

3. Nexus with an Armed Conflict? Most commentators today note that crimes against humanity do not contain an element of a nexus with an armed conflict.[19] At the time of Nuremberg, such a nexus was part of the definition used. One of the issues that will arise in the KRT will be whether or not a nexus with an armed conflict was an element of crimes against humanity in 1975–1979 when the alleged offenses were committed by the Khmer Rouge. The lawyers and judges will research and deliberate on the development of customary international law on this point. As a matter of fairness to the defendant, the acts committed must have been a crime at the time they were commit-

---

19. *See, e.g.,* Antonio Cassese, International Criminal Law 90–91 (2003); Phyllis Hwang, *Defining Crimes Against* *Humanity in the Rome Statute,* 22 Fordham Int'l L.J. 457 (1998).

ted. This is a basic, legal principle of *ex post facto* in American jurisprudence and *nullum crimen sine lege* in international parlance.[20]

4. War Crimes. War crimes are the other major crimes prosecuted at an international level. War crimes include grave breaches of the Geneva Conventions and violations of the laws and customs of war. Grave breaches include:

[T]he following acts against persons or property protected under the provisions of the relevant Geneva Convention:

(a) wilful killing;

(b) torture or inhuman treatment, including biological experiments;

(c) wilfully causing great suffering or serious injury to body or health;

(d) extensive destruction and appropriation of property, not justified by military necessity and carried out unlawfully and wantonly;

(e) compelling a prisoner of war or a civilian to serve in the forces of a hostile power;

(f) wilfully depriving a prisoner of war or a civilian of the rights of fair and regular trial;

(g) unlawful deportation or transfer or unlawful confinement of a civilian;

(h) taking civilians as hostages.

ICTY Statute, Article 2: Grave breaches of the Geneva Conventions of 1949.

Violations of the laws and customs of war is a broader category than grave breaches. The crimes can occur in either an international or an internal conflict. The crimes also cover the conduct of war as well as harm to individuals. Illustrative of this crime is the ICTY statute:

Such violations shall include, but not be limited to:

(a) employment of poisonous weapons or other weapons calculated to cause unnecessary suffering;

(b) wanton destruction of cities, towns or villages, or devastation not justified by military necessity;

(c) attack, or bombardment, by whatever means, of undefended towns, villages, dwellings, or buildings;

(d) seizure of, destruction or wilful damage done to institutions dedicated to religion, charity and education, the arts

---

20. The legal principle of *ex post facto* and *nullum crimen sine lege, nulla poena sine lege* protects an accused against a prosecution and punishment for a crime that did not exist (or whose elements were different) at the time of the acts of the accused.

and sciences, historic monuments and works of art and science;

(e) plunder of public or private property.

ICTY Statute, Article 3: Violations of the laws or customs of war

What is the likelihood that the defendants in the KRT Problem would be criminally culpable for war crimes?

5. Superior Orders. Soldiers who commit crimes during war will often claim that they did so because of an order from a superior to do the act. The defense of superior orders has typically either not been allowed or not prevailed when the crimes are as serious as war crimes or crimes against humanity. For example, in the *Llandovery Castle* case, Germany, Reichsgericht, 16 July 1921, Cmd 1422, 2 Am. Dig. 436, a German court found two German sailors guilty of violations of the laws and customs of war for firing on lifeboats from a British hospital ship, despite an order from the German commander to fire on the boats. The court found that the order in a case such as the lifeboats was clearly contrary to law and no defense could be maintained. Reflecting the inability to raise a superior orders defense to genocide, crimes against humanity, and war crimes, the statutes of the ICTY and ICTR provide that superior orders can only serve as mitigation of a punishment, not as a defense to a crime. *ICTY Statute, Article 7(4); ICTR Statute, Article Article 6(4).* The statute of the ICC takes a more liberal stance, allowing in theory for a defense of superior orders. However, the ICC statute provides that there is no defense if the orders were "manifestly unlawful," and further provides that orders to commit genocide or crimes against humanity are manifestly unlawful. *ICC Statute, Article 33.*

6. Revisiting the Definition of Genocide. As you know from preparing the KRT problem, only certain mass killings are "genocide" due to the limitations in the definition of genocide. Specifically, the limitation to an "intent to destroy, in whole or in part a *national, ethnical, racial, or religious group* as such" precludes a finding of genocide in the context of many mass atrocities.

Many commentators have criticized the limitations in the definition of genocide, both on a legal level and on a political level. In a recent article, Professor David Luban has pointed out the mismatch between the legal consequences of actions not constituting genocide and the public's reaction to such a conclusion. In the context of an evaluation of the devastation in Darfur, Sudan, Professor Luban wrote:

> On January 25, 2005, the International Commission on Darfur presented its report to U.N. Secretary–General Kofi Annan. The Commission, chaired by the eminent international jurist Antonio Cassese, did a meticulous job of investigating possible international crimes in Darfur. Newspaper headlines summarized the Cassese Commission's basic findings a few days later:

"U.N. Finds Crimes, Not Genocide, in Darfur"—New York Times, February 1.

"U.N. Panel Finds No Genocide in Darfur but Urges Tribunals"—Washington Post, February 1.

"Murder—But No Genocide"—The Scotsman, Feb. 2.

"Darfur 'Criminal But Not Genocide' "—the Australian, Feb. 2.

"Sudan's Darfur Crimes Not Genocide, Says U.N. Report"— The Guardian (London), Feb. 1.

And nearly identical headlines appeared in the Chicago Tribune, the Independent, the Queensland Courier Mail, the St. Petersburg Times, the Irish Times, and the Financial Times.

Most revealing are headlines from the Herald–Times in Melbourne—"Horrors Short of Genocide" (Feb. 2)—the Glasgow Herald—"UN 'clears Sudan of genocide' in Darfur" (Feb. 2)(with a nearly identical headline in The Mercury of Australia), and London's Daily Telegraph: "UN confusion as Sudan conflict is no longer 'genocide' " (Feb. 2). Plainly, "short of genocide" means "not as bad as genocide." "Clears Sudan of genocide" means exoneration—and, coming just two days after headlines declaring that Sudanese officials denied bombing a village in Darfur, headline-scanners could be excused for believing that the U.N. report had disproven atrocity reports in Darfur. And "U.N. confusion" as the Darfur catastrophe is "no longer 'genocide' " shows the baleful results. The U.N. no longer knew what to do, because without the word 'genocide', the mandate for action disappears. * * *

Strikingly, however, all those damaging headlines actually reflected a horrible misunderstanding of the U.N. Commission's conclusions. The Report contained no factual exonerations. More importantly, the Report insisted that the war crimes and crimes against humanity that it found in Darfur are just as evil and just as legally significant as genocide. However, the Commission made this point in a maddeningly legalistic manner: it pointed out that trial chambers in the Yugoslav and Rwanda Tribunals had referred to genocide as the "crime of crimes"—but they were reversed by their Appellate Chambers, which held that there is no hierarchy among international crimes. This pettifogging mode of argument vividly demonstrates how disconnected the law of genocide has become from the generally accepted meaning of the word. To everyone in the world other than a handful of international lawyers, genocide *is* the "crime of crimes," regardless of what the judges on Appellate Chambers in The Hague say. And the Commission's effort to insist that the crimes in Darfur are not genocide, but it doesn't matter because they are as bad as genocide, not only swims upstream against the force of language, but argues its conclusion not on moral or factual grounds, but merely because a handful of judges say so. Its conclusion that Darfur is not a genocide turned on fine points of the technical definition of genocide contained in the Genocide Convention and subsequently incorporated into the ICC Statute and national legislation. Thus, when the Melbourne Herald–Times said that Darfur falls "short of genocide" it actually misrepresented the U.N. Commission Report, which goes out of its way to insist that genocide is not the "crime of crimes," and that crimes against humanity are every bit as significant. * * *

We may understand the difference between the legal definitions of genocide and crimes against humanity in the following way: the law of crimes against humanity focuses on the political, organized, group character of the *perpetrators*, while genocide focuses on the group character of the *victims*. To be sure, by definition crimes against humanity must be committed against civilian populations, that is, against groups. But for the Nuremberg framers, the victims could be *any* civilian population under attack, including populations that mix multiple groups. There is in fact a studied vagueness in the concept of a "civilian population," but the most natural way to think of it is *territorially*: the civilian population of the village of Amaki Sara, in Darfur province, Sudan has been attacked and the crimes against humanity of murder and rape have been committed.

From a group-pluralist point of view, the concept of crimes against humanity fails precisely because it ignores the specific character of the target groups, and the specific intention to diminish humanity by annihilating the group as such. To be sure, the crimes against humanity include a crime called "extermination." But the legal definition, though it requires extermination committed in a planned, systematic attack, does not require a specific intent to exterminate, nor does it require the targeting of a racial, ethnic, religious, or national group "as such." From Lemkin's point of view, it misses the distinctive pluralist dimension of human value that genocide assaults.

Ultimately, Professor Luban proposes a revision to the definition of genocide that would include the concept of extermination from crimes against humanity. His suggestion is:

The idea is not to water down the concept of genocide, but to "upgrade" the legal category of extermination by recognizing that it has the same core meaning as genocide, and equal claim to designate the "crime of crimes." Article II of the Genocide Convention would now read:

In the present Convention, genocide means

(A) any of the following acts committed with intent to destroy, in whole or in part, a national, ethnical, racial or religious group, as such: (i) Killing members of the group; (ii) Causing serious bodily or mental harm to members of the group; (iii) Deliberately inflicting on the group conditions of life calculated to bring about its physical destruction in whole or in part; (iv) Imposing measures intended to prevent births within the group; (v) Forcibly transferring children of the group to another group; *or*

(B) the crime against humanity of extermination.

David Luban, *Calling Genocide by Its Rightful Name: Lemkin's Word, Darfur, and the U.N. Report,* 7 CHI. J. INT'L L. 303 (2006).

Compare Professor Luban's proposal with this commentary by Professor William Schabas, who advocates keeping the definition of genocide in its present, narrower form:

Although the Convention is principally about the punishment of the crime—a matter addressed in most of its substantive provisions—the treaty also imposes an obligation of prevention. The term is an enigma, and there is essentially nothing in the Convention to designate the scope of the duty to prevent genocide. How states behave when confronted with genocide may give some clues on this. In 1994, as the Rwandan genocide unfolded, several members of the Security Council, and in particular the permanent members, were extremely reluctant to use the word "genocide" in a resolution directed to the Rwandan crisis. In the view of many, including the Secretary–General Boutros Boutros–Ghali, this was because a finding of genocide would impose an obligation to act to prevent the crime. The United States was foremost among those who were uncomfortable with the word genocide. At a press briefing on June 10, 1994, Department of State spokeswoman Christine Shelley said that the United States was not prepared to declare that genocide was taking place in Rwanda because "there are obligations which arise in connection with the use of the term." The position of the United States is still not entirely clear on the subject, although obviously there has been considerable soul-searching about the obligations that flow from the Convention in terms of preventing genocide. In a speech at Kigali airport, on March 25, 1998, President Bill Clinton said, contritely: "We did not immediately call these crimes by their rightful name: genocide." It is reasonable to deduce that American hesitation at the time was in some way connected with a perception that there was indeed an obligation under the Convention. If genocide is to be stopped in the future, it is imperative that the vague obligation to prevent set out in article I of the Convention be made more robust. But enhancing the obligations states are prepared to assume when faced with genocide, up to and including military intervention, will never be achieved if they are unsure about the crime's parameters. Strict definition of the crime explains why, in 1948, the international community was able to achieve a Convention, something that proved elusive for the broader concept of crimes against humanity. And it remains the price to be paid for recognition of a positive duty to act in order to prevent genocide.

William A. Schabas, *Problems of International Codification—Were the Atrocities in Cambodia and Kosovo Genocide?*, 35 NEW ENG. L. REV. 287 (2001).

What do you think of Professor Luban's proposal to include the crime against humanity of extermination as a form of genocide? What are the advantages or disadvantages of this approach? Do you agree that there is no difference between "extermination of a population within a territory and intentional destruction of a group within a territory?" Does the definition of genocide as presently written require a mass killing of a population? Do you agree with Professor Schabas that a strict definition of genocide is necessary in order to achieve intervention by the international community?

Index

†